HUMAN RIGHTS
and
Health Care Law

HUMAN RIGHTS
and
Health Care Law

by EUGENE I. PAVALON, B.S., J.D.

Medical Consultant:
David Birnbaum, M.D.

AMERICAN JOURNAL OF NURSING COMPANY, NEW YORK
EDUCATIONAL SERVICES DIVISION

TO MY FAMILY

ACKNOWLEDGEMENTS

The input of others contributed greatly to the completion of this book.

My sincere thanks and appreciation to Linda Smith, Esq., now a practicing attorney in Florida, for her indefatigable work in the research of the manuscript.

My appreciation to Ena Morris, my editor, whose facility with the written word helped make intelligible much of what is written here.

My gratitude to my secretary, Ann Maksymiw, who typed, retyped, and retyped again, much of the original manuscript.

Contents

Preface

"We hold these truths to be sacred and undeniable; that all men are created equal and independent, that from that equal creation they derive rights inherent and inalienable, among which are the preservation of life, and liberty and the pursuit of happiness." (Original draft of the Declaration of Independence, by Thomas Jefferson)

Only recently have people begun to question vociferously the authoritarian approach of the health care professions, aided and abetted by legislative directives concerning individuals' rights to make the ultimate decision as to what is to be done with and to their bodies. Those inalienable rights, so well stated in the cornerstone document of this country, have long been regarded lightly in the delivery of medical treatment and other health care services.

The advent of consumer activism has had its fallout in the health care field. That, together with rapid medical and scientific advances, has resulted in a plethora of varying legal responses, both legislative and judicial, to the many resulting complex issues.

Indeed, social scientists, philosophers, and religious leaders often differ dramatically concerning the answers to the many questions raised generally by concerns of patients' rights and such specific issues as abortion, euthanasia, rights of minors and the mentally ill, and artificial insemination. The legal response has frequently been a reflection of such controversy.

Certainly, the consuming public should be aware of the issues concerning their rights as patients and the basic legal principles concerning such issues. It is equally important that health care practitioners be conversant with these issues and the general principles of applicable law to enable their professional performance to be at an optimum level. Furthermore, each health care practitioner is also a potential consumer of health care services.

It has been my intention to provide an overview of pertinent contemporary issues concerning the legal rights of people in various situations presented by the health care milieu. The topics that I have selected frequently arise in the health care setting, affecting providers and consumers alike. The courts and legislatures have recently been confronted with the many issues presented in these areas.

Controversy is a common element to all of these topics. Indeed, a simple declaratory statement concerning abortion may well transform an otherwise placid conversation into a heated debate. Bearing this in mind, I have attempted restraint in editorializing on the many controversial issues discussed. Human frailty, however, has prevented a complete purging of personal opinions.

A detailed analysis of a number of judicial decisions and statutory provisions has been provided in those instances in which I believe it necessary for a better understanding of the problems and issues under consideration. I have purposely omitted an in-depth discussion of the issues and legal doctrine concerning malpractice. It is a subject that I believe has been given excess attention during the past several years.

For those readers who are interested in further pursuing any of the issues and topics discussed, citations are provided for material referred to in the text. For those untrained in deciphering legal citations, I suggest obtaining a small paperbound manual called *A Uniform System of Citation*, 12th ed. 1976, published and distributed by the Harvard Law Review Association, Cambridge, Mass. This "bluebook" is available in most college bookstores and certainly in every law-school bookstore. The glossary of legal terms and abbreviations has been included in the book as Appendix A, and most lay readers should be able to understand the legal terminology used in the text and citations.

It is my hope that this volume will serve as a vehicle for more people to become aware of and involved with the issues and appreciate the difficulties lawmakers and judges face. As the myriad problems and points of view concerning human rights in the health care setting are confronted, more enlightened and universally accepted solutions should result.

E.I.P.

Chicago
March 11, 1980

Part ONE

PATIENTS' RIGHTS IN GENERAL

Introduction

The patients' rights movement has been rather slow to emerge in this country. In the past decade, virtually every minority in society has been pushing courts and legislatures to uphold the basic rights of freedom and self-expression guaranteed by the Bill of Rights of the United States Constitution. Patients as a group have been more hesitant than other groups to push for change, mainly as a result of many cultural and psychological factors in their relationships with the medical profession.

An almost mystical aura has surrounded the healing arts for centuries. The medicine man or shaman of old tribal societies has been traditionally represented as an awesome character clothed with magical powers of healing, living apart from other tribal members. He held a highly respected place when his power worked, when the gods were pleased, and the person recovered. The great healer had the power to communicate with the gods and beg for their mercy to cure the diseased and injured. Thus, healing was strictly between the gods and the man, with the shaman as mediator. Healing took on almost supernatural overtones.

Reverence for the healer of yesterday has persisted long after healers became licensed physicians and nurses, schooled in a more structured and scientific and less supernatural manner. The secret potions and magical remedies formerly achieved through ritualistic chants and dances survive today in our wonder drugs. It is not unusual to see a person recovering from an operation or a heart attack who has an incredible number of pills to ingest daily and who does not even know what the pills are for. With such a cultural and psychological pattern of relating to the healing arts, it is no wonder that so many mortals unhesitatingly place their trust in the medical profession.

In addition, the most powerful drive in a normal human being is the will to live. When life is threatened by sickness, disease, or injury, a person will do virtually anything to be cured. A person who seeks the aid of a doctor or nurse is not primarily concerned with preserving any basic rights but simply wants to be well. As Oliver Wendell Holmes, M.D., once said,

> The persons who seek the aid of the physician are very honest and sincere in their wish to get rid of their complaints.... There is nothing men will not do, there is nothing they have not done, to recover their health and save their lives. They have submitted to be half-drowned in water, and half-cooked with gases, to be buried up to their chins in earth, to be seared with hot irons like slaves, to be crimped with knives, like codfish, to have needles thrust into their flesh, and bonfires kindled on their skin, to swallow all sorts of abominations, and to pay for all of this, as if to be singed and scaled were a costly privilege, as if blisters were a blessing, and leeches were a luxury.[1]

It is difficult to say whether this undying confidence and trust, overstepping all reason and logic, placed in the medical and health professions, mainly the physician, is a result of the awe with which people have looked at the healer or the strength of a human being's will to live. The fact remains that people as patients have been slow to step forward and demand basic rights in the treatment process.

Aside from cultural and psychological factors, there is the reality of the hospitalization process and the attitude of the patient and toward the patient that has existed for a long time. Much of the treatment for sickness takes place in the hospital, which many persons view as a confinement. The person is confined to his bed, a wheelchair, or a hospital for a certain length of time until released by the physician and the hospital. The use of the terms confinement and release in themselves indicate a person's loss of control and subsequent loss of rights.

The hospitalized patient is under the almost total control of the doctors and staff. He or she is told what to wear, what to eat, when to sleep, when to arise, and when visitors are allowed. Often, patients need assistance in bathing, eliminating, and walking. As one writer put it, "A stay in a hospital exposes an individual to a condition of passivity and impotence unparalleled in adult life."[2] In such a setting where nearly all control is placed in the hands of the doctors and staff, it is no wonder that people forget their rights, if they ever knew them.

Since the agitation of the sixties stirred a general increase in concern for human rights, patients have gradually been pulled into the whirlwind of change. With abortion, euthanasia, and a current increase in malpractice litigation in the public eye, patients' rights have become an important issue. An issue such as public school integration for blacks has been expanded to include adequate medical care and facilities for the poor and the blacks. The struggle for equality in job opportunities and equal pay for women has spread the struggle for the person's inviolability and the right to control her own destiny by choosing abortion, sterilization, or natural childbirth in the hospital. The elderly are concerned with such issues as mandatory retirement and the right to die with dignity without the use of extraordinary life-sustaining apparatus. With the ever increasing concern about privacy in this age of computer records on every aspect of life, the right to privacy in both patient treatment and medical records is a growing concern. Religious groups, ever concerned with upholding the First Amendment guarantee of freedom of worship, have moved into the legal arena to demand the right to refuse the treatment that conflicts with their religious beliefs.

The current concern with the rights of patients is not easy to trace or explain simply. Nevertheless, an increase in patients' rights is happening and is an ongoing concern of the nursing and medical professions, hospital associations, state legislatures, and courts. The body of rights due a patient have developed through (1) case law arising as various groups fight through the legal system to preserve their bodily integrity, (2) legislation, and (3) medical and hospital ethics committees.

The American Hospital Association's House of Delegates has codified a set of patient's rights that reflects, to some degree, the rights of all patients in general and those specifically available to hospital patients. Some of these rights are legal rights, tested and preserved by the courts, and made into law by state legislatures. Others are hospital policy that are probably legal rights, developed by regulatory boards but not yet tested in a court of law. Others are basic human rights due patients because they are human beings and because our society and the natural law demand that they be respected. Still others are a result of medical ethics, necessary for a doctor and nurse to be aware of in order to live up to their responsibilities and duties as healers, and necessary because of the trust placed in them by the people seeking their services.[3]

Patients' rights differ from state to state, making it difficult to determine how strong and effective these rights are in any given instance.

A broad overview of rights in general will help insure that future medical treatment and hospitalization will become a more comfortable and less humiliating or debasing experience. Perhaps the discussion on the constitutional rights of privacy and basic respect for human dignity that the legal profession is determined to uphold, along with the discussion from the viewpoint of the medical profession and their dedicated and persevering struggle to insure adequate and competent treatment for individuals seeking medical aid, will assure the general public that their rights as patients have firm support.

Notes and References

1. Holmes, Oliver Wendell, "The Young Practitioner," In *The Good Physician*, edited by W. H. Davenport (New York: Macmillan, 1962), quoted in Annas, George J., *The Rights of Hospital Patients* (New York: Avon Books, 1975), p. 3.
2. Gaylin, W., The patient's bill of rights (editorial), *Saturday Review of the Sciences* 1:21, Mar. 1973, quoted in Patient's rights, nursing responsibilities, *Hospitals J.A.H.A.* 47 (No. 12): 104, June 16, 1973.
3. Ideas from Annas, George J., and Healy, The patient rights advocate: redefining the doctor-patient relationship in the hospital context, *Vanderbilt Law Review* 27:243 (1974); and Annas, *The Rights of Hospital Patients*, supra at ch. 1.

CHAPTER 1

Admission, Continuity of Care, Discharge

To say that a person has certain rights implies that another has the duty to provide certain things or to treat the possessor of the rights in a certain manner. To say that patients have rights necessarily implies that physicians, nurses, and hospitals have requisite duties. The foundation for most of the patients' rights we will be discussing lies in a court, legislature, or the determination of a board of ethics that a duty exists on the part of the health care provider to act in a certain manner.

EMERGENCY CARE

It is appropriate to begin by discussing admission practices, whether admission be to a hospital, clinic, or private physician's office. A person who seeks medical care is not legally a patient of a hospital, clinic, or private physician until the agency's personnel or the physician take steps to accept the patient. A patient is considered to have been admitted when the appropriate admission forms are completed or when a hospital employee or a physician or nurse practitioner has begun examining or treating the person so as to lead the person to believe he or she has been accepted as a patient.[1]

Most laymen might be surprised to learn that a person seeking medical care does not have an absolute right to be admitted to a hospital. Although the stated standards of the medical profession direct its members toward providing aid to emergency patients, several state courts have held that there is no absolute duty to admit or treat anyone.[2] Nevertheless, when hospital staff members or physicians have been tried for negligence for refusing to treat an emergency patient whose condition worsened as a result of the refusal, the majority of courts have found them liable for negligence.

Where there is a duty to treat, there is a subsequent right to treatment. So it can be said that, in an emergency, where there is a threat of death, disability, or serious illness if the condition is not immediately treated, a person has the right to adequate and competent care in the hospital. The following are examples of emergency situations, determined as such by various courts: heart attack, hemorrhage, poisoning, shock, pneumonia, wounds, fractures, and frostbite.

Private hospitals are not required by law to have emergency room facilities. If the hospital does not have an emergency room, it may not be duty bound to accept emergency patients because of the lack of adequate facilities to care for such patients.

If the hospital is a public hospital, that is, supported by government funds and open to the public regardless of ability to pay, various states require it to have an emergency room. The Arizona Supreme Court declared that if any hospital, public or private, does have an emergency room, then it is obliged to admit emergency patients.[3]

Two Mexican children, who lived near the border of Arizona, were taken to a private hospital in Arizona after they had been burned. Hospital personnel refused them first aid and emergency care. They were taken to a county hospital later and treated there. The Arizona Supreme Court predicated its finding of liability of Copper Queen Hospital on public policy grounds via its interpretation of a state regulation that required general hospitals to maintain emergency facilities. The court determined a general hospital could not deny emergency care without good cause, and citizenship and domicile were not acceptable excuses for denying assistance.

The holding in Guerrero v. Copper Queen Hospital has been codified in various state statutes. Illinois requires hospitals that give general medical and surgical service and are licensed by the department of public health to be equipped with emergency facilities and to furnish such services to any applicant whose injury or medical condition is liable to cause severe injury, serious illness, or death.[4] New York and California codes have similar provisions.

In New York State, in cities with a population of one million or more, general hospitals must provide emergency care to all persons but can transfer them to other facilities if the hospital is not properly equipped or is short on personnel. Every general hospital must admit to the inpatient service any person in need of immediate hospitalization. They must do this without first obtaining financial data, provided the patient or his family agrees to supply this information after admission. Whether the patient is admitted from the hospital's emergency department of transferred to another hospital, the attending physician has the right to evaluate whether there is in fact an emergency.[5]

Likewise, California hospitals are required to provide emergency services to any person where there is the danger of loss of life or serious illness or injury, provided the hospital maintains and operates an emergency department and has the appropriate facilities and personnel. As with the New York statute, no questions concerning the patient's finances are to be asked before admission or before treatment begins, when such information will be supplied after the services are rendered. In California, if the hospital or health care facility does not have an emergency room, and an emergency exists, hospital authorities must take reasonable care to direct the patient to another facility and, where reasonable, provide transportation.[6]

Federal law provides that no hospital can deny emergency services to the poor or discriminate against a person because of race, color, or creed.[7] Since a hospital is forced to institute an "open door" policy for emergency care (i.e., open to everyone regardless of their ability to pay) the federal government has attempted to ameliorate the consequent financial burden through various means. The Hill-Burton Act makes available large federal loans, which are interest free, for hospital building and expansion. In return, the recipient of the funds must provide a certain quota of free medical care to the poor.

Likewise, the Internal Revenue Service awards hospitals a tax-exempt status for providing open-door emergency services, even where all inpatients are required to pay for hospital care.[8] The Supreme Court made this ruling almost impossible to challenge in a case involving an organization of indigents who challenged it on the basis that it encourages hospitals to deny other medical services to the poor.[9]

Although hospitals have a duty to provide emergency services without regard for a person's ability to pay, they can require a deposit from persons to be admitted as inpatients in nonemergency situations. Since there are county and other charitable hospitals available, a private hospital has no such duty to render nonemergency services free except to fulfill its Hill-Burton quotas.

Courts have stated that a medical decision that a situation is a nonemergency, based on a reasonable exercise of judgment, will absolve a hospital from liability for failure to admit a patient.[10] On the other hand, the reasonable exercise of judgment must be based on a competent examination including obtaining a history and attempting a diagnosis.[11]

Once the hospital personnel begin examining and treating the patient, they become responsible for rendering adequate and competent care. Furthermore, the patient has a right to be seen by a physician within a reasonable time.[12] Where persons have been seriously injured by gunshot or automobile accidents and have remained untreated for several hours before being transferred to another hospital, courts have found the first hospital liable for the aggravation of the patient's condition, the prolonged pain and suffering, or the wrongful death.[13]

Courts have also held hospitals liable where an emergency patient was transferred or discharged to another hospital in such serious condition that the condition was worsened, aggravated or caused death.[14] Thus, it can be said that a patient has the right to continuity of treatment until he is transferred or discharged without harm.

ABANDONMENT

Once the doctor-patient relationship is established, the doctor cannot indiscriminately terminate it unilaterally. Such a unilateral severance without the patient's consent or reasonable notice of withdrawal is abandonment. When a patient still needs continuing medical attention, the doctor or the hospital that abandons the patient may be held liable for damages resulting from complications or changes in the patient's condition.[15]

A New York case illustrates this point. An eight-year-old boy was treated surgically by a specialist for osteomyelitis, and both legs were placed in plaster casts. The boy was discharged from the hospital on the orders of the specialist when the father was unable to pay past medical bills. The boy's legs had not healed at the time of discharge, and he had a high temperature. The specialist advised the father to take the boy to the family doctor and said he could properly care for the child.

The family's physician attempted to care for the child, but he was not adequately qualified. The boy's condition worsened considerably and he was left severely crippled. The court determined there was sufficient evidence to warrant a trial on the merits as to the willful abandonment of the patient by the hospital and the specialist.[16]

Even after a patient has been discharged from the hospital, a physician may face a charge of abandonment if he refuses to help the patient after a relapse, unless another physician takes over the patient's care.[17]

Abandonment, for which consequences the physician or hospital may be liable, can also occur if a patient is discharged prematurely from a hospital.[18] In one case, a doctor treated a patient for multiple facial fractures and discharged him from the hospital without telling him that his facial bones needed to be set by a specialist. A court held that there was sufficient evidence to submit to a jury.[19]

DISCHARGE

A patient has the right to be discharged at will from a hospital unless he is suffering from a communicable disease or is dangerous to himself or others.

If a patient wishes to be discharged against the judgment of the physician, the hospital or physician will usually request the patient to sign a release of liability for leaving against such advice. The patient, however, has no legal obligation to sign such a document.

Public health statutes of the states govern the duty of hospitals and physicians regarding communicable diseases. If a patient is mentally ill and dangerous to himself or others, then the hospital or physician must take the necessary steps to see that he is committed to an institution or get a declaration of incompetency from a psychiatrist. Such circumstances are subject to the provisions of state mental health statutes.

The general duty of a hospital to discharge a patient at his request arises from the patient's constitutional civil rights. A breach of that duty gives rise to action for false imprisonment, which could result in the hospital's liability for money damages to the patient. In 1925, an Alabama hospital was found liable for $1,500 in an action for false imprisonment where a patient was detained against her will for failure to pay her hospital bill.[20] Just as a hospital cannot refuse aid to an emergency patient who lacks the ability to pay, it also cannot refuse to discharge any patient for lack of ability to pay.

If a patient cannot pay the hospital bill, a hospital administration does have recourse. The administration can bring a civil action against that person for the money due or can apply that money toward their Hill-Burton funding quota for free medical care to the impoverished.

Sometimes the problem is that a patient insists on remaining in the hospital contrary to the treating physician's judgment. A patient has no right to remain in a hospital after being discharged by the physician and can be removed as a trespasser for failure to leave when requested.[21] The patient, however, can demand a consultation with another physician before his discharge.[22] The discharge order must be in writing and come from a physician who is familiar with the patient's case.

The source of the foregoing rights—the right to admission in emergency situations, the right to continuity of care, and the right to be discharged when well enough and not before—is in court decisions, constitutional provisions, and state statutes. More important, however, is the attitude of the health care provider with regard to the implementation of these rights. Legal guarantees alone will not insure patients adequate and humane treatment in hospitals and clinics. Many patients have died or have been seriously disabled as a result of improper and inhumane treatment. Yet these people were in possession of such "legal rights." The assurance that these rights will be given meaning comes from the consciousness of health care providers that they are doing a service for humanity by functioning in their professions. Their jobs are not average. They cannot often afford to let personality fluctuations affect their performance when peoples' lives are at stake. Absent an abiding respect for life and human dignity by the health care provider, no amount of legal rights will provide quality health care.

Notes and References

1. *Le Jeune Road Hospital, Inc. v. Watson,* 171 So.2d 202 (Fla. 1965).
2. Id.; *Campbell v. Mincey* 413 F.S. 16 (D.C. Miss. 1975); see also, Powers, Emergency services and the open door, *Michigan Law Review* 66:1455 (1968); *Birmingham Baptist Hospital v. Crews* 229 Ala. 398, 157 So. 224 (1934).
3. *Guerrero v. Copper Queen Hospital,* 537 P. 2d 1329 (Ariz. 1975).
4. Ill. Rev. Stat. 1976 ch. 111½ § 86.
5. McKinney's Consol. Laws of N.Y., Public Health Law § 2805-b(1) and(2).
6. Cal. Health and Safety Code, § 1317 (amended 1973).
7. 42 U.S.C.S. § 2000a; see also, *Simkins v. Moses H. Cone Memorial Hospital* 323 F.2d 959 (4th Cir. 1963).
8. U.S. Internal Revenue Service, Revenue Ruling 69-545 § 501 (c) (3).
9. *Simon v. Eastern Kentucky Welfare Rights Organization,* 426 U.S. 26 (1976).
10. *Wilmington General Hospital v. Manlove,* 54 Del. 15, 174 A.2d 135 (1961).
11. *Bourgeois v. Dade County,* 99 So.2d 575 (Fla. 1956).
12. *O'Neill v. Montefiore Hospital,* 11 App. Civ. 2d 132, 202 N.Y.S. 2d 436 (1960).
13. *New Biloxi Hospital v. Frazier,* 245 Miss. 185, 146 So.2d 882 (1962); *Citizen's Hospital Association v. Schoulin,* 262 So.2d 203 (Ala. App. 1972).
14. *Jones v. New York Hospital for Joint Diseases,* 134 N.Y.S. 2d 779 (1954), rev'd on other grounds, 286 App. Div. 825, 143 N.Y.S. 2d 628.
15. *Capps v. Valk,* 189 Kan. 287, 369 P.2d 238 (1962).
16. *Meiselman v. Crown Heights Hospital,* 285 N.Y. 389, 34 N.E.2d 367 (1941).
17. Annas George J., *The Rights of Hospital Patients* (New York: Avon Books, 1975), p. 96.
18. *Meiselman v. Crown Heights Hospital, supra.*
19. *Doan v. Griffith,* 402 S.W.2d 855 (Ky. 1966).
20. *Gadsden General Hospital v. Hamilton,* 103 So. 553 (1925).
21. Annas, *The Rights of Hospital Patients, supra at 52.*
22. *Meiselman v. Crown Heights Hospital, supra.*

CHAPTER 2

Medical Records: The Right to Access and Privacy

MEDICAL RECORDS

At the time of a patient's discharge, questions of financial responsibility and access to hospital records often given rise to controversy. As has been noted previously, a hospital cannot detain a person merely because the hospital bill has not been paid and no third-party payer appears to have responsibility. Such detention by the hospital would be, under the law, a false imprisonment.

Contrary to the law covering emergency situations, a hospital may withhold nonemergency services until a deposit is secured or some proof of payment by a third party is presented. Legislation has been enacted in some states to insure that public (not-for-profit or county) hospitals and physicians working within such institutions have protection by means of liens.

A lien is an interest in property that must be satisfied before the property can be traded or sold. Under the law, a lien is said to "attach" to the property. Some examples are mechanics' liens on equipment, plumbers' or carpenters' liens on buildings, and hotel liens on guests' baggage. A hospital's or a physician's lien attaches to any judgment, verdict, or decree of a court or a compromise settlement awarding money damages to the patient. If a person is injured in an automobile accident and is treated in a county hospital and the medical expenses are not paid in full, the physician or hospital, by following established civil procedure, can have a lien attached on any judgment or settlement the injured party may receive from the other driver, the person whose negligence caused the accident, or his insurance carriers. In Illinois, the total amount of all liens cannot exceed one-third of the sum paid to the injured party.[1] In addition to the lien procedures, the hospital or physician can bring suit to collect the funds directly from the patient.

Hospitals may also validly charge patients for a copy of their hospital bill, as an Illinois attorney-patient discovered after an unsuccessful court battle waged in protest against the $5.00 fee he was required to pay as a condition for receiving a copy of his hospital bill.[2]

Patient's Access to Medical Records

Patients request examinations of their medical records for a wide variety of reasons, ranging from curiosity to the discovery of grounds for a malpractice action against the physician or hospital. The relevant issues regarding the viewing of medical records are the right to access as opposed to the confidentiality afforded medical records.

Hospitals accredited by the Joint Commission on Accreditation of Hospitals (JCAH), a private accreditation agency, are required to record all necessary and pertinent identification information, consent forms, medical histories, physical-examination and laboratory reports, all diagnostic and therapeutic orders, notes on observation of the patient's condition and progress, and reports on treatments and consultations. They must include all preoperative, operative, and postoperative reports and all conclusions and the diagnosis. State statutes and hospital licensing regulations also mandate the contents of hospital records.

Because of the confidentiality basic to the physician-patient relationship, access to these records is restricted. The relationship is said to be fiduciary, one of trust, where, because of the respective inequality in knowledge, the patient is placed in a dependent position. Thus, the physician has the fiduciary duty to treat interactions with patients confidentially.

This relationship has been protected by the courts in the handling of evidence at trial, by providing a physician-patient privilege that prohibits the court from receiving as evidence facts learned in the physician-patient relationship. This is like the privilege enjoyed in the attorney-client and clergyman-penitent situations. The physician is not allowed to testify in court regarding any information gleaned from the diagnosis or treatment of that patient without the patient's express permission. The privilege belongs to the patient, as a means of providing the confidentiality of the relationship, so that the patient will openly disclose all information necessary for the physician to provide adequate treatment.

Because of this confidentiality, access to medical records, which contain much of this confidential communication between the physician and the patient, is restricted by the written, express direction of the patient. A waiver of this privilege occurs when the patient causes a lawsuit to be filed which places in issue his physical condition.

Medical records are, in fact, the property of the hospital, while the information contained in them is subject to the property right of the patient. A hospital could not function properly without the ability to keep its records intact and available for various administrative and substantive purposes. Thus, only the copies of these original records or summaries of the information contained in them need be passed on to those interested parties who have a right to them.

X-rays (roentgenograms) are owned by the radiologist or the hospital where they were produced. A patient has no legal right to see them or have a copy of the x-ray unless a written agreement to the contrary has been executed beforehand.[3] Many states, however, have enacted statutes that provide the patient with the right to view and obtain copies of x-rays. Ownership does provide immunity to subpoena. Thus, it is usually the right of the radiologist to dispense the films and his reports to the physician at the patient's request, and all films are considered on loan when they leave the office.

The rationale of this principle of ownership is to preserve the records of the radiologist in the event his diagnosis or findings are challenged. Also, unlike the situation where a person has a photograph taken, when a patient has x-rays taken he is seeking advice and opinion and not ownership of the negative.[4]

While the hospital owns the medical records, some courts have held that a duty exists to disclose relevant information to the patient or his physician or attorney on request. Most states, however, allow access to medical records only through the subpoena process whereby the court orders the records produced after a lawsuit is instituted.

The records must be relevant to the suit. Some states require hospitals to furnish patients with copies of their records, on their written authorization.[5] Almost all hospitals will copy a patient's records for a physician with the patient's written permission.

Court decisions regarding access to hospital records demonstrate the diversity of approaches to this issue from state to state. In Texas, an appellate court found a common-law right of a patient to inspect his own medical records, whereas a member of the public (other than the patient) would be precluded from doing so by statute.[6] An opposite result appeared in a New York case, where a district court upheld a hospital's denial of mental health records to a patient.[7] The woman requested her records for the purpose of writing a book about her hospital experiences. The court found no statute recognizing an unrestricted property right to mental health records nor any deprivation of constitutional rights in denying access to the records in the absence of good cause. New York's statute regarding release of medical records applies only where a physician or another hospital requests the records with written authorization from the patient or the patient's legal guardian.[8] Thus, a patient's request or his attorney's request for access to medical records for his own information is not governed by statute and is left to the discretion of the hospital or a court of law in the event a subpoena is requested for the records.

Illinois, as mentioned previously, takes a different approach, permitting broad access to medical records by the patient and his physician or attorney.[9] Illinois courts have followed an earlier decision of the United States Court of Appeals, District of Columbia Circuit, which determined that the fiduciary characteristics of the physician-patient relationship placed a duty on the physician to reveal to patients what they should know in their best interest. This duty extends to the hospital, which is the repository of such knowledge.[10] Thus, in Illinois, if hospital authorities in private or public hospitals refuse to allow a patient or the patient's physician or attorney to examine and copy the medical records, a cause of action can be maintained against them for breach of their statutory duty.[11]

Of course, while a patient is still hospitalized, all hospital personnel involved in the patient's treatment must have access to the medical records. Such permission is implied by the patient's presence in the hospital under the staff's care. The patient's written permission is needed, however, for the release of confidential information from the medical records to any other person, including the patient's spouse. Exceptions are for minors and incompetents.

Statutory exceptions also exist for reporting the following information to the police or public health officials: dangerous diseases, acute poisoning, child abuse, motor-vehicle accidents, and firearm and knife wounds. Many states also require that venereal diseases, chronic drug addiction, and other public health problems be reported to the local and state departments of health.

Disclosures from Medical Records

Along with access to medical records, the extent of disclosure is an important issue. Patients have a right to privacy with regard to the facts of their personal life revealed in these records. The right of privacy is a right that has developed recently from old roots. This right was first referred to in 1890 in a *Harvard Law Review* article concerning the right to privacy at common law.[12]

Historically, the first major decision with regard to this right appeared in 1965, with the Supreme Court decision declaring unconstitutional a Connecticut statute banning the use of contraceptives by married persons, as well as prohibiting the aiding or abetting of such use.[13] In this decision (*Griswold v. Connecticut*) the court found a zone of privacy emanating from from the First, Third, and Fifth Amendments to the Constitution, into which the government could not intrude without some compelling justification or the person's consent. Thus, a "legal island of personal autonomy" and intimacy was recognized extending the common-law torts of physician intrusion upon seclusion and solitude to a constitutionally protected right of privacy.[14]

The right of privacy has blossomed from its humble beginnings in the discussion in the 1890 article to an important right people often assert to protect their private lives. In *Roe v. Wade*, the Supreme Court further extended this right in terms of autonomy, intimacy, and identity to "encompass a woman's decision whether or not to terminate her pregnancy."[15] The right to privacy with regard to information has been asserted more frequently in the past several years and has carried over into patients' rights with a concern to protect the confidentiality of the physician-patient relationship as pertaining to a patient's medical records.

The duty not to disclose confidential information concerning patients is set out in the Hippocratic Oath, taken by many physicians upon entering the medical profession: "*Whatsoever I see or hear concerning the life of man, in any attendance on the sick or even apart therefrom; which ought not to be noised about, I will keep silent thereon, counting such things to be professional secrets.*"[16]

The American Medical Association, in their "Principles of Ethics," address this topic as follows:

A physician may not reveal the confidences entrusted to him in the course of medical attendance, or the deficiencies he may observe in the character of patients, unless he is required to do so by law or unless it becomes necessary in order to protect the welfare of the individual or the community.[17]

A recent case illustrates the concern with privacy in the treatment of medical records. A psychiatrist's book was published eight years after he terminated the treatment of several patients. He reported their thoughts, feelings, emotions, sexual fantasies, biographies, intimate personal relationships, and the disintegration of their marriages. Although the patients' names were withheld and no pictures were used, a New York court found a breach of privacy based on both public policy and the implied promise of confidentiality that exists between a physician and his patients. The court went on to say that although in some cases there is a valid purpose for confidential disclosures to public agencies as for communicable diseases or gunshot wounds, the curiosity or the education of the medical profession has never superseded this duty of confidentiality.[18]

Such unauthorized use of a patient's records may give rise to a cause of action for libel. In a 1958 Utah case, the Supreme Court reversed a lower-court decision and granted the plaintiff a new trial to prove that the unauthorized submission of information about the plaintiff, a former patient of the psychiatrist-defendant, constituted libel.

In this case, the parents of the prospective bride of the plaintiff became concerned about their future son-in-law's character after finding out he had been a patient of a psychiatrist. They prompted a doctor friend to write to the psychiatrist-defendant to obtain information about their future son-in-law. The psychiatrist answered the letter stating that the man was a manic-depressive psychopath, gambled, never supported his former wife or children, and was an irresponsible and unsavory character.

He went on to add, "My suggestion to the infatuated girl would be to run as fast and as far as she possibly could in any direction away from him. Of course, if he doesn't marry her, he will marry someone else and make life hell for that person." The psychiatrist had an incredible recall, considering that he had not seen the patient for seven years, and in fact had seen him professionally only a few times. The psychiatrist's defense to the charge was that all the statements were true. The plaintiff-patient, however, was allowed the opportunity to prove the statements false and maintain an action for damages.

Several cases have arisen with respect to public law and medical privacy. In Pennsylvania, plaintiffs successfully blocked a school program that used psychological testing to identify eighth-grade students who were potential drug abusers. Part of this controversial program included compulsory counseling to modify the behavior of those students identified as part of the high-risk group.[19] In another case, physicians and patients were unsuccessful in their attempts to strike down a New York City ordinance requiring that abortion patients have their names and addresses put on "termination of pregnancy" certificates, which were later filed in a central registry.[20]

A patient need not have his case history delved into by anyone except the physician or other members of the medical staff involved in his care and treatment. The American Hospital Association (AHA), in its "Patient's Bill of Rights," declares that the patient has the right to every consideration of privacy in the medical care program and to confidential treatment of all communications and records pertaining to his care.

Aside from case law and hospital policy, many states have passed legislation dictating confidential treatment of medical records and other communications between physicians and patients. Many of these statutes apply to evidence admissible in a courtroom. There is said to be a physician-patient privilege available to a patient whereby he can refuse to disclose and prevent anyone else from disclosing a confidential communication between himself and his physician. In California, such a confidential communication includes any information obtained in a physical examination of the patient and the diagnosis and advice given by the physician.[21] In Illinois there are seven exceptions in the statute defining this privilege:

1) *in trials for homicide when the disclosure relates directly to the fact or immediate circumstances of the homicide;*

2) *in actions, civil or criminal, against the physician for malpractice;*

3) *with the expressed consent of the patient, or in case of his death or disability, of his personal representative or other*

person authorized to sue for personal injury or of the beneficiary of an insurance policy on his life, health, or physical condition;

4) *in all civil suits brought by or against the patient, his personal representative, a beneficiary under a policy of insurance, or the executor or adminstrator of his estate wherein the patient's physical or mental condition is an issue;*

5) *upon an issue as to the validity of a document as a will of the patient;*

6) *in any criminal action where the charge is either murder by abortion, attempted abortion or abortion; or*

7) *in actions, civil or criminal, arising from the filing of a report in compliance with the "Abused and Neglected Child Reporting Act," enacted by the 79th General Assembly.*[22]

As for medical records, most statutes protect the right of privacy by limiting access to the records without written authorization of the patient.[23] A New York statute words it this way: "An unwarranted invasion of personal privacy includes, but shall not be limited to... disclosures of items involving the medical or personal records of a client or patient in a medical facility."[24]

Another New York statute permits medical records to be released only upon the written authorization of the patient, or parent or guardian of a child or incompetent, and only to another physician or hospital. It also provides that information about any treatment for venereal disease or the performance of an abortion on a minor patient shall not be released or in any way made available to the patient's parent or guardian.[25]

Of particular concern are mental health records, which most states deal with separately in the mental health section of their statutes. Confidentiality is most important in mental health treatment. For the relationship between a psychiatrist or psychologist and a patient to be at all effective, an open flow of communication is necessary. Unless a person has assurance that his most private expressions are kept in strict confidence, the requisite openness will be difficult to establish or maintain.

Interesting cases have arisen over confidentiality in the psychiatrist-patient relationship. Some psychiatrists feel more strongly about the privilege than patients do, although most courts have held that the privilege exists for the benefit of the patient and not to protect the therapist. One psychiatrist was jailed for contempt when he refused to disclose any mental health records or even admit that the plaintiff in a lawsuit had been his patient. The plaintiff did not claim the privilege here. In fact, in the course of a deposition, the plaintiff lost the privilege when he put into issue the very information the psycho-therapist refused to disclose. The California Supreme Court refused to allow the psychotherapist to assert the confidentiality privilege unilaterally, for fear a patient might not be able to waive the privilege if it were advantageous for him or her to do so. The court required only a very limited admission, that of the existence of the relationship itself, thus preserving the confidentiality of subsequent communications.[26]

Release forms, waiving a patient's privilege, are construed strictly against the drafter of the form. To release mental health information, the form must refer specifically to such records. If a form authorizes a doctor or hospital to release records regarding a patient's "physical condition" or "treatment rendered," the court will deem the psychotherapist-patient privilege not to have been waived.[27] Nevertheless, where a patient is involved in a lawsuit and brings his mental condition into issue, for example, by suing for damages for emotional or mental distress or pleading insanity as a defense, the patient or therapist cannot invoke the privilege.[28]

Patients have increasingly fought for and won the right to compel disclosure and to protect confidentiality of medical records about both physical and mental health. Thus, both the right of access to a patient's medical records and, on the other hand, an increased right to privacy in the way information in those records is treated have become stronger as patients have asserted their rights more frequently.

The advent of computerized records has brought concern about confidentiality and privacy into focus. The advantages of computerization are great. Records previously spread out over doctors' offices, hospitals, and clinics can be conveniently linked to increase the quality and consistency of a patient's medical care. Prescriptions can be compared more easily against average dosage levels. Files can be scanned quickly to find patients who are susceptible to certain diseases.

One of the main problems with computerized systems for medical records is that they are too costly to maintain for a single purpose. There is economic pressure to use large-scale computerization of records for purposes other than direct patient care including policy analysis, financial accounting, and biomedical research.[29] Thus, confidential treatment of information in medical records dictated by common law and state statutes cannot be insured in such a system.

One author discusses a computerized data bank operated by Medical Information Bureau (MIB), which is a trade association of over 700 life insurance companies.[30] Most of the insurers have a computer terminal in their offices. For a nominal fee, an inquiry can search directly any one of over 12 million health records. Insurance companies may be examining distorted data. Health data that comes directly from an applicant may be distorted because of his desire to withhold data that might raise the insurance rates. Likewise, an insurance agent, eager to get a commission, may distort data in his desire to make sure the client is insurable.

Aside from using these data gathered directly from applicants, MIB employs the Retail Credit Company to gather more information concerning the applicants' finances, health history, profession, and alcohol consumption. This information may be inaccurate and may have damaging effects on an applicant's chances of obtaining not only life insurance, but also credit and other insurance.

This is just one illustration of how dealing with large-scale computer services can subject medical information to a wide range of sources that may have adverse effects on a person and a loss of confidential treatment of this information.

Information systems run by federal agencies or government contractors performing an agency function (as Medicare) are governed by the Privacy Act of 1974.[31] The act attempts to assure public accountability of system operations and avoid the growth of secret-data systems by requiring the agencies to publish annual notices in the *Federal Register* describing the general characteristic of their data systems. Such agencies must give notice to individuals who are data subjects of the following: (1) the source of the agency's authority to collect personal information, (2) the uses to be made of this information, (3) the consequences to the subject for refusal to supply the requested data, and (4) the agency's rules regarding disclosure of the data to other sources.

The data subject has a right to find out whether an agency has information about him, to gain access to the records, and to obtain a copy.[32]

The Privacy Act establishes four actions for civil remedies:

1) An individual can bring an action to compel production of his record if he is refused access, and the burden is on the agency to sustain its refusal; 2) A subject can obtain a trial de novo if the agency refuses to amend the record which the person claims is inaccurate and the court may order the record amended; 3) the subject can obtain damages for other violations; 4) if an individual is injured because the agency failed to maintain records with such accuracy, relevance, timeliness, and completeness as necessary to assure fairness, he can recover actual damages, costs and attorney's fees if he can show the action was intentional or willful.[33]

Thus, while the computerized medical records have acted to diminish the right of privacy, federal legislation is attempting to control and remedy the situation.

OTHER RIGHTS TO PRIVACY AND CONFIDENTIALITY

Aside from the right of privacy in treatment of medical records, confidentiality must likewise be afforded in consultation, examination, and treatment of the patient. The patient has the right to considerate and respectful care as well. People do not have to subject themselves to dehumanization merely because they find themselves as patients. Both physicians and nurses are compelled by professional ethics to treat their patients with the dignity and respect they are due as human beings. The American Hospital Association's "Patient's Bill of Rights" states: "The patient has the right to every consideration of his privacy concerning his own medical care program. Case discussion, consultation, examination, and treatment are confidential and should be conducted discreetly. Those not directly involved in his care must have the permission of the patient to be present."

Teaching hospitals are often the scene of much abuse in this area, as physicians appear at the bedsides of their patients with an army of interns or student nurses to poke, prod, and gape at the "disease" occupying the bed. At some county hospitals, young medical students bring their dates along to watch a delivery. Even at a teaching hospital, a patient must give express permission under the AHA "Patient's Bill of Rights" before his case can be presented to "outsiders."[34] Annas points out some of the rights of hospital patients:

As a patient in a hospital you have the following rights based on the right of privacy:

1) *to refuse to see anyone or all visitors;*
2) *to refuse to see anyone not officially connected with the hospital;*
3) *to refuse to see persons officially connected with the hospital who are not directly involved in the patient's care and treatment;*
4) *to refuse to see social workers and to forbid them to view his records;*
5) *to wear your own bedclothes so long as they do not interfere with your treatment;*
6) *to wear religious medals, etc.;*
7) *to have a person of your own sex present during a physical examination by a medical professional of the opposite sex;*
8) *not to remain disrobed any longer than is necessary for accomplishing the medical purpose for which you were asked to disrobe;*
9) *not to have the case discussed openly in the hospital;*
10) *to have your medical records read only by those directly involved in their treatment or monitoring of its quality;*
11) *to insist on being transferred to another room if the person sharing it with you will not let you alone or is disturbing you unreasonably by smoking or other actions.*[35]

Notes and References

1. Ill. Rev. Stat. 1976 ch. 82 § 97 et seq.
2. *Rabens v. Jackson Park Hospital Foundation,* 40 Ill. App. 3d 113, 351 N.E.2d 276 (1976).

3. Annas, George J., *The Rights of Hospital Patients* (New York: Avon Books, 1975), p. 115.
4. Id. at 82.
5. Ill. Rev. Stat. ch. 51 § 71 et seq.
6. *Hutchins v. Rehabilitation Commission* 544 S.W.2d 802 (Civ. App. Tex. 1976).
7. *Gotkin v. Miller*, C.A. N.Y., 1975, 514 F.2d 125 (1975).
8. McKinney's Consol. Laws of N.Y. vol. 44 § 17 1977.
9. Ill. Rev. Stat. 1976 ch. 51 § 71 et seq.
10. *Emmett v. Eastern Dispensary and Casualty Hospital*, 396 F.2d 931 (D.C. Cir. 1967).
11. *Rabens v. Jackson Park Hospital Foundation*, supra: *Cannell v. Medical and Surgical Clinic*, 21 Ill. App. 3d 383, 315 N.E.2d 278 (1974).
12. Warren, Samuel D., and Brandeis, Louis D. Harvard Law Review, 193, 1890.
13. *Griswold v. Connecticut*, 381 U.S. 479 (1965).
14. Gerety, Redefining privacy, *Harvard Law Review*, 12:217, 1977.
15. *Roe v. Wade*, 410 U.S. 113, 153 (1973).
16. *Hippocratic Oath*, quoted in Annas, *Rights of Hospital Patients*, supra at p. 125.
17. American Medical Association, "Principles of Ethics," quoted in Annas, id. at 125.
18. *Doe v. Roe*, (N.Y. Sup. Ct. 1977). 46 Law Week 2301.
19. *Merriken v. Cressman*, 364 F. Supp. 913 (E.D. Pa. 1973).
20. *Schulman v. New York City Health and Hospital Corporation*, 44 App. Div. 2d 482, 355 N.Y.S. 2d 781 (1st Dept. 1974).
21. Cal. Evidence Code vol 29B § 992, 994.
22. Ill. Rev. Stat. 1976 ch. 51 § 5.1.
23. Ill. Rev. Stat. 1976 ch. 51 § 71 et seq.
24. McKinney's Consol. Laws of N.Y., Public Officer's Law, book 46 § 89 (b)(ii).
25. McKinney's Consol. Laws of N.Y., Public Health Law, vol. 44 § 17.
26. *In re Lifschutz*, 2 Cal. 3d 415 (Cal. 1970); discussed in Bernstein, Law in brief, *Hospitals J.A.H.A.* 47(19):100, Oct. 1, 1973.
27. *Roberts v. Superior Court*, 9 Cal. 3d 330 (Cal. 1973).
28. *Hall v. Alameda County*, Super. Ct. 20 Cal. App. 3d 652 (1971).
29. Creighton, Helen, The diminishing right to privacy: computerized medical records, *Supervisor Nurse* 9(2):58–61, Feb. 1978.
30. Boyer, Barry B., Computerized medical records and the right to privacy: the emerging federal response, *Buffalo Law Review* 25:37, 49, 1975.
31. United States Privacy Act of 1974, 88 Stat. 1897.
32. 5 U.S.C.A. § 552 (a) (f) (1); see also, Creighton, The diminishing right to privacy, supra.
33. Creighton, id. at 60.
34. Annas, *The Rights of Hospital Patients*, supra at 132.
35. Id. at 131–32.

CHAPTER 3

Informed Consent and the Right to Refuse Treatment and Experimentation

The foundation for the right to an informed consent, to refuse treatment, and to refuse to take part in experimentation lies in the concept of inviolability of the person, a legal concept that preceded and became the basis of the right to privacy. The law protects individuals from nonconsensual contact or battery by imposing civil or criminal liability or both on the one who makes such contact. The remedy afforded the victim-plaintiff is money damages, paid by the defendant, who may also be subject to criminal fine or imprisonment depending on the seriousness of the harm to the victim.

INFORMED CONSENT

The protection afforded individuals from nonconsensual contact is carried over into the area of medical treatment by the requirement that before a physician begins a treatment plan that may involve some risk to the patient, the risks and the alternatives must be disclosed to the patient. A patient's voluntary, understanding, and competent *consent* is required before a physician can proceed with the treatment or operation. The rationale behind this doctrine of informed consent was stated by one court:

> Anglo-American law starts with the premise of thorough-going self determination. It follows that each man is considered to be master of his own body, and he may, if he be of sound mind, expressly prohibit the performing of life-saving surgery, or other medical treatment. A doctor might well believe that an operation or form of

treatment is desirable or necessary, but the law does not permit him to substitute his own judgment for that of the patient by any form of artifice of deception.[1]

The basic elements of an informed consent are voluntariness, competency, and knowledge. "The Nuremberg Code" addresses the element of voluntariness:

[T]he persons involved... should be so situated as to be able to exercise a free power of choice, without the intervention of any element of force, fraud, deceit, duress, over-reaching or other ulterior forms of constraint or coercion; and should have sufficient knowledge and comprehension of the subject matter involved so as to enable him to make an understanding and enlightened decision.[2]

For consent to be voluntary, the patient must feel that he or she has a real choice whether to agree to the treatment, free from any physical or psychological coercion. The element of voluntariness is an important issue when determining whether patients who are prisoners are capable of giving true informed consent, with all the intense pressures on them to conform to the wishes of the prison officials.

For consent to be competent, a patient must be an adult, of sound mind, and legally and mentally capable of making a decision that will affect his physical well-being. A drugged or drunk person or a child in most situations is incompetent to consent to a medical procedure that carries any risk of serious bodily harm or death.

The third and final element for an informed consent is that the patient must have adequate knowledge concerning the disease or infirmity and the treatment prescribed. The United States Department of Health, Education, and Welfare has published the following regulations stipulating the amount of knowledge necessary to be imparted to the patient:

1. A fair explanation of the proceaures to be followed and their purposes, including an identification of those that are experimental;
2. A description of any expected discomfort and risk;
3. A description of the benefits of the treatment;
4. A disclosure of appropriate alternative procedures.[3]

Thus, both the content of the disclosures and the context surrounding the expression of consent are important in determining whether a patient has given informed consent. The philosophy behind informed consent is that the patient has the right and responsibility to determine whether he wishes to risk the corrective treatment or operation. If a patient's decision is to be intelligent, he must understand both the risks and the results of the failure to undergo treatment.

The doctrine of informed consent has generated scores of articles and case law, mostly in the past 15 years, during which the term became firmly entrenched in medicolegal jargon.[4] The courts have generally agreed that the basis for obtaining a patient's consent before treatment lies in the individual's right to the inviolability of his person. Without such consent, a physician or hospital may be found guilty of battery, negligence, or breach of a fiduciary duty. The majority of courts award damages on the grounds of negligence where there is a failure adequately to inform a patient of alternatives and risks to the prescribed treatment.

Because of the resulting liability of the hospital and physician for negligence, battery, or breach of fiduciary duty, depending on the jurisdiction, the patient's consent for any operation or major treatment program is secured in writing by means of a consent form, which becomes part of the hospital records. Oral consent is effective but difficult to prove.

For a consent form for an operation to be valid, it must designate with some specificity the nature of the operation. Courts give no weight to a consent form that authorizes a surgeon to do any medical or surgical procedure he believes to be in the patient's best interst. Such a form is considered "blanket consent" and is invalid.[5] In addition, a patient cannot, on such a form, waive his right to sue for negligence.[6]

There are two exceptions to disclosing inherent risks before securing consent: one in certain emergency conditions, the other where risk-disclosure poses a threat to the patient.

The first is an emergency situation where a patient is unconscious or otherwise incapable of consenting, and failure to treat would cause imminent risk of death or such serious bodily harm that the risk would outweigh any harm threatened by the proposed treatment. If there is a relative available to consent for the patient, the physician or hospital employee should attempt to secure his or her consent.[7] If the relative refuses to consent to lifesaving treatment in an emergency, the physician or hospital authorities may petition a court to order the treatment.

The interplay between the concepts of consent and emergency has required courts to strike a delicate balance between the patient's right to choose the treatment he wishes to undergo and the freedom of the physician to follow the dictates of his ethical convictions and to practice responsible medicine without fear of frequent litigation.[8] Many states have passed "Good Samaritan" statutes to protect physicians and nurses from liability for giving first-aid and emergency treatment without a patient's consent. Unfortunately, such measures have been deemed necessary to prompt the members of the medical profession to follow the dictates of medical ethics.

The second exception for informed consent exists where risk disclosures poses such a detriment to the physical condition or well-being or both of the patient as to constitute unsound medical practice. This exception arises when the physician can reasonably predict from past experiences with a patient that the patient would become so emotionally distraught by a disclosure of the risks that he would be unable to make a rational decision about a medical procedure. In such a case, courts have armed the physician with the privilege of keeping the information from the patient.[9] The physician may not remain silent simply because divulgence might prompt the patient to forego the therapy. Also, as in an emergency situation, disclosure to a close relative to secure consent may be necessary if one is available.[10]

Many physicians try to extend this second exception broadly. If a patient sues, the usual result is the physician's being found liable for failure to secure the person's informed consent. Many physicians believe that the average patient is not capable of understanding various procedures and is too suspicious to consent to a procedure that carries any risk, after having been informed of those risks. Testimony from a plastic surgeon reflects the feelings of many doctors as to risk disclosure:

> Now, if we go into risks involved, I would be talking the rest of the day about the risks... risks are minimal, and they are never mentioned to a patient.... A patient would walk out of everybody's office if you say there is a danger of anything. This is never done.... It is not good practice to frighten a patient by telling them a dozen different things that might happen as a result of dermabrasion.[11]

Despite this surgeon's testimony, the Supreme Court of Washington State found that the patient, a Korean woman who had undergone dermabrasion to remove facial scarring and discoloration, presented a prima facie case of medical malpractice, because the surgeon had not disclosed the probability of success or failure.

Litigation brought by patients for failure to secure their informed consent has been abundant. The complaints range from allegations that the operation went beyond the scope of the consent given (e.g., an appendix was removed when consent was given for an exploratory operation) to the patient's not having been made aware of the risks. Sometimes, surgical untoward effects become grounds for litigation, as in allegations that no mention was made that the operation might not be successful.

Courts, depending on the jurisdiction, generally use one of two inconsistent tests to determine if disclosures are legally sufficient: an objective test and a subjective test.

The majority of courts use an objective test whereby the standard for disclosure is the disclosure practices of other competent surgeons. Thus, the standard is set by other physicians in that locale.

Applying the objective test, a Massachusetts court found in favor of a physician who performed an appendectomy but left a portion under one inch in length. The patient-plaintiff produced an expert witness who testified that it was standard appendectomy procedure to remove the organ completely, leaving no stump or vestige. The court found that this testimony did not prove the "knowledge and understanding in

1949 of members of the medical profession in the community about the extent of risk to the patient involved where a small vestige of the appendix was not removed."[12] The patient's failure to satisfy the burden of proving such current medical standards in the community for risk disclosure caused the plaintiff to lose this case.[13]

Fewer courts use a subjective test, which focuses on a particular patient's needs. The patient-plaintiff needs only to convince the jury that his consent would have been withheld had the physician provided certain information describing the risk or consequence that in fact materialized, even if remote and not ordinarily discussed.[14]

The dermabrasion case demonstrates this second test. The plaintiff successfully sued the plastic surgeon for malpractice, after having undergone long and intensely painful recovery, only to find that her face was even more severely discolored than before. The surgeon had failed to inform her that the probability of success was only 50 percent generally and was even lower for Orientals. The court did not determine a recognized medical standard for disclosure of dermabrasion risks. The court found that where an elective operation is for improvement of appearance only, the necessity for disclosure is too clear to require medical testimony to establish it.[15]

Likewise, in a case where the patient died from a thyroid operation and informed consent was questionable, the court determined that disclosure of alternative treatment necessarily includes the alternatives applicable to that particular patient's own particular circumstances.[16]

Some general principles concerning informed consent can be gleaned from the many cases in this area:

1. The person actually administering the test or treatment must obtain the patient's informed consent.
2. The physician has the duty to disclose the probable consequences of the treatment and the dangers incident to it.[17]
3. An informed consent is necessary where there is any risk of death or serious bodily harm or where the probability of success is low.[18]
4. The duty to disclose the potential of death or serious bodily harm should be explained in lay terms, so that the patient is adequately informed.[19]
5. The duty to disclose is a function of the patient's right of self-decision, measured by whatever information is reasonably necessary for that patient to make a decision.[20]
6. The more elective a treatment, the more disclosure is necessary.
7. There is no duty to disclose risks that would so alarm a patient as to constitute bad medical practice.[21]
8. Where a reasonable person would have consented to the operation or treatment even if informed of such risks, there is no liability on the part of the physician or surgeon.[22]

9. No liability will result for the physician for lack of written consent where the patient knows the general course of the treatment and the risks involved[23] or where relatively minor risks are involved in common procedures.[24]

Some states, Texas for one, have taken the doctrine of informed consent a step further and passed legislation defining the requisite elements and subsequent liabilities for failure to obtain an informed consent. The Texas legislature took from judges the determination of the scope of the duty to disclose by creating the Texas Medical Disclosure Panel, a panel of three lawyers and six physicians. One of their functions was to determine the medical and surgical risks that health care providers must disclose to their patients. Another was to establish the general form and substance of the disclosure, including the degree of disclosure.[25]

The panel decreed that consent for those treatments found to require disclosure must be given in writing, signed by the patient or the person authorized to consent for the patient (as with minors or incompentents), and a witness. Where the panel has dictated the form and degree of disclosure, the form and content must be incorporated into the consent form. Where they have set no requirements, the physician or health care provider is under the duty imposed by law.

Texas limits the theory of legal recovery to negligence for failure to disclose the risks or hazards that would have influenced a reasonable person while making a decision to consent. Thus, the other grounds of recovery previously mentioned, battery or breach of fiduciary duty, are not recognized in this jurisdiction.

Aside from liability to the physician, in certain circumstances a hospital may be found liable for failure of its employees to obtain an informed consent before a treatment. In most jurisdictions, where a patient makes no allegations that hospital employees acted independently without his consent, the hospital's liability will be governed by laws regarding hospital liability for the negligent acts of its medical and nonmedical personnel.[26] In a 1914 decision by the famous New York judge, Benjamin Cardozo, a hospital escaped liability for an unauthorized operation. The court determind that where there was no actual knowledge of the lack of consent for the operation, there could be no liability imposed on the hospital.[27]

In this case, a woman was admitted into a charitable hospital for a stomach disorder. The house physician discovered a lump in her left breast. She consented to an examination under ether but testified that she gave no consent for any operation. The doctors and nurse involved repudiated her testimony. Following an allegedly unauthorized removal of the lump, gangrene developed in the patient's left arm. Consequently, several fingers had to be amputated.

The patient sued the hospital for pain and suffering and compensation for the loss of her fingers. In holding for the hospital, the court rationalized that (1) charitable institutions are not liable for the negligence of physicians and nurses in patient care; and (2) under an agency theory, a physician is an independent contractor, liable for his own wrongs, but the hospital is not liable provided he was hired with due care.

A New York court reiterated this view in 1967. An orthopedic specialist used a radical and relatively novel operation to alleviate a 14-year-old boy's scoliosis. He had developed the operation, called a spinal-jack, and had performed it 35 times with questionable success. One patient had died and four others had experienced serious complications.

The procedure was a radical departure from the usual treatment of spinal fusion, but if successful, should have shortened the convalescent time a great deal. The boy died of a massive hemorrhage 18 days after the five-and-one-half-hour operation.

The jury found the surgeon liable on the grounds that he had never explained sufficiently to the child's mother the hazards and the novelty of the operation, the available alternatives, or the risk of death. The court stated the common-law rule that the plaintiff must establish that the hospital was guilty of malpractice through its *own* agents, because the physician was an independently retained healer. A hospital's liability was limited unless authorities had reason to know that the act of malpractice would take place. The court determined the physician-patient relationship to be an independent one into which the hospital should not meddle. The court, however, alluded to the fact that if the operation were per se an act of malpractice, the hospital might share in the responsibility of advising the patient of the novelty and the risks attending the procedure.[28]

Another New York case determined that the liability is limited by the actual damages when a hospital participates in a nonconsensual operation. Thus, if the treatment is necessary and beneficial to the patient, he can recover only a small amount, or nominal damages.[29]

One recent case, *Darling v. Charleston Community Memorial Hospital*, reversed the trend of not imposing liability on a hospital for the acts of physicians and nurses.[30] The court imposed liability on a hospital for the negligent application of a plaster cast to a broken leg. But in this case, the attending medical and nursing personnel aside from the physician who applied the cast were also negligent. The cast prevented adequate circulation. Resultant swelling and hemorrhaging led to a leg amputation.

The Illinois Supreme Court held that the jury verdict of negligence for the hospital was supportable on either of the plaintiff's theories: (1) that the defendant hospital was negligent in permitting that particular doctor to do orthopedic work and not requiring him to bring his operative procedures up-to-date, and (2) by failing through its medical and nursing staff to adequately supervise the patient. The temperature and color of the toes should have been checked to evaluate the circulation of the leg, but they were not. The case did not deal in particular with informed consent. Only future litigation will show whether the trend of not holding hospitals liable where there is a lack of informed consent will be reversed.[31]

One last case, *Canterbury v. Spence*, shows the interplay of informed consent, the standard arguments physicians make to defend against disclosing risk, the factors that a court considers in deciding if disclosure was adequate, and ways a hospital may become involved in litigation.[32]

A 19-year-old boy underwent a laminectomy to correct a ruptured disk. The defendant, a neurosurgeon, had represented the spinal operation to the patient as being necessary and to his mother as being no more serious than any other operation. The youth did not object to the operation and never asked for any details. His mother signed a consent form the day of the operation but not until the operation was over. There was conflicting testimony as to the mother's having given oral consent by telephone prior to the operation.

After the operation, the patient fell while voiding unattended and became paralyzed from the waist down. A subsequent operation improved the condition somewhat. At the time of the trial, some 13 years later, the patient was still on crutches, suffering from urinary and fecal incontinence.

The neurosurgeon testified that risk of paralysis from the operation was negligible, only 1 percent. He believed it was unsound medical practice to communicate such a slight risk, because communicating risks might have deterred the patient from undergoing the needed operation and might have produced adverse psychological reactions, which in turn might have precluded the success of the operation.[33]

The Circuit Court in the District of Columbia traced the origins and rationale of the physician's duty to inform a patient of alternatives and risks of treatments available.

For liability to ensue, there must be a causal relationship between the physician's failure adequately to divulge risks and the resulting damage to the patient. The patient must prove that disclosure of the risk that materialized would have resulted in a decision against the treatment. To protect against a patient's taking a subjective hindsight approach, tinged with remorse and bitterness, this court chose an objective approach, that is, what a prudent person in the patient's condition would have decided if informed of all the significant risks.[34]

The district court determined that when the case was tried in a lower court, the jury should have been entitled to determine whether a 1 percent risk of paralysis would warrant disclosure by the defendant neurosurgeon. Also, as to the liability of the hospital, the court held that the jury should have been allowed to decide whether there was a breach of duty to exercise reasonable care for this patient's safety by providing bedrails and supervision while the patient was voiding. The court ordered a new trial wherein the doctor and hospital would have the burden of proving that they were not responsible for the harm to this patient.

The doctrine of informed consent has developed over the.years to insure a patient the freedom to decide for himself what treatment he will choose. This right is an important one and remains one of the strongest grounds for litigation in negligence actions. This right also forms a foundation for the next two rights to be discussed: the right to refuse treatment, and the right to refuse to participate in experimentation.

THE RIGHT TO REFUSE TREATMENT

The right to refuse treatment has been litigated mainly by the Jehovah's Witnesses, whose religious beliefs preclude them from consenting to blood transfusions. This right follows from the doctrine of informed consent. Generally, an adult person who is conscious and competent has the legal right to refuse any medical or surgical procedure. The courts, however, have limited the right when the treatment is necessary to save that person's life.

The right of refusal is governed by state law and thus varies from state to state. There are relatively few cases in this area for several reasons. If a patient refuses to consent to a treatment or an operation that is not essential to preserve his life, it is simply not performed, or the physician or hospital risks a lawsuit for negligence or malpractice. In emergency situations, where most lifesaving treatment is administered, no consent need be obtained by the physician or hospital if the patient is unconscious and there is no other person on hand qualified to give such consent.

Thus, there is only a narrow situation in which such cases have been litigated. In these, a physician or hospital is faced with a seriously ill or dying person who is conscious and will not consent to treatment necessary to save his life. Since most people have a strong will to live, they freely give their consent for lifesaving treatment. The cases that have arisen have usually dealt with persons who have refused treatment on grounds of their religious convictions, which may call into question the right to die.

The vast majority of cases have been concerned with the refusal of blood transfusions by the Jehovah's Witnesses. The foundation of their belief that blood transfusions are impermissible is in the following quotations from the Bible:

> Hence my decision is not to trouble those from the nations who are turning to God, but to write to them to abstain from things polluted by idols and from fornication and from what is strangled and from blood. (Acts. 15:19–20)

> As for any man of the house of Israel or some alien resident who is residing as an alien in your midst, who eats any sort of blood, I shall certainly set my face against the soul that is eating the blood, and I shall indeed cut him off from among his people. (Lev. 17:10)[35]

The prohibition against the consumption of blood supersedes any dietary law. Jevohah's Witnesses see it as a sin against God that "draws upon the soul of the transgressor the enmity of God."[36]

Their refusal is based also on the substantial risk to health and life inherent in transfusions, because of the possible transmission of syphilis, malaria, hepatitis, and allergic conditions in blood from commercial blood banks.[37]

The freedom of religion in the First Amendment is one of the fundamental rights of our society and is used by such groups as the Jehovah's Witnesses to substantiate their right to refuse blood transfusions. One judge traced the history and basic principles behind this important right with these words:

> The motivating factors underlying the constitutional separation of church and State and the prohibitions against governmental interference in matters of religion emanated from the circumstances prevailing in many European countries during precolonial ages, and from the practices among the colonies themselves prior to federation. The cruel and oppressive measures adopted, and the punishments imposed to compel conformity of all religious beliefs to those held by the most numerous or powerful groups are too well known to require documentation. Even the colonial governments legislated in this area, or attempted to do so, taxing inhabitants against their will for the support of religion or a particular sect, compelling attendance at worship meetings with various penalties including death provided for those who failed or refused to comply, and punishing those nonconformists whose opinions were considered heretical. The controversy culminated in the First Amendment's guarantee to the individual of freedom from governmental domination in his religious beliefs and practices.[38]

Government interference in such freedom of religion was found necessary in certain situations when, in the words of Thomas Jefferson at the proceedings of the Virginia House of Delegates, "principles break out into overt acts against peace and good order."[39]

Courts are hesitant to intrude on the practice of a person's religious convictions, but in circumstances where the public health, welfare, or morals are endangered, such practices have not been upheld. Courts distinguish between freedom to believe, which is absolute, and freedom to act, which is not and remains subject to regulation for the protection of society.[40]

The delineation of the difference between constitutionally protected expressions of religious conviction and those acts that do not enjoy such protection is illustrated in the famous case of *Prince v. Commonwealth of Massachusetts*.[41]

In this case, the United States Supreme Court upheld a Massachusetts statute that made it a misdemeanor, as a violation of the child-labor laws, to knowingly permit a child to sell magazines on the public streets. The plaintiff, the aunt of two Jehovah's Witnesses children, was fined under the statute after her niece and nephew were caught selling *The Watchtower*, the organizational magazine, on the streets at night.

The aunt protested her arrest and fine on the grounds that such activity was protected by the freedom of religion in the First Amendment. The majority of the court, in a five-to-four decision, expressed the belief that a state action interfering with a claimed religious freedom is sustained where the state can show its necessity to protect against a "clear and present danger." Thus, although one is free to be a Jehovah's Witness, one is not free to violate child-labor laws in propagating one's religious convictions.

A more timely example of a state's restriction on acts expressing religious convictions is seen in a Pennsylvania case, where members of the Hare Krishna sect were compelled to obtain permits to solicit contributions for their group in public places such as airports. Such permits were limited to two per day and areas of solicitation were restricted to certain booths.[42]

In the majority of blood-transfusion cases, courts became involved after a patient had been hospitalized for an emergency condition and the physician or hospital authorities could not obtain consent for the treatment from either the patient or next of kin. The hospital authorities then applied for an emergency writ ordering the transfusion over the objection of the patient or family. In some cases, the courts have respected the patient's wishes finding no compelling state interest to ignore the patient's wishes. Yet where the patient was pregnant, had minor children, or was found to be incompetent to make such a decision, the courts have ordered the transfusions.

Court-Ordered Transfusions and Operations

In a 1965 New York case, the patient's husband sought an injunction ordering the blood transfusion for his wife, a mother of six. She needed blood after a Caesarian section. The judge ordered the transfusions based on his determination that she did not actually object to receiving them but was precluded by her religious beliefs from directing the use of the transfusion.[43]

In an earlier District of Columbia case, in an opinion by J. Skelly Wright, which has received wide attention, the court ordered a series of transfusion necessary to save the life of the mother of a seven-month-old child.[44] She was dying because of the quantity of blood she lost through a perforated ulcer. He based his order on a number of factors, which neatly summarize the rationale of many of the decisions in this area:

1. The woman was not in the mental condition to make her own decision;

2. A husband has no right to order doctors to treat his wife in a way that she would die;
3. A state does not allow a mother to abandon her child;
4. Where suicide is unlawful, refusal of necessary medical assistance is likewise unlawful;
5. Since the woman came to the hospital for treatment she obviously did not want to die;
6. The hospital may be exposed to civil and/or criminal liability if they let her die.

What prompts a hospital administration to seek such an order? Hospitals today require a written statement from a dying patient who refuses treatment, releasing the physician and hospital from liability for failure to institute recommended treatments to save that person's life.

In *United States v. George*, the court added another factor, that a doctor's conscience and professional oath must be respected.[45] Other courts as well have taken the view that a patient who voluntarily submits to medical care by placing herself in a hospital should not then dictate a course of treatment amounting to medical malpractice.

In New Jersey, a case concerned a 22-year-old, single woman, who had been injured in an auto accident. The patient herself, being unconscious and then extremely disoriented, was incompetent to decide about treatment. Her mother was the one who refused the treatment and signed the release-of-liability forms for the hospital and medical personnel.

The Appeals Court in New Jersey expressed this position: "The medical and nursing profession are consecrated to preserving life. That is their professional creed. To them, a failure to use simple, established procedure in the circumstances of this case would be malpractice."[46]

This case was decided after the transfusion had already been given, and the patient had survived. The court substituted the "clear and present danger test," used by the Supreme Court in *Prince v. Commonwealth of Massachusetts* (supra), for the test of a "compelling state interest in preserving life," upholding the lower court order for the transfusions.

Another case in which the court ordered the transfusions is an unusual one, which steps outside the prior case law on thinner grounds. The New York commissioner of health brought a neglect petition charging that a 15-year-old boy was neglected because his mother, a Jehovah's Witness, would not permit blood transfusions, which were necessary with an operation to correct a gross facial and neck disfiguration. The disfiguration had given the boy personality, educational, and employment problems.[47] The mother did not object to the operation but gave permission only for the use of plasma. The surgeons insisted on a consent to use blood transfusions for this major surgical procedure, which carries substantial risk.

This court used a whole new set of rights to justify the adjudication of this child as neglected and the mandate to his mother that she must permit the operation and the necessary blood transfusions, the necessity for the transfusions to be determined upon the advice and recommendation of a qualified surgeon.

This court determined that a child's life need not be in danger before a court can act to safeguard his health or general welfare. The child has the "right to live and grow up without disfigurement," and the state has the duty to protect "his right to live and grow up with a sound mind in a sound body."[48]

This case illustrates an instance in which a court went beyond a life-and-death situation to order treatment that carried with it substantial risk. This was a nonemergency situation. The child was in no danger of dying, and his sight and hearing functioned normally. This court left it up to the discretion of the surgeons involved to exercise their own professional judgment as to the nature, extent, and timing of the operations and gave the mother no choice but to consent. The case report never mentioned whether the child wanted the operations.

The court could have waited until the patient reached his majority to let him decide for himself. Apparently, the court was convinced that the psychological effects of his impairment were a major concern. This case obviously would never have come up had the patient been a competent adult, so the holding of this case cannot be extended beyond minors and incompetents, who are, for the most part, legally incapable of consenting to medical treatment.

This decision was followed by two similar rulings in Pennsylvania and New Jersey. In one case, a spinal fusion was ordered to correct defects left by poliomyelitis in a 16-year-old child, to preserve for him some chance of normal life. His mother, a Jehovah's Witness, opposed blood transfusions necessary for the operation to take place.[49] Transfusions were also ordered for an infant who was not in danger of death but would have suffered brain damage and mental retardation were they to be withheld.[50]

Two final cases demonstrate judges deciding in favor of giving patients opportunities for a longer and fuller life, overstepping the doctrine of informed consent and precedent in this area. A judge in the Pittsburgh Common Pleas Court acted without precedent and "in favor of life" by ordering the amputation of a 67-year-old man's right leg over the expressed objections of both the man and his adult daughter. Though the man's chances of recovery were slight even with the operation, the judge granted the order protecting the right to operate.[51]

In *The Matter of Eugene Weberlist*, a New York Supreme Court judge granted the physician's request to permit extensive head surgery on a mentally defective person, a resident of the Manhattan Developmental Services.[52] The patient was 22 years old at the time of the proceeding. He had been born hydrocephalic and with a cleft palate and webbed fingers and toes. The Manhattan Developmental Services had lost contact with his parents five years prior to this proceeding.

The man was severely retarded but could function somewhat normally. The proposed treatment included dental work, operations on his hands, cleft palate, and jaw, and an intracranial operation for facial restoration. This man had the potential to be educable or at least trainable, and with a change in his appearance he could possibly live a more normal life outside the institution. A guardian ad litem was appointed and, after speaking with the physician in charge and visiting the patient and observing his defects, the guardian recommended that the court authorize the operations.

The court stated that it was faced with the possibility that this patient might serve as an object for experimentation. With some reluctance, the court authorized the requested operations; because, as the judge put it, if he were in the place of the patient, he would want to have his full potential as a human being realized.[53]

Court-Upheld Right to Refuse Treatment

On the other hand, in many decisions, courts have preserved the patient's right to refuse treatment where the patient is an adult, of sound mind, and with no dependents relying on him for support. The Illinois Supreme Court, in 1965, handed down a landmark decision in this area.

The plaintiff was a Jehovah's Witness, a mother of two adult children. This woman was being treated for peptic ulcer. She had been a patient of the same physician for over two years and informed him of her religious beliefs and had signed release-of-civil-liability forms for failure to administer the transfusions. She was competent and fully informed of the hazards involved in refusing blood transfusions.

Her doctor solicited the aid of several assistant state's attorneys and the attorney for the public guardian of Cook County and petitioned the probate division of the circuit court asking for the appointment of a guardian to consent to the transfusion. The probate court ordered a conservator, who authorized blood transfusions. This was done with no notice to the patient or her family. Thus, it was after the fact that the patient appealed to have the prior orders vacated and to then ask the Illinois Supreme Court to take a stand in this matter.

The court held her constitutional rights had been abused. After reviewing the case law, the Illinois Court took the following position on the case of In re Brooks, Aste v. Brooks:

Even though we may consider appellant's beliefs unwise, foolish or ridiculous, in the absence of an overriding danger to society we may not permit interference therewith in the form of a conservatorship established in the waning hours of her life for the sole purpose of compelling her to accept medical treatment forbidden by her religious principles, and previously refused by her with full knowledge of the probable consequences. In the final analysis, what has happened here involves a judicial attempt to decide what course of action is best for a particular individual, notwithstanding that individual's contrary views based upon religious convictions. Such action cannot be constitutionally countenanced.[54]

The court went on to quote two Supreme Court decisions and comment:

[F]or the courts to attempt to distinguish between religious beliefs or practices on the ground that they are reasonable or unreasonable would be for them to embark upon a hopeless undertaking and one which would inevitably result in the end of religious liberty.... The religious freedom guaranteed by the 1st and 14th Amendments means that he shall have the right to do this, whether his belief is reasonable or not, without interference from anyone, so long as his action or refusal to act is not directly harmful to the society of which he forms a part.[55]

The makers of our Constitution... sought to protect Americans in their beliefs, their thoughts, their emotions, and their sensations. They conferred, as against the Government, the right to be let alone—the most comprehensive of rights and the right most valued by civilized man.[56]

Nothing in this utterance suggests that Justice Brandeis thought an individual possessed these rights only as to sensible beliefs, valid thoughts, reasonable emotions, or well-founded sensations. I suggest he intended to include a great many foolish, unreasonable and even absurd ideas which do not conform, such as refusing medical treatment even at great risks.[57]

A New York court likewise upheld a 23-year-old, single woman's right to not submit to transfusions. She was competent, not pregnant, and childless.[58]

Likewise, the Court of Appeals for the District of Columbia Circuit in 1972 upheld a Jehovah's Witness's right to refuse blood transfusions. A tree had fallen on him causing internal bleeding, and he found himself in the emergency room of a hospital.[59] This man was the father of two young children, but the elements of a close family relationship and a thriving family business were found as adequate support for the children. The court distinguished the situation where a patient is comatose or otherwise incompetent to make a decision to refuse lifesaving treatment. In this plaintiff's circumstances, the court stated, "it may be better to give weight to the known instinct for survival which can, in a critical situation, alter previously held convictions," and not allow other concerned persons to speak for the patient.[60]

The District of Columbia Court applied a two-part test to make their decision: (1) has the patient validly and knowingly chosen this course for his life, and (2) is there a compelling state interest that justifies overriding that decision?[61] After resolving previously that the patient fulfilled the first half of the test, the court went on to say "the role of the state... is to ensure a maximum of individual freedom of choice and conduct."[62] The court affirmed the lower court order refusing to appoint a guardian. One last point is that just prior to handing down this decision, the court had been informed that the patient had recovered and had been discharged from the hospital without receiving the transfusions.[63] Thus, as in the *Brooks* decision, which was just described, the patient had been treated or had survived before the judge determined the extent of his right to refuse treatment.

There is no telling how these decisions might have been altered had these judges been faced with a dying patient and their own personal convictions regarding the sanctity of human life. Although these opinions used rather strong, forceful language in support of their decisions, had they chosen to go the other way, such strong support could be gleaned from the numerous holdings we have discussed on the other side.

One judge faced with such a dying patient did rule similarly to these two decisions. In an unreported 1972 case, a Milwaukee judge declined to appoint a temporary guardian for a 77-year-old woman who had refused consent for the amputation of a gangrenous leg. The court noted her clear determination, although she was in a physically weakened condition, to avoid the operation. The opinion upheld the prerogative of a competent adult to make life-and-death medical decisions about her own body. The judge expressed his view that "I believe we should leave the patient depart in God's own peace." She died several weeks later.[64]

A New York court, in a 1962 decision, allowed a man to refuse blood transfusions necessary for an operation for gastrointestinal bleeding, giving him the say because ours is "a system of government which gives the greatest possible protection to the individual in the furtherance of his own desires."[65]

Treatment Against a Patient's Will

In a 1978 case, the Tennessee Court of Appeals, acting at the request of the Tennessee Department of Human Services, entered an order that a responsible person should be named and given authority to consent to the amputation of both feet of a 72-year-old woman. She was suffering from gangrene due to frostbite.[66] Such an authorization to consent to the operations would occur only on the urgent recommendation by the physicians that there was imminent danger of her dying. In the opinion, the court stated:

> The patient has not expressed a desire to die. She evidences a strong desire to live and an equally strong desire to keep her dead feet. She refuses to make a choice.
>
> If the patient would assume and exercise her rightful control over

her own destiny by stating that she prefers death to the loss of her feet, her wish would be respected. The doctors so testified, this Court so informed her; and this Court here and now reiterates its commitment to this principle.[67]

Various causes of action have arisen from the adminstration of treatment against a patient's will. In *Winters v. Miller*, a patient brought an action for damages under federal Civil Rights Statute section 1983.[68] The patient was a 59-year-old, single woman who had been involuntarily admitted to Bellevue Hospital in New York for observation after her landlord called the police because she refused to change rooms as he requested.

She gave the hospital and doctor notice that she was a Christian Scientist and refused all treatments and medications, per her religious convictions. In spite of this and over her continual objections, doctors gave her heavy doses of tranquilizers orally and intramuscularly for the one-and-one-half months she was hospitalized. She was never adjudged mentally incompetent or mentally ill by any court, but merely had been labeled to be suffering from a mental illness by two staff physicians who examined her on admittance.

The court reversed the granting of the defendant hospital's motion for summary judgment and remanded the case for a hearing on the merits, thus finding a cause of action for damages resulting from the forced medication.

The court based its holding on the grounds of freedom of religion. Before a patient's right to exercise her religious views can be infringed upon by the state, the court determined, some compelling interest must be present. The court found "no evidence... that in forcing the unwanted medication on Miss Winters the state was in any way protecting the interest of society or even any third party."[69] Thus, the court's holding points to this result: physicians and hospitals may be held liable for damages for ignoring a patient's refusal of treatment based on religious grounds.

Balancing Individual Liberty and State Interest

In all of these cases, the patients' right to refuse treatment based on their bodily integrity and religious liberty was balanced against a state interest. Cantor analyzed five separate state interests that have been weighed in this balance:

1. The preservation of society
2. The sanctity of life
3. The respect for and preservation of public morals
4. Protection of the individual against himself
5. Protection of third parties.[70]

Cantor weighs individual rights against each of the foregoing state interests. According to Cantor, the first interest, preservation of society, does not outweight bodily integrity or religious liberty. He says,

> Any significant diminution in population might be a matter of real concern, but no one has ever suggested that the volume of persons declining medical treatment constitutes a threat to the maintenance of population levels. Nor is the refusal of treatment an act likely to be widely imitated or duplicated if openly allowed, it is unlike narcotics addiction in that respect. In short, society's existence is by no means threatened by patients' refusals of treatment.[71]

The second interest, sanctity of life, is held by many to be the foundation of a free society. By denying a patient the opportunity to choose death, the court supposedly promotes a general respect for life. Cantor counters this argument by saying that an individual's right to refuse treatment represents a deeply personal or religious conviction and does not represent any depreciation of life. Human life has no sanctity unless human dignity is preserved and "human dignity is enhanced by permitting the individual to determine for himself what beliefs are worth dying for."[72]

As far as the state's interest in public morals, Cantor traces the public views on suicide that are based on religious objections. These views are that only God or a divine power can control the withdrawal of the life force from an individual. In English common law, suicide was considered an offense against nature, God, society, and the king. Today, attitudes toward suicide have changed and, in a majority of states, suicide is no longer a criminal offense. Thus, to Cantor, there is no need to rule against the right to refuse treatment to give credence to public morals that no longer exist in this area.

The fourth state interest, that of protection of the individual against himself, has been labeled as "paternalism" by some authors.[73] Paternalism exists where a society legislates to protect the individual from himself. Some examples of paternalism include the "snake cases," where courts interfered with the religious expression of various sects in dealing with live snakes because of the harm to those individuals and to spectators.[74]

The cases involving the use of motorcycle helmets required by state statute represent another example of state imvolvement compelling individuals to act for their own benefit. Other examples included food and drug laws, licensure schemes, regulation of noxious substances, seat-belt requirements, and federal regulations of flammable fabrics. Cantor distinguishes these situations that require regulatory schemes from the right-to-treatment cases on the basis that persons compelled to act in their own behalf are impelled by conditions that preclude real individual choice.[75]

> Thus, while precedents may be cited for governmental efforts to preclude individual risk-taking, none sanction judicial intervention to protect a patient against his own decision to

decline treatment. Clearly, there are limitations on attempts to guarantee the individual's safety, for otherwise an individual's personal habits, including eating and sleeping would be potentially subject to governmental dictates. The rights to freedom of religion and personal privacy circumscribe paternalistic impulses in the context of compelled medical treatment.[76]

As for the fifth interest, protection of third parties, Cantor discusses four groups of people who might be affected by the patient's decision: surviving adults, fellow patients, physicians, and surviving minors. The grief or any emotional harm suffered by the patient's relatives and friends certainly cannot outweigh the patient's interest in preserving his bodily integrity or religious liberty. Many decisions a person makes, such as divorce or separation or a child's decision to marry against his parent's wishes, cause others some grief. Cantor points out the temporary nature of these emotions and the fact that they must be "tempered by respect for the patient's principled decision."[77] The informed-consent doctrine is "grounded in the premise that a physician's judgment is subservient to the right to self-determination" of the patient, and thus, in this regard the decision of the physician is not more important than the rights of the patient.

Courts have often acted under the *parens patriae* doctrine to order medical treatment for a parent of a minor child. The child benefits emotionally and economically from having the parent kept alive, and thus the state, in preserving the best interests of minor children, has a compelling interest in ordering the treatment over the patient's objection. Cantor says that loss of a parent may not always cause emotional upheaval, and he challenges the public-ward theory, which the state asserts as grounds to order treatment where there is a fear that the child will have to be supported by public funds if a parent is lost. He says they may not be valid grounds to ignore important rights. Thus, Cantor is taking a hard-set approach in refusing to regard any of these state interests as compelling enough to outweigh the individual's right to bodily integrity or religious liberty.

THE RIGHT TO REFUSE TO PARTICIPATE IN EXPERIMENTATION

Another right, the right to refuse to participate in experimentation, is an extension of the informed-consent doctrine that a patient's consent must be obtained before any treatment is instituted. The primary focus here is on the duty of the physician or hospital authorities to inform a patient that a treatment is in an experimental stage.

The problem arises most frequently in teaching hospitals or in county or charitable institutions, where patients have not always been adequately informed about medical procedures and the requisite rights involved. Also, the major classes of patients involved in the controversy over experimentation have been minors, prisoners, and incompetents, whose rights will be dealt with in detail in the next chapter.

One Massachusetts case demonstrates the scope of the problem. A staff doctor brought a lawsuit against the clinic that employed him, on the grounds that his freedom-of-speech rights under the First Amendment were being violated by clinic policy. Policy restrained the doctors from informing clinic patients of dangers inherent in certain medical procedures or dangers from being operated on by residents with less experience than attending doctors. The doctor alleged that hospital policy required that information communicated for informed consent differed significantly for paying patients of the hospital and clinic patients, who were in general much poorer.[78]

The court held that the doctor had established a cause of action to bring suit for the violation of his own First Amendment rights but had no standing to represent the patients, whose rights he attempted to bring into focus at the trial.

The poor, Annas points out, are the most likely to be experimented upon in the hospital setting. They are more often ward and clinic patients and their handicaps make them more available to such treatment.[79] Even paying patients of high socioeconomic rank, however, may find themselves unwitting subjects of experimentation.

Experimentation has been defined as departure from standard medical practice in treating a patient for the purpose of obtaining new knowledge or testing a hypothesis.[80] No patient can legally be experimented upon without obtaining his informed consent. This principle has been incorporated into the American Hospital Association's "Patient's Bill of Rights," which states: "The patient has the right to be advised if the hospital proposes to engage in or perform human experimentation affecting his care or treatment. The patient has the right to refuse to participate in such research projects."

Chalmers and MacDonald address the divergent views of the legal and medical professions concerning experimentation and the necessity for the two to be reconciled for the benefit of society.[81] The legal critics of medical research, according to Chalmers and MacDonald, look only to research abuses of the past and ignore the substantial progress that has been made to correct abuses and prevent further abuse. They note progress by such groups as the National Institutes of Health and the National Commission for the Protection of Human Subjects of Biomedical and Behavioral Research, which was formed by the National Research Act of 1973.[82] Physicians, on the other hand, do not give the issues of individual choice and consent the credence they deserve, often ignoring the safeguards developed to protect individual rights.[83]

There can be no denying the benefits to society in the form of disease prevention and advances in treatments that extensive medical research has made possible. Such advances often require the use of human subjects, as animals do not always provide effective models due to the difference in physiological structures.

On the other hand, past abuses have been shocking. A study was discovered in Tuskegee Institute in which patients suffering from syphilis went untreated for 40 years for research purposes.[84] The major issue or concern is that persons who participate as study subjects in such experiments do so with the knowledge, voluntariness, and competence required for informed consent to *any* medical procedure. Experimentation is useful and in many cases ethical but only where the protection of an individual patient's rights to bodily integrity is preserved and upheld by the medical researchers.

Aside from the issue of consent, physicians and medical researchers are held to another test to escape liability; that is, whether the use of the experimental procedure was reasonable under the circumstances. If it is medically unreasonable, a patient cannot lawfully consent to it.[85]

Notes and References

1. *Natanson v. Kline*, 186 Kan. 383, 406, 407, 350 P2d, 1093, 1104 (1960).
2. "The Nuremberg Code," quoted in Bronstein, Prisoners of research, *Trial* 11(6):17, Nov.-Dec. 1975.
3. DHEW Regulations on Informed Consent, reprinted in Brown, Behavior modification in the right hands, *Trial* 11(6):32–36, Nov.-Dec. 1975.
4. Epstein, Richard L. and Benson, David J., The patient's right to know, *Hospitals J.A.H.A.*, 47(15):47–57, Aug. 1, 1973.
5. *Rogers v. Lumberman's Mutual Casualty Company*, 119 So.2d 649 (1960).
6. *Tunkl v. Regents of the University of California*, 60 Cal. 2d 92, 383, P.2d 441 (1963).
7. *Canterbury v. Spence*, 464 F.2d 772, 788 (D.C. Cir. 1972).
8. *Dunham v. Wright*, 423 F.2d 940, 942 (3rd Cir. 1970).
9. *Roberts v. Wood*, 206 F. Supp. 579, 583 (S.D. Ala. 1962); *Nishi v. Hartwell*, 52 Haw. 188, 473 P.2d 116, 119 (1970).
10. *Canterbury v. Spence*, supra at 789.
11. *Hunter v. Brown*, 81 Wash. 2d 465, 502 P.2d 1194, 1196 (1972).
12. *Haggerty v. McCarthy*, 181 N.E.2d 562, 565 (1962).
13. See also, *Nishi v. Hartwell*, supra at 116; and *Niblach v. United States*, 438 F. Supp. 383 (E.D. Col. 1977).
14. Hershey, Nathan, and Bushkoff, Stanley H., *Informed Consent Study* (Pittsburgh, Pa.: Aspen Systems Corporation, 1969), pp. 3–4.
15. *Hunter v. Brown*, supra.
16. *Dunham v. Wright*, supra.
17. *Archer v. Galbraith*, 18 Wash. App. 369, 567 P.2d 1155 (1977).
18. *Canterbury v. Spence*, supra.
19. *Cobbs v. Grant*, 8 Cal. 3d 229, 502 P.2d 1 (1972).
20. Subjective test: *Hunter v. Brown, Cobbs v. Grant, Canterbury v. Spence*, supra.
21. *Natanson v. Kline, Cobbs v. Grant*, supra; *Miceikis v. Field*, 37 Ill. App. 3d 763, 347 N.E.2d 320 (1976).
22. *Percle v. Saint Paul Fire and Marine Insurance Company*, La. App. 349 So.2d. 1289 (1977), rehearing denied La. Court of Appeals 1st Cir. 1977;

Schroeder v. Lawrence, 359 N.E.2d 1301 (Mass. 1977).

23. Parr v. Palmyra Park Hospital, Inc., 139 G. App. 457, 228 S.E.2d 596 (1976).

24. Cobbs v. Grant, supra.

25. 13 Tex. Stat. art. 4590(i) § 6.01, 6.03(a); further details on the panel are found in § 6.02, 6.07(2), and 6.07(b).

26. Epstein and Benson, The patient's right to know, Hospitals, supra at 50.

27. Schloendorff v. Society of New York Hospitals, 211 N.Y. 125, 105 N.E. 92 (1914).

28. Fiorentino v. Wenger, 19 N.Y.2d 407, 227 N.E.2d 296 (1967).

29. Garzione v. Vassar Brothers Hospitals, 36 App. Div. 2d 390, 320 N.Y.S. 2d (1st Dept. 1971).

30. Darling v. Charleston Community Memorial Hospital, 33 Ill. 2d 326, 211 N.E.2d 253 (1965).

31. Epstein and Benson, The patient's right to know, Hospitals, supra.

32. Canterbury v. Spence, supra at 772.

33. Id. at 778.

34. Id. at 791.

35. The quotations from Acts and Leviticus are found in Jevohah's Witnesses in the State of Washington v. King County Hospital Unit No. 1, 278 F. Supp. 488 (1967) (W. D. Wash. N.D. 1967) affirmed 390 U.S. 598 (1968), rehearing denied 391 U.S. 961.

36. In the Matter of Sampson, 317 N.Y.S. 2d 641, 644 (1970); the court cited I Samuel 14:32,33 and Leviticus 17:10.

37. Id. at 644.

38. In re Brooks, 32 Ill. 2d 361, 205 N.E.2d 435, 438–39 (1965).

39. Id. at 439.

40. Cantwell v. State of Connecticut, 310 U.S. 296, 299 (1940).

41. Prince v. Commonwealth of Massachusetts, 321 U.S. 158 (1944).

42. International Society for Krishna Consciousness of Western Pennsylvania Inc., v. Griffin (U.S.D.C. W. Pa.) 46 Law Week 2176 (9/23/77).

43. Powell v. Columbia Presbyterian Medical Center, 49 Misc.2d 215 (S. Ct. N.Y. 1965).

44. Application of the President and Directors of Georgetown College, Inc., 331 F.2d 1000, cert. denied 377 U.S. 978 (1964).

45. United States v. George (U.S.D.C. Conn. 1965).

46. John F. Kennedy Memorial Hospital v. Heston, 279 A.2d 670 (S. Ct. N.J. 1971).

47. In the Matter of Sampson, supra at 641.

48. Id. at 645.

49. In re Green, 220 Pa. Super. 191, 286 A.2d 681 (1971).

50. Muhlenberg Hospital v. Patterson, 128 N.J. Super. 498, 320 A.2d (1974).

51. Kaimowitz, patient or victim? Trial 11(6):18, 11/12/75, citing a release of the United Press International, June 5, 1975, of an opinion, which was unreported in the legal reporter.

52. In the Matter of Eugene Weberlist (MDS).

53. Id. at 18.

54. In re Brooks, Aste v. Brooks, 32 Ill. 2d 361, 205 N.E. 2d 435, 442 (1965).

55. Id. at 442, quoting Barnette v. West Virginia State Board of Education D.C. 47 F. Supp. 251, 253, affirmed 319 U.S. 624.

56. Id. at 442, quoting Olmstead v. United States, 277 U.S. 438, 478 (1928) (dissenting opinion).

57. Id. at 443.
58. In the Matter of Melido, 88 Misc. 2d 974, 390 N.Y.S. 2d 523 (1976).
59. In the Matter of Osborne, 294 A.2d 372 (1972).
60. Id. at 373.
61. Id. at 374.
62. Id. at 374, n. 5.
63. Id. at 375, n. 6.
64. In re Raasch, No. 455–996 (Probate Div., Milwaukee County Ct., Jan. 21, 1972) cited in Cantor, A patient decision to decline life-saving medical treatment: bodily integrity vs. the preservation of life, Rutgers Law Review 26:228, 235 (1973).
65. Erickson v. Dilgard, 44 Misc. 2d 27, 27 (1962).
66. State Department of Human Services v. Northern, 563 S.W.2d 197 (1978) cert. denied U.S. (1978).
67. Id. at 207.
68. Winters v. Miller, 446 F.2d (2d Cir. 1971), cert. denied 404 U.S. 985 (1971); Civil Rights Stat. 42 U.S.C. § 1983.
69. Winters v. Miller, id. at 70.
70. Cantor, A patient decision, Rutgers Law Review, supra at 242–54.
71. Id. at 242.
72. Id. at 244.
73. See Dwarkin, Gerald, "Paternalism," In Morality and the Law.
74. State v. Massey, 229 N.C. 734, 51 S.E.2d 179 (1949), appeal dismissed 336 U.S. 942 (1949); Harden v. State 188 Tenn. 17, 216 S.W.2d 708 (1948); Hill v. State, 38 Ala. App. 623, 88 So.2d 880 (1956).
75. Cantor, A patient decision, Rutgers Law Review, supra at 248.
76. Id. at 249.
77. Id. at 250.
78. Meyer v. Massachusetts Eye and Ear Infirmary, 330 F. Supp. 1328 (D. Mass. 1971).
79. Annas, George J., The Rights of Hospital Patients (New York: Avon Books, 1975), p. 100.
80. Id. at 100.
81. Chalmers, Thomas C., and MacDonald, Michael G., Worlds apart, Trial 11(6): 27, Nov. 12, 1975.
82. National Research Act of 1973, P.L. 93–348.
83. Chalmers and MacDonald, Worlds apart, supra at 27.
84. Loew, Charles U., and Mishkin, Barbara F., Science fiction or non-fiction? Trial 11(6):22–25, Nov. 12, 1975.
85. Annas, Rights of Hospital Patients, supra at 105.

Part TWO

THE MENTALLY ILL AS PATIENTS

Introduction

Historically, the mentally ill have been treated with the most contempt and abuse of any group of patients. Societies throughout the ages have displayed an irrational fear of "madness" and "insanity," viewing mental disturbance as either punishment by a divine power or possession by a demon.

This attitude was reflected in the treatment these people received from both peers in their communities and the medical community. The mentally ill were banished or ostracized or subjected to exorcism rituals to oust the "demon" possessing them. In seventeenth century England, the king had the duty to care for the insane under the *parens patriae*, the right to care for those legally unable to care for themselves. If the mentally ill were wealthy, this usually meant that the king took control of all their worldly possessions and had them committed to an institution. Indigent mentally ill patients were not provided for.

Puritans in colonial America expected families to take care of their own members, and the mentally ill without family or financial means became social outcasts or drifters. An early Massachusetts statute, probably the earliest piece of American legislation in this area, provided for restraint of "violent persons."[1]

Hospitalization of the mentally ill in this country for detention and treatment began sometime in the late eighteenth century. With the advent of hospitalization, some innovative and rather horrifying forms of treatment were developed.

An early nineteenth century psychiatrist, Benjamin Rush, promoted the use of mechanical restraints and corporal punishment. He developed several devices including the "tranquilizer," a chair to which the patient was strapped. The patient's head was held in a fixed position with the arms and legs secured to reduce the pulse and, consequently, reduce stress. The "bath of surprise" was another device Rush developed, and it certainly lived up to its name. The unsuspecting patient was positioned over a trap door, which was suddenly opened, flinging the patient into a bath of icy water.[2]

Aside from the influx of such "creative" treatment devices, an abundance of social and legal problems developed with the hospitalization of the mentally ill. Much of the abuse they suffered and still suffer has centered on the commitment process. Since mental illness does not always have external manifestations, standards set to define mental disorders can potentially serve to promote grave injustices.

One noted reformer in this area was Mrs. E. P. W. Packard, a woman who had been committed involuntarily to an Illinois institution. Her husband had her committed under an 1851 statute, which reads as follows:

> Married women and infants who in the judgment of the medical superintendent are evidently insane or distracted, may be received and detained in the hospital on the request of the husband... or guardian of the infants without the evidence of insanity or distraction required in other cases.[3] [Emphasis added]

Mrs. Packard wrote several books on her commitment, which sparked a public concern for the plight of the mentally ill and the railroading of people into institutions by uncaring, greedy, or malicious relatives. Packard's campaign led to several changes in state commitment laws, such as introducing the right to a jury determination of the need for hospitalization. The gross inadequacies of the treatment facilities for the mentally ill were brought to light during this time by another reformer, Dorothea Dix.[4]

Until World War II, there was a stigma of criminality attached to the civil commitment for mental health care. Commitment laws contained many criminal procedures such as arrest by a sheriff with a warrant, a charge of dangerous insanity, detention in a jail pending a vacancy in the state asylum, and transportation under sheriff's guard to the asylum.[5]

It is only since World War II that legislatures in this country have acted to remedy the plight of the mentally ill and only since the 1960s that courts have played a role in bringing about needed reform. Development of mental health laws with patients' rights more in focus occurred during the post-World War II era. Commitment before the 1960s was for an indefinite time (and still is in some states). Patients had to bear the burden of proof that they were sound and the responsibility for retaining their own legal counsel in petitioning for discharge. Up until the 1960s, the medical consideration of need for treatment without court action was the normal procedure. Then legal considerations became predominant.

A realistic view of "treatment" afforded the mentally ill has led courts to insist on the standard of "dangerousness to self or others" rather than relying solely on a medical determination of "need for treatment" to justify commitment. Courts have likewise taken a more realistic look at the extent of the loss of liberty involved in civil commitment and have extended certain due process safeguards to patients involved in such hearings.

Notes and References

1. Records of the Governor and Company of the Massachusetts Bay in New England 80 (1854); cited in Schneider, Joseph, Civil commitment of the mentally ill, *American Bar Association Journal* 58:1059, Oct. 1972.
2. Plotnick, Robert, Limiting the therapeutic orgy, *Northwestern U. Law Review* 72: 465–66, 1978.
3. Shlensky, Ronald, Constitutional problems with mental commitments in Illinois, *Illinois Bar Journal* 62:552 at 557, June 1974.
4. Schneider, Civil commitment of the mentally ill, supra 1059.
5. Flaschner, Franklin N., Legal rights of the mentally handicapped; a judge's viewpoint, *American Bar Association Journal* 60: 1371, Nov. 1974.

CHAPTER 4

Civil Commitment

COMMITMENT UNDER TWO SYSTEMS

There are two systems through which a person can be committed to a hospital or state institution for mental health care: the criminal justice system and the civil commitment system.

Criminal Justice System. In this system, a defendant charged with a crime and awaiting trial can be found, after having been examined by two psychiatrists, unfit or incompetent to stand trial. Commitment can also result from the defendant's successfully pleading insanity as a defense against a criminal charge.

Also, when a defendant is found guilty of a sexually motivated crime, the criminal court or a court in subsequent civil proceedings may adjudge the defendant a sexual psychopath or a sexually dangerous person. The court may commit the defendant indefinitely to a state mental institution or a prison with a hospital facility.

Civil Commitment Statutes. Persons can voluntarily commit themselves for mental health care. Also, friends, relatives, a state department of mental health, hospital authorities, or the police may institute involuntary-commitment proceedings, as outlined by the statutes of the particular state.

THE CIVIL COMMITMENT SYSTEM

The power to commit a person for mental health care via the civil-commitment system lies with the state under the common law *parens patriae* doctrine or under police power extended to the state by the United States Constitution. *Parens patriae* is a Latin phrase meaning "father of his country." In England, the *parens patriae* was the king, in whom was vested the power to act as guardian of all "infants, idiots and lunatics" and the duty to act in their best interest.[1]

In America, this term refers to the power of guardianship that the state as sovereign possesses of people with disabilities. Under this power, the state has the authority to take custody of children who are neglected or abused. In this context, the state is like an extension of the parents, supervising the care and treatment afforded its minor citizens. Likewise, under *parens patriae*, the state has the authority to appoint a guardian or order commitment to protect the best interests of those citizens who are unable to care for themselves. This power can be viewed as one delegated by the citizens to the state to protect their own well-being.[2]

Under the police power, the state has the authority to enact legislation to preserve the life and health of its citizens. When a person is judged to be dangerous to himself or others, commitment may be ordered if there is mental illness involved or incarceration under criminal processes if there is not. Civil commitment of persons in this category has been questioned by many legal authorities as constituting preventive detention, since the "dangerous" standard in many commitment statutes is a prediction of future acts rather than past overt acts.

Preventive detention has been absolutely forbidden in the criminal legal system of this country as a denial of the fundamental fairness guaranteed by the due process clause of the Fifth and Fourteenth Amendments of the United States Constitution. To imprison a person for a crime, the state has the burden of proving the defendant guilty beyond a reasonable doubt. The state must offer proof that a crime has been committed and that this particular defendant committed the crime.

In a civil commitment, however, persons may be committed because of their potential for doing harm rather than because of any harm they have actually caused. Examining psychiatrists are asked to predict the potential of a particular person for being dangerous. This raises the issue of whether the commitment of a person based on psychiatrists' predictions is, in fact, preventive detention.

Prompted by litigation and criticism in legal commentaries, legislatures and courts, modern civil commitment statutes and decisions are dealing with this criticism. In the controversial *Lessard v. Schmidt* decision, a Wisconsin federal court held that the standard of dangerousness that must be met is "an *extreme* likelihood that if the person is not confined he will do *immediate* harm to himself or others."[3] [Emphasis added]

The proof of dangerousness must include a "finding of a *recent overt act, attempt* or *threat* to do *substantial harm* to oneself or another."[4] [Emphasis added] These standards resemble those adopted in the civil-commitment statutes of Massachusetts, California, North Carolina, and Washington.[5]

In Massachusetts, a new mental health code[6] defines dangerousness as the likelihood of serious harm "(1) to the person himself, as *manifested by evidence* of threats of or attempts at suicide or serious bodily harm; (2) to others as *manifested by evidence* of homicidal or other violent behavior or serious harm to them."[7] [Emphasis added]

This upgraded standard of dangerousness, however, has not been universally upheld, as one Illinois respondent found on appealing his commitment order. His order was based on a medical opinion that he was "reasonably expected to engage in dangerous conduct."[8] The Illinois Mental Health Code defines a person in need of mental treatment as including one who "is reasonably expected at the time the determination is being made or within a reasonable time thereafter to intentionally or unintentionally physically injure himself or other persons."[9]

The court dismissed the contention that the absence of evidence of dangerous conduct constitutes preventive detention when ordered because of the mentally ill person's status. The court discussed the U.S. Supreme Court decision in *Robinson v. California,* which referred to imprisonment based on the status of drug addiction as unconstitutional under cruel-and-unusual punishment.[10] The Illinois court distinguished this case from *Robinson* in that detention for criminal punishment could not be compared with the detention under laws that required medical treatment. Since the purpose of the Mental Health Code was to provide treatment and not to punish, the Court held, the *Robinson* concept of cruel-and-unusual punishment did not apply. The court held that "a finding of 'in need of mental treatment', absent evidence of prior harmful conduct, is not per se violative of due process."[11] This court left open the argument that if, in fact, no treatment was being provided, a respondent might have grounds to charge preventive detention or cruel-and-unusual punishment in civil commitments under this standard.

To support a finding of dangerousness for a police-power commitment, courts show a trend toward limiting the type of harm and increasing the severity of harm necessary. As the right-to-treatment issue is further litigated and the *Lessard* rationale is applied in other jurisdictions, more state commitment-statututes can be expected to reflect this trend.[12]

The source of the state's power to commit an individual lies under the *parens patriae* doctorine, developed in common law, and the police power, derived from the United States Constitution. The state, however, cannot arbitrarily commit a person. Since every individual has the fundamental right to liberty, the state must present a compelling reason to limit this right. The state must provide legitimate reasons or grounds for civil commitment. Each state sets standards in the civil commitment sections of its mental health code. These standards or grounds for commitment vary from state to state.

In the majority of states, proof of mental illness, along with either a finding of dangerousness to self or others or inability to care for oneself, is ground for civil commitment. The requirement of some finding of mental illness is universal in commitment statutes. The definition of mental illness, however, is by no means universal.

A comprehensive study of mental health codes by the *Harvard Law Review* in 1974 revealed the disparity of these definitions.[13] In some states (Delaware, District of Columbia, and Kentucky), mental illness is defined as "any condition which substantially impairs an individual's mental health," a definition which at best seems dangerously broad.[14] Other states (Colorado, Connecticut, and Idaho) define mental illness based on the need for care, supervision, protection, and treatment or confinement or both.[15]

A few others are more specific yet equally inadequate. For example, in Ohio, a disorder which "substantially impairs the capacity of the person to use self-control, judgment, and discretion in the conduct of his affairs and social relations," is labelled "mental illness." To understand the problem such a definition raises, one has only to apply the same definition to an alcoholic or the victim of a stroke or heart attack.

In New Hampshire, the statutory definition attempts to more precisely define mental illness as "maladaptive behavior and/or recognized emotional symptoms that can be related to psychological, physiological, and/or sociological factors."[16]

To clearly define mental illness would be difficult if not impossible in view of the elusiveness that surrounds the diagnosis and treatment and considering that the drafters of the mental health codes are not psychiatrists. Some states, for instance Illinois, have not even attempted to define the term *mental disorder* but have only defined a person in need of mental treatment in relation to other grounds, which will be discussed hereafter.

In 1975, the United States Supreme Court produced a landmark opinion in the case of *O'Connor v. Donaldson*, which was the first time this court addressed the problems of the mentally ill.[17] Since this decision, many states have amended their commitment laws to require a finding of dangerousness to self or others to justify an involuntary civil commitment. The language in the *O'Connor v. Donaldson* decision, which initiated such change, follows:

> A finding of "mental illness" alone cannot justify a State's locking a person up against his will and keeping him indefinitely in simple custodial confinement. Assuming that that term can be given a reasonably precise content and that the "mentally ill" can be identified with reasonable accuracy, there is still no constitutional basis for confining such persons involuntarily if they are dangerous to no one and can live safely in freedom.

• •

> May the State confine the mentally ill merely to ensure them a living standard superior to that they enjoy in the private community? That the State has a proper interest in providing care

and assistance to the unfortunate goes without saying. But the mere presence of mental illness does not disqualify a person from preferring his home to the comforts of an institution. Moreover, while the State may arguably confine a person to save him from harm, incarceration is rarely if ever a necessary condition for raising the living standards of those capable of surviving safely in freedom, on their own, or with the help of family or friends.

• •

May the State fence in the harmless mentally ill solely to save its citizens from exposure to those whose ways are different? One might as well ask if the State, to avoid public unease, could incarcerate all who are physically unattractive or socially eccentric. Mere public intolerance or animosity cannot constitutionally justify the deprivation of a person's physical liberty.

• •

In short, a State cannot constitutionally confine without more a nondangerous individual who is capable of surviving safely in freedom by himself, or with the help of willing and responsible family members or friends.[18]

Thus, a finding of mental illness alone can no longer be used to justify an involuntary commitment. This decision clearly mandates some finding of dangerousness to self or others before a state can deprive an individual of liberty.

Several federal courts have struck down commitment statutes as being unconstitutional on due process and equal protection grounds, holding that the mentally ill person must pose a serious threat of substantial harm to himself or others, and that the threat must have been evidenced by a recent overt act or threat. The "dangerous to self" standard as implied in *O'Connor v. Donaldson* may be evidenced by patients' neglect or inability to care for themselves.[19]

There are many mentally ill people who are not dangerous to themselves or to others in so far as inflicting serious physical harm, but they may be incapable of feeding and clothing themselves properly or keeping a job, paying rent, getting medical attention, et cetera. While standards for life-style differ, there are people who cannot maintain even a basic level of health and cleanliness and who may require some custodial care to protect them from wandering the streets and being subject to attack from others. Hence, many states provide another ground for commitment, that of mental illness coupled with the inability to care for oneself. The *O'Connor v. Donaldson* decision includes this ground for commitment under the "dangerous to self" category, but many states list this ground separately. In Illinois, one category of person in need of mental treatment includes one afflicted with a mental disorder (other than mental retardation) who is "unable to care for himself so as to guard himself from physical injury or to provide for his own physical needs."[20]

In the Interest of Love demonstrates the application of this standard for commitment.[21] The person in question was diagnosed as a chronic schizophrenic with chronic tuberculosis. The department of mental health filed the petition for hospitalization alleging Mr. Love was in need of mental treatment after he had earlier been found unfit to stand trial.

The psychiatrist testified that he doubted Mr. Love's present ability to "provide himself with the necessary nutrients to maintain good health" and since he was "unable to hold a job, communicate with others, or function meaningfully in the community," he was unable to care for himself within the meaning of the Mental Health Code.[22]

The appellate court upheld the commitment order on the basis of the inability of the respondent to care for himself owing to his present physical and mental health, noting "it is present and future, and not past ability to care of oneself that is to be considered."[23] The court was concerned that this man, "sorely in need of medical treatment for a serious physical ailment," might, because of his mental illness, "potentially refrain from seeking help." The court quoted another Illinois decision explaining the rationale and necessity for having such a ground for commitment:

> [T]he hazards and stresses of everyday life can strain the coping mechanisms of the average citizen. The person who is distressed by a crippling mental illness is sadly deficient in the resources required to meet the challenges of everyday living and is highly vulnerable to these pressures. A person who may not be overtly suicidal or homicidal may nevertheless still require the protections which legal processes afford if his mental illness renders him incapable of functioning in a responsible fashion.[24]

Likewise, the California Code defines a "gravely disabled person" as including one who is "unable to provide for his basic personal needs for food, clothing, or shelter (not including the mentally retarded)."[25]

A disparity of situations may occur if commitment laws are, on the one hand, too lax about applying such a standard as inability to care for oneself and, on the other hand, too stringent about requiring a finding of dangerousness only as justification for commitment.

In one case, the Texas American Civil Liberties Union won the release of a college student who had been committed to a mental institution by his father without a hearing or legal counsel. The allegation was that the student was "crazy" as demonstrated by his conduct in having spent the previous summer traveling around the country on a motorcycle and working on an Indian Reservation.

The other side is reflected in a *Washington Post* article in which Paul Hodge reported the brutal murder of a young woman who had been living homeless, penniless, and shoddily clad for almost a week in

Union Station in Washington, D.C. The reporter had attempted to have her committed to a hospital, after he realized the seriousness of her situation and mental condition. The examining psychiatrist explained that she could not be forcedly detained, since, in his determination, she was not a threat to herself or others and she refused voluntary commitment.[26]

A final ground for commitment is that of "in need of care or treatment and lacking sufficient capacity to make a responsible application for care on his own behalf." This ground is demonstrated in the commitment laws of 16 states including Florida, Alaska, Utah, and Vermont.[27] This fourth ground seems much more arbitrary than any of the others and may be eliminated by the current trend to upgrade standards to include a finding of dangerousness.

CIVIL COMMITMENT PROCEDURES

Although civil commitment procedures differ from state to state, procedures from the Illinois Mental Health Code provide a starting point for discussing the types of commitments and the differences between states. The majority of states have the same categories for civil commitments.

In Illinois, a person can commit himself or herself for mental health care under either *informal, voluntary* admission procedures or admission may be involuntary.

In the informal process, a person can sign himself in and out of a hospital almost at will, although the signing is restricted to daytime working hours. This procedure is seldom used because of the lack of hospital control and the potential for frequent interruption of a treatment plan. Since the new Illinois Mental Health Code became effective on January 1, 1979, hospitals have been mandated to use informal admission whenever possible.

Under a voluntary admission, a patient signs an application for admission and can request release at any time. Hospital authorities have five working days to honor the application for discharge or file for a petition for involuntary commitment, if they think the person is not well enough to leave. A person must be legally competent to voluntarily admit himself for mental health care.

Those involuntarily committed are committed under one of three procedures outlines by statute: emergency admission, admission on physician's certificate, or petition for examination and hearing upon court order.

Emergency Admission

Illinois Revised Statutes set out the procedures for emergency admissions, which may be followed where a person is "mentally retarded or in need of mental treatment and in such a condition that immediate hospitalization is necessary for the protection from physical harm of such person or others."[28] Thus, there is an underlying requirement of dangerousness as a justification for civil commitment under this emergency provision. Rules that protect the patient's rights are outlined in Figure 4-1.

This statute attempts to provide a means of immediate admission for people who really need help quickly, without going through the more formal, lengthy procedures for involuntary admission. At the same time, however, this statute allows enough protection so that a person will not be railroaded into a hospital by a relative who "paid-off" a psychiatrist to certify him as mentally ill since an adversarial court hearing is ultimately required. The goals of such emergency admissions also are to protect the person from harming himself or others and to confine him temporarily until the more formal procedures for involuntary commitment are begun.

States differ as to how long a person may be detained under the state's emergency power to commit and before the procedural due process safeguards of nonemergency commitments come into play.

In the District of Columbia, 48 hours are the limit of emergency detention unless a petition is filed and a court order authorizes continued hospitalization (for up to seven days) for observation and diagnosis.[29]

Likewise, a patient must be released after 48 hours under the Florida law, unless he agrees to remain voluntarily for evaluation, treatment, or hospitalization, or unless a proceeding is initiated for a court-ordered evaluation of involuntary hospitalization.[30]

New York, on the other hand, allows a 15-day period for emergency admission if there is a likelihood of serious harm meaning,

1) *substantial risk of physical harm to himself as manifested by threats of or attempts at suicide or serious bodily harm or other conduct demonstrating that he is dangerous to himself, or*
2) *a substantial risk of physical harm to other persons as manifested by homicidal or other violent behavior by which others are placed in reasonable fear of serious physical harm.*[31]

Within 48 hours, however, a patient in New York must be examined by another psychiatrist to confirm the findings of dangerousness. If the patient, relative, friend, or mental-health-information service gives notice to the director of the hospital that a court hearing is requested on the issue of the need for immediate observation, care, and treatment, the hearing must be held within five days. If the court orders retention of the patient, it can only be for a maximum of 15 days, unless involuntary admission proceedings are instituted.

California has a provision for immediate detention of dangerous or gravely disabled persons (but specifically excluding the mentally retarded) for 72 hours of treatment and evaluation.[32]

Fig. 4-1. Mentally Ill Patients' Rights Under Two Civil Commitment Procedures in Illinois

EMERGENCY ADMISSION AND
ADMISSION BY PHYSICIAN'S CERTIFICATE
Rules that Apply to Both Procedures
Patients' rights before admission

An applicant who asks a superintendent of the hospital to admit a patient must be at least 18 years old.

The petitioner must state the reasons for concluding the patient needs treatment in the hospital.

The petition must contain the names and addresses of the patient's nearest relative or friend, guardian if any, and witnesses by whom asserted facts can be proved.

No longer than 72 hours before admission, the patient must have been examined by a physician who is not employed by and has no financial interest in the hospital where admission is sought.

The examining physician must certify the need for the recommended hospitalization and give the reasons for the conclusions. In an emergency, if procuring a certificate is impossible, the petitioner must secure one within 24 hours after the patient's admission. If admission is by certificate, the applicant has 10 days.

Patients' rights within 12 hours after admission

The superintendent or his agent must give the patient
—a copy of the petition
—a written statement explaining that he will be examined and given a court hearing within five days (excluding Saturdays, Sundays, and holidays)
—an oral explanation of his rights on request or if necessary.

Patients' rights within 24 hours after admission

A copy of the petition and written statement of rights must be given personally or mailed to
—the patient's attorney
—the nearest relative other than the petitioner
—two other persons designated by the patient.

The patient is entitled to make a reasonable number of telephone calls (not fewer than two).

The patient must be examined by a psychiatrist other than the one who issued the certificate. If the patient is to be held, the psychiatrist must certify the need for mental treatment.

Rules that Apply to Emergency Admission Only

To justify hospitalization under the emergency provision, there is an underlying requirement of the patient's dangerousness to self or others.

Although state laws vary, the majority of states have the same categories for civil commitment. The other two categories are (1) involuntary or informal admission and (2) petition for examination and hearing upon court order.

Admission on Physician's Certificate

"Admission on Certificate of a Physician" is another procedure in Illinois for involuntary civil commitment.[33] It is similar to an emergency admission, except that the time periods differ, as Figure 4-1 shows.

Within five days after a patient is admitted, a judge must meet with the patient and explain his rights to have a hearing with representation by counsel. If the patient so desires, the hearing must be scheduled within five working days. This is known as a "probable cause" hearing, in which the judge personally determines that there is or is not probable cause for continued hospitalization and orders discharge if there is not. The patient has 60 days to request a hearing after meeting with the judge.

After 60 days, to retain the patient, the superintendent of the hospital must apply for a court order authorizing continued hospitalization. Notice of the hospital's application for continuation of treatment must be given to the patient, his attorney, nearest relative, and, at the patient's request, two other persons. The patient or any of the persons given notice of the application may request a hearing within 10 working days, or the court may, on its own motion, schedule such a hearing to determine the need for continued hospitalization. The court may order the transfer of the patient from a private hospital to a state-operated hospital under the care of the mental health department of the state.

Petition for Examination and Hearing

The remaining method of involuntary commitment in Illinois is the Petition for Examination and Hearing upon Court Order. The petition for hospitalization is filed with the court and the person remains at home pending examination, unless the court orders otherwise.

The petition must contain the name and address of the spouse or nearest relative or guardian of the respondent (the patient to be) or, if they are unknown, notice that diligent inquiry was made to learn the names of such persons and of witnesses to prove the asserted facts as a basis for the need for mental treatment. A certificate of a physician certifying the need for mental treatment, based on an examination within 72 hours of filing the petition, must accompany the petition. If the court orders an examination and the chosen psychiatrist or psychologist further certifies the need for hospitalization, the court sets a hearing date.

Hospitalization prior to the hearing occurs only upon court order, unless the hospital authorities deem it necessary to admit the person on the basis of the petition and certificate. If they do, they must inform the court as soon as possible. The Illinois statute requires that a copy of the petition and order for examination—and notice of admission to the hospital for examination, if ordered—be delivered personally and within 36 hours to the patient, his attorney, and, if the patient is mentally retarded, two close relatives. Notice of a hearing must similarly be delivered within 48 hours and may be delivered to other persons and witnesses the court deems necessary. The hearing must be set within five working days after receipt of the petition and certificate by the court.

The major difference between this and the other methods of involuntary hospitalization is that the person is not detained (unless court ordered or the hospital authorities determine it necessary and alert the court). Thus, the person remains at home until the final determination of need for mental treatment. Obviously, this method is used where the element of dangerousness is not an issue.

Other states do not have Illinois's liberal notice requirements. Florida has a similar statute.[34] An example of a less liberal notice is seen in Nebraska. A 1971 Nebraska statute provided that notice be served only when an application for commitment is filed and that it be in the form of a warrant issued by the county board of mental health.[35] A New Jersey statute requires notice only of the time and place of the final hearing.[36] More stringent notice requirements are bound to be put in effect, at least in jurisdictions favoring the ruling of *Lesard v. Schmidt* (supra), which held that the prospective patient must be given notice of his rights under the statute to facilitate his preparation of a defense against commitment.[37]

Not all commitment statutes have a provision for a probable-cause hearing as Illinois does under the second method of involuntary civil commitment, admission upon certificate of a physician. Several cases have come down in the District of Columbia and in Wisconsin holding such a hearing to be a constitutional requirement. *In re Barnard* held that such a hearing was necessary for emergency detention.[38] *Lessard* held that such a hearing must be held within 48 hours for any civil commitment that is against the patient's will.[39] Virtually all statutes provide for a full hearing with representation by counsel on the issue of mental illness and need for treatment.

The Illinois Mental Health Code has set up the foregoing procedures "in recognition that civil commitment is a deprivation of personal liberty, and... to provide adequate safeguards against unreasonable detention and commitment."[40] The inclusion of these due process safeguards represents years of litigation and lobbying efforts to implore judiciaries and legislatures to apply criminal due process safeguards of the Fifth and Fourteenth Amendments to civil-commitment proceedings, closely paralleling a similar struggle in the area of juvenile delinquent adjudications.

Notes and References

1. 3 W. Blackstone, Commentaries 47, quoted in Civil commitment of the mentally ill, *Harvard Law Review*, 87:1190 at 1207–08, April 1974.
2. Civil commitment of the mentally ill, *Harvard Law* Review, id. at 1208.
3. *Lessard v. Schmidt*, 349 F. Supp. 1078, 1093 (E.D. Wis. 1972).

4. Id. at 1079.
5. Civil commitment of the mentally ill, *Harvard Law Review*, supra at 1206, n. 29.
6. Mass. Gen. Laws, Mental Health Code, ch. 123 § 1 et seq.
7. Flaschner, Franklin N., Legal rights of the mentally handicapped: a judge's viewpoint, *American Bar Association Journal*, 60:1371 at 1373, Nov. 1974.
8. *People v. Sansone*, 18 Ill. App. 3d 315, 309 N.E.2d 733 (1974).
9. Ill. Rev. Stat. ch. 91½ § 1–11 (1973).
10. *Robinson v. California*, 370 U.S. 660 (1962).
11. Id. at 739.
12. *Lessard v. Schmidt*, supra.
13. Civil commitment of the mentally ill, *Harvard Law Review*, supra.
14. Del. Code Ann. tit. 16 § 5125 (4) (Cum. Supp. 1970); D.C. Code Ann § 21–501 (1973); Ky. Rev. Stat. Ann. § 202.010 (1) (1972).
15. Col. Rev. Stat. Ann. § 71-1-1 (1963); Conn. Gen. Stat. Ann. § 17–176 (Supp. 1973); Idaho Code § 66–317 (Supp. 1972).
16. Ohio Rev. Code Ann. § 5122–01 (A) (Page Supp. 1972); N.H. Rev. Stat. Ann. § 135–B:2 (Supp. 1973); see, Civil commitment of the mentally ill, *Harvard Law Review*, supra at 1202–03.
17. *O'Connor v. Donaldson*, 422 U.S. 563 L. Ed. 2d 396 at p. 407 (1975).
18. Id. at 450.
19. *Doremus v. Farrell*, 407 F. Supp. 509 at 515, 55 (D.C. Neb. 1975); *Stamus v. Leonhardt*, 414 F. Supp. 439 (D.C. Iowa 1976); *Suzuki v. Yuen*, U.S.D.C. Hawaii, 46 Law Week 2181 (7/26/77).
20. Ill. Rev. Stat. ch. 91½ § 1–11 (1973).
21. *In the Interest of Love*, 48 Ill.App.3d 517,363 N.E.2d 21 (1977).
22. Id. at 23.
23. Id. at 25.
24. *People v. Williams*, 47 Ill. App. 3d 861, 365 N.E.2d 404 (1977).
25. Cal. Code § 5008 (h) (1); see also, codes in La., Mont., N.H., N.C., Ariz., D.C., Ga., Me., Nev., Wash., Idaho, Md., and Mass.
26. Shlensky, Ronald, Constitutional problems with mental commitments in Illinois, *Illinois Bar Journal* 62:552, June 1974.
27. Fla. Stat. Ann. Vol. 14A § 94.467 (1) (b).
28. Ill. Rev. Stat. 1973 ch. 91½ § 7–1 to 7–6.
29. D.C. Code Encycl. § 21–523 (1973).
30. Fla. Stat. Ann. § 394.463 (1) (d).
31. McKinney's Consol. Laws of N.Y. art. 9 § 9.39 (1977).
32. Cal. Code vol. 73A § 5150.
33. Ill. Rev. Stat.; § 6–1 to 6–6 cover rules on "Admission on Certificate of a Physician" and § 8-1 to 8-8 cover "Petition for Examination and Hearing upon Court Order."
34. See, Fla. Stat. Ann. § 394·459 (12).
35. Neb. Rev. Stat. § 83–325.
36. N.J. Stat. Ann. § 30:4–41.
37. Civil commitment of the mentally ill, *Harvard Law Review*, supra at 1274–75, Apr. 1974.
38. *In the Matter of Barnard*, 455 F.2d 1370 (D.C. Cir. 1971).
39. See discussion, Civil commitment of the mentally ill, *Harvard Law Review*, supra at 1278–79.
40. *People v. Sansone*, 18 Ill. App. 3d 294, 309 N.E.2d 730, 738 (1974).

CHAPTER 5

Due Process: From Criminal to Civil

Until the 1960s, courts held that involuntary civil commitment was not such a loss of liberty as to fall within the due process clause of the Fifth Amendment that protected criminal defendants.[1] The criminal-justice system, on the other hand, was continually being subjected to such further constitutional constraints as procedural safeguards and beyond-the-reasonable-doubt standard of proof, while the civil-commitment system went relatively ignored until the *O'Connor v. Donaldson* decision in 1975.[2]

The major obstacle to the extension of constitutional restraints in noncriminal areas, according to one author, was the *parens patriae* concept of the state acting "benignly" toward the mentally ill. The concept caused courts to believe that procedural safeguards were unnecessary and would possibly distort the benefit of hospitalization and treatment.[3] This argument was used to deny due process safeguards to juveniles in delinquency adjudications until the Supreme Court interceded, as will be shown.

Many authors argued the need for due process safeguards based on the extent of a person's loss of liberty under civil commitment. A person is committed to possible lifetime confinement in a mental institution and, even further, to certain areas of certain wards within that institution.

The maximum-security wards of state mental hospitals almost always contain barred windows, armed guards, and individual "cells," with restricted periods for exercise and socialization with others. They are so much like prisons that the word *hospital* seems completely out of place in describing them.

A civilly committed person encounters considerable restriction of other rights, too. A person's right to refuse treatment, his right to privacy, and basic civil rights are restricted. A judgment of "need for mental treatment" can result in the person's loss of the right to be with his or her children, to vote, to be a candidate, to retain public office, to serve on a jury, to practice a profession, to obtain a driver's license, or to make a contract or a will.[4] Furthermore, civil commitment bears a stigma "as debilitating as a criminal conviction."[5]

In light of such "a massive curtailment of liberty" the need for the due process safeguards available to criminal defendants have been fought for and won by legal reformers over the past 15 years.[6]

A list of procedural due process rights has been extended to civil-commitment procedures by a number of courts, the most extensive of which came down with the *Lessard v. Schmidt* decision.[7] In this decision, the Wisconsin District Court laid the foundations for the right-to-notice of "charges" justifying detention, the right to a jury deliberation of the need for commitment, the right to a full hearing on the necessity for commitment, the privilege against self-incrimination, required proof of mental illness and dangerousness beyond a reasonable doubt, and confinement to the least restrictive alternative.[8]

All of these rights did not originate with this decision but were merely extended and applied to the Wisconsin commitment statutes and have influenced courts and legislatures in other jurisdictions. The right to notice, a hearing, and counsel have existed for a long time in many states, Illinois for one; but the *Lessard* decision went much further in applying due process safeguards, such as the privilege against self-incrimination and the beyond-a-reasonable-doubt standard, from the criminal system to the civil-commitment system.

Many authors have commented on the effect on the civil-commitment system and the practicality of applying such due process requirements. To Schneider, "the legal trappings of due process often turn out to be more ceremonial than protective of the person before the court."[9] Stone discusses three of these legal safeguards in depth and presents an honest analysis of their usefulness. The safeguards include (1) the objective definition of conduct leading to loss of freedom (attempt to somehow standardize the grounds for the adjudication of "in need of mental treatment"), (2) the right to counsel, and (3) the privilege against self-incrimination and the right to remain silent.[10]

In discussing grounds for commitment, Stone challenges the objectivity required of psychiatrists in predicting the "imminence" of dangerous behavioral events. Such events or their immediate likelihood must be proved beyond a reasonable doubt or by clear and convincing evidence in most states. He comments, "This may be good law, but in my view it is bad medicine. Because most psychiatric treatment is based on the patient's condition rather than his behavior, this method of selecting involuntary patients inevitably undermines the treatment orientation of the hospitals charged with the care of these patients."[11]

Stone argues that the effectiveness of the therapeutic relationship between the patient and the doctor depends a great deal on trust and confidentiality. A system of involuntary commitment based on the therapist's testimony as to the dangerous propensities of his patient's conduct serves to destroy this alliance from the start.

The right to counsel for involuntary commitments presents an unusual problem. The most common source for this right is state statutes, although the role and the stage of the proceedings when the right emerges are not always clearly specified.

Under the *Lessard v. Schmidt* decision, the mentally ill respondent has the right to counsel as soon as feasible after commitment proceedings are instituted. The role of the attorney is that of an active advocate and not merely an amicus curiae (friend of the court).[12]

Criticism of the practicality of counsel at such proceedings has come from two sides, one arguing the uncertainty of the role while the other focuses on the lack of a counterbalance in the form of a prosecutorial figure.

Two authors studied the role and effectiveness of counsel at civil-commitment proceedings in several cities in the United States where there was a statutory right to counsel. Their findings were rather disheartening. In several cities, the hearings lasted from five to 40 minutes and the lawyers met with their clients for only a few minutes, if at all, before the hearing began. In one city, the attorneys viewed their role primarily as insuring that the client received the doctor-recommended treatment. In another city, the role was viewed primarily as one of preventing the relatives from railroading the client into an institution. Throughout the study, the theme revolved around the lack of advocacy in these proceedings, in spite of the rationale for having an attorney present to fulfill due process requirements.[13]

The staff of the *Harvard Law Review*, in their article cited previously, differentiate between the attorney's role in a *parens patriae* and a police-power commitment.[14] In the former, the role of counsel is uncertain both under the statutes and in practice. Since the structure of the hearing is less combative and more informal and lacking the "punitive atmosphere of a criminal trial," an adversarial role seems out of place. If the "best interest of the client" standard is applied, the attorney may act against his client's wishes to fight an involuntary commitment if, in the opinion of the attorney, his client actually needs the treatment. An adversary role seems only appropriate and possible in police-power commitments where the primary purpose of the commitment is the protection of society and where confinement in a maximum-security setting is often the result.[15]

Stone attacks the system from another perspective. His concern is that there is no effective counterbalance to the patient's advocate in the form of a prosecutorial figure at the hearing. He points out that the psychiatrist, present to offer testimony as to the person's mental condition and propensities for dangeousness, may find himself fulfilling a prosecutorial role. To Stone, this results in the "mutilation of one's professional identity" and serves to "undermine the possibility of a therapeutic alliance" in the future when that same person becomes the patient of the psychiatrist.[16]

The patient's privilege against self-incrimination and the right to remain silent have long served to protect the criminal defendant from coercion and force the state to prove its own case. The *Lessard* decision extends such a right to a person who is subject to a psychiatric interview to determine the need for treatment.

This decision requires both the attorney and the psychiatrist to inform the person that his statements may be the basis of commitment and that he does not have to speak to the psychiatrist. In other words, a person may not be committed on the basis of evidence gathered at the psychiatric examination unless he had knowledge of his right to refuse to answer the psychiatrist's questions.

Other courts, however, have ruled differently. An Illinois court held that the privilege against self-incrimination applied in civil-commitment hearings only to the extent of statements that would expose the speaker to criminal liability.[17] In *United States ex rel. Matthews v. Glass*, however, the Illinois Department of Mental Health, in a "Motion to Dismiss Certain Issues and File Amended Complaint," agreed to inform patients orally and in writing that they did not have to talk to doctors and social workers if they did not wish, and that everything they said might be repeated later at the hearing.[18] Not all judges in Illinois, however, have recognized this decision.[19]

Several Supreme Court decisions cast doubt on whether the *Lessard* position on this point will be upheld. In their decision whether to apply the Fifth Amendment to the quasi-criminal proceedings of deportation, the Court focused on whether the legislature's intent in imposing such a sanction was *to punish*.[20]

In another case involving a juvenile-delinquency proceeding, the Court, in deciding whether the privilege against self-incrimination should apply, focused on the impact of the proceeding and *not* whether the intent of the legislature was to punish.[21] Here the state was relying on "benevolent intent" to argue against applying the privilege, however, and the Court saw through such a statement since, in reality, the only difference between juvenile-delinquency commitment and criminal incarceration was that in the former there was indefinite commitment while in the latter there was not, although at times even confinement to the same facility was ordered.[22]

Civil commitment under *parens patriae* is arguably in the person's best interest and not intended to be punitive. Likewise, under police-power commitments, where only those with "substantially reduced criminal responsibility" because of their mental illness may be committed, there is no moral culpability and thus no punitive or retributive intent in confinement.[23] Absent this punitive intent in confinement, it is doubtful (but not totally unlikely) that the Supreme

Court would extend the Fifth Amendment privilege to involuntary civil commitments. Nevertheless, if someone made a strong case that commitment would result in confinement to a maximum security ward which is, in reality, a prison, and where there is no real treatment offered to cure the patient's mental illness, such a privilege might be extended.

As to the right to remain silent, one author suggests its inappropriateness in civil commitments and that *Lessard* was erroneous in holding such a right necessary for due process. The exercise of this right would prevent the state from obtaining from a psychiatric interview the evidence it needs to confine the dangerous mentally ill and those who are unable to care for themselves.

A better solution might be "vigorous representation by an attorney, the right to examination by an independent psychiatrist, and other assurances that he would have the opportunity to effectively contest the evidence produced by the state."[24] There would be less disruption of the commitment process if patients who wished to do so simply refused to be interviewed rather than granting all persons this privilege and informing them before the examination of their right to remain silent.[25]

Several other due process safeguards warrant mention. At the commitment hearing, there is a burden of proof that the state must bear in proving the grounds for commitment. In criminal cases, the state always bears the largest burden of proof, beyond a reasonable doubt. In most civil cases, the burden is the preponderance of the evidence.

Legal reformers have fought for years to raise the standard in quasi-criminal proceedings (those which can result in incarceration, detention, or loss of liberty). Such a label has been placed on juvenile-delinquency hearings, civil commitments, commitments under the Sexually Dangerous Persons Act, and hearings on child abuse and neglect. In many states, in involuntary civil-commitment hearings, the standard is clear-and-convincing evidence, a degree higher than the preponderance of the evidence. "It requires a high level of certainty before finding an individual in need of mental treatment and curtailing his liberty, but does not place an impossible burden on the State in proving its case."[26] Another court went on to further develop the definition of this standard of proof:

> Where the issue involved is not the occurrence of an event, but the determination of an individual's mental condition, the state must prove that the individual is in need of mental treatment by clear and convincing evidence. The facts upon which a medical opinion is based must be established by clear and convincing evidence, and the medical testimony upon which the decision to commit is based must be clear and convincing.[27]

Several courts have heard arguments and held in favor of the beyond-a-reasonable doubt standard for civil commitments.[28] The majority of courts, however, have rejected arguments along this line, as an Illinois Appellate Court reasoned:

> While both civil commitment procedures and criminal proceedings may result in confinement, a person involuntarily committed pursuant to the Mental Health Code is entitled to treatment, to review of his condition and to release when he is no longer in need of treatment. Our legislature has made a considerable effort to differentiate between persons in need of mental treatment and persons who have transgressed our criminal laws. The Mental Health Code not only utilizes civil labels and good intentions, but affords the individual a full panoply of due process protections.... [I]t may well be true that the difficulty in proving an individual state of mind, combined with a stringent reasonable doubt standard, may work a hardship on the individual who has a right to treatment and on society which has a right to protection.[29]

Other courts, as the New Hampshire Supreme Court, have found the "workability" arguments weak at best. In holding in favor of the reasonable-doubt standard, the court in *Proctor v. Butler* noted:

> The loss of liberty and stigmatization involved are fully comparable to the deprivations attending a criminal conviction. This deprivation of liberty is not, as to the person mistakenly committed, ameliorated by the fact that "treatment" may be dispensed. Nor is the potential deprivation rendered significantly less threatening by the fact that an involuntary commitment order is limited to a two-year period and may actually extend only for a matter of months. Days and months are precious commodities to one erroneously confined. Moreover, an enlightened view of mental illness does not yet prevail and a former mental patient is likely to be socially ostracized and victimized by employment and educational discrimination.
>
> •
>
> [T]he certitude required reflects the severity of the deprivation imposed, not the difficulties that may inhere in the proof of the commitment criteria.[30]

The Supreme Court has yet to settle the differences just described. In *Murel v. Baltimore City Criminal Court*, the Supreme Court dismissed the writ of certiorari after briefs were filed on the ground that the writ was improvidently granted.[31] The case involved Maryland state prisoners who were convicted and sentenced to fixed prison terms and subsequently committed for indeterminate periods to Patuxent Institute under the Maryland Defective Delinquency Law.[32] One of the contentions presented was that they were entitled to the government's being responsible for providing the burden of proof beyond a reasonable doubt rather than the preponderance of the evidence, the standard that was used. In his dissent, Justice William O. Douglas explained proceedings under this law: "Individuals who have demonstrated persistent aggravated anti-social or criminal behavior, who have a propensity toward criminal activity, and who have either such intellectual deficiency or emotional imbalance as to present an actual danger to society may be confined at Patuxent."[33]

Under the Maryland law, the judge makes the determination of defective delinquency, which can be reviewed at three-year intervals for those confined. If no treatment is rendered or if treatment proves ineffective, the person might remain there for life.[34] The opinion goes on to discuss the Maryland standard of fair preponderance of the evidence for this procedure and all civil commitments, and it comments:

> Petitioners have thus been deprived of their constitutional protected liberty under the same standard of proof applicable to run-of-the-mill automobile negligence actions.
>
> •
>
> The right to liberty is one of transcendent value. Without it, other constitutionally protected rights become meaningless. Yet Maryland has deprived petitioners of this right, using a burden of proof which fails to give sufficient weight to the interests involved.
>
> •
>
> [A]n individual personal liberty is an interest of transcending value for the deprivation of which the state must provide its case beyond a reasonable doubt. I would follow established precedent and hold that a state may not subject an individual to lengthy if not indefinite incarceration under a lesser burden of proof.[35]

A Texas case was filed with the Supreme Court in 1978 and probable jurisdiction noted, but as of this date, has not been granted in *Addington v. Texas*.[36] The Supreme Court has been presented with the question whether the standard of proof of less than beyond a reasonable doubt is a due process violation in an indefinite-commitment situation. The grant of certiorari and a decision on the merit will offer a resolution of this issue.

Finally, the doctrine of the least-restrictive alternative has been applied to civil commitments. "Under this principle, the state is required, when legislating in an area affecting rights deemed fundamental, to accomplish its purpose by means least restrictive of those rights."[37] This doctrine has been applied previously to freedom of speech, the right to travel, and freedom of assembly. It has been carried over into civil commitments. Several states now mandate investigation into alternatives to hospitalization in their mental health codes.[38]

One of the earliest cases on least-restrictive alternative cases came before the U.S. Court of Appeals in the District of Columbia Circuit in 1966. In *Lake v. Cameron* the court was presented with an appeal from denial of release in habeas corpus from a 64-year-old woman who had been involuntarily committed to St. Elizabeth's Hospital as an "insane person."[39] The real problem was that the woman was senile and would wander the streets at all hours. She believed she was able to be released, and her husband and sister offered to provide a home for her. The district court found that her mental illness, cerebral arterioisclerosis, combined with her need for care and supervision, warranted her commitment unless other facilities were made available. The court determined that her husband and sister were not capable of caring for her and were without funds to employ another to do so.[40]

The court of appeals refused to accept the rationale of the lower court and ordered the lower court to make an inquiry into alternative courses of treatment, relying on the new District of Columbia Code, which provided for the court "to order any alternative course of treatment... in the best interests of the person or of the public."[41] Four judges wrote strong dissents, expressing their abhorrance at turning the district court into "an administrative agency for proceedings involving the mentally ill."[42]

Stone also expressed a negative reaction to such a decision, which, in reality, was attempting to force the District of Columbia to provide nursing homes, day care, and foster-care centers to deal with elderly people who have been deprived of their liberty simply because such community mental-health facilities are lacking. Stone made the following point:

> [The District of Columbia] may seek to avoid the enormous
> expense involved in establishing the full panoply of community
> services by either no longer seeking to commit patients who need
> less restrictive alternatives or by discharging the patients now
> confined or changing their legal status. ... If that happens the least
> restrictive alternative, rather than improving care, may simply
> become another gambit in the libertarian strategy of abolishing
> civil commitment.[43]

Many subsequent decisions, several in the District of Columbia circuit, have upheld the requirements for seeking the least-restrictive alternative despite this criticism and the strong dissent in *Lake v. Cameron*.[44] As Judge Bazelon of this circuit stated, "It makes little sense to guard zealously against the possibility of unwarranted deprivations prior to hospitalization, only to abandon the watch once the patient disappears behind the hospital doors."[45]

The courts have ordered the hospitals in several cases to furnish them with a report concerning the treatment plan and the exploration of alternative courses within and without the hospital.[46]

Several cases concern transfers within a hospital from a minimum- to a maximum-security ward. In *Eubanks v. Clarke*, the court reasserted the right to the least-restrictive setting and held that in-hospital transfers to maximum-security wards without a hearing violated patients' due process rights.[47]

An earlier Pennsylvania decision mandated a "specific finding" that placement in a maximum-security setting was necessary, based on a preponderance of the evidence, regardless of whether this placement resulted from initial commitment or by transfer.[48]

Several cases have also held that a prisoner subsequently transferred to a state mental hospital has the same rights as those civilly committed, including the right to treatment under the least restrictive conditions possible.[49]

In the past decade, courts have stepped with full force into the areas of mental health care reform and patients' rights. Many writers argue that, as the dissent in *Lake v. Cameron* expressed, the courts are not social service agencies that should concern themselves or even have the power to concern themselves with institutional policy. One cannot help but admire the spirit of these judges, however, taking an almost personal responsibility to see that certain rights are given the weight they deserve, even if it takes a great deal of court supervisision and time, two things most courts refuse to give quite so easily. If civil-commitment of the mentally ill is to be at all effective, to be at all adequate in dealing with the realities of these individuals' conditions, and to preserve the individual rights that our society so carefully guards in other areas, the courts must take a staunch stand.

Legislatures are political bodies, intent on saving taxpayers' dollars to "keep the peace" back home. Institutional reforms and alternatives to confinement take money and personnel to become a reality. The right-to-treatment cases, discussed in another chapter, will show the extremes to which courts have gone to see that this important right is guaranteed for the mentally ill. For these basic rights to become a reality, the criticisms concerning preventive detention and all the arguments for the full set of criminal due process safeguards being afforded mentally ill people must be resolved in their favor.

The civil-commitment hearing must become as adversary as a criminal trial, because the reality of incarceration in a prison for the criminal defendant will be the fate of the individual committed to a mental institution. If the fact of the matter is that civilly committed persons are given the same treatment as prisoners, then they are entitled to the same type of trial and the same standard of proof in proving the need for commitment.

Notes and References

1. *Prochaska v. Brinegar*, 251 Iowa 834, 838, 102 N.W.2nd 870, 872 (1960).
2. *O'Connor v. Donaldson* 422 U.S. 563 (1975); Stone, Alan A., Recent mental health litigation: a critical perspective, *American Journal of*

Psychiatry 134(3):273–79 Mar. 1977.

3. Reisner, Ralph, Psychiatric hospitalization and the Constitution: some observations of emerging trends, *University of Illinois Law Forum* 1973: 9.

4. Civil commitment of the mentally ill, *Harvard Law Review* 87: 1190 at 1198–99, n. 22–28, Apr. 1974.

5. Id. at 1201.

6. *Humphrey v. Cady*, 405 U.S. 504, 509 (1972).

7. *Lessard v. Schmidt*, 349 F. Supp. 1078 (E.D. Wis. 1972).

8. See also, *Bell v. Wayne County General Hospital at Eloise*, 384 F. Supp. 1085 (E.D. Mich., 1974).

9. Schneider, Joseph, Civil commitment of the mentally Ill, *American Bar Association Journal* 58: 1059 at 1060, Oct. 1972.

10. Stone, Recent mental health litigation, *American Journal of Psychiatry*, 134: supra at 273–79.

11. Id. at 274.

12. Bleis, Edward, *DePaul Law Review* 23: 42 at 56, 1973.

13. Andalman, Elliot, and Chambers, David L., Effective counsel for persons facing civil commitment: a survey, a polemic, and a proposal, *Mississippi Law Journal* 45:43, Jan. 1974.

14. Civil commitment of the mentally ill, *Harvard Law Review*, supra.

15. Id. at 1289–90.

16. Stone, Recent mental health litigation, *American Journal of Psychiatry*, supra at 275.

17. *People ex rel. Keith v. Keith*, 38 Ill. 2d 405, 231 N.E.2d 387 (1967); *In the Matter of Ciancanelli*, 26 Ill. App. 3d 884, 326 N.E.2d 47 (1975).

18. *United States ex rel. Matthews v. Glass*, (D.C. N.D. Ill. 1972).

19. Bleis, Edward, *DePaul Law Review*, supra at 79.

20. *Kennedy v. Mendoz Martinez*, 372 U.S. 144 (1963).

21. *In the Matter of Gault*, 387 U.S. 1 (1967).

22. Civil commitment of the mentally ill, *Harvard Law Review*, supra at 1305.

23. Id. at 1366.

24. Id. at 1308–12.

25. Id. at 1313.

26. *In the Matter of Deiter*, 55 Ill. App. 3d 7, 370 N.E.2d 84 (1977).

27. *People v. Sansone*, 18 Ill. App. 3d 315, 309 N.E.2d 733 (1974).

28. *Lessard v. Schmidt*, supra; *In the Matter of Ballay*, 482 F.2d 648 (D.C. Cir. 1973); *Proctor v. Butler*, 46 380 A2d 673 (N. Hamp. 1977).

29. *People v. Sansone*, supra at 740–41; see also, *In the Matter of Stephenson*, 67 Ill. 2d 544, 367 N.E.2d 1273 (1977).

30. *Proctor v. Butler*, supra at 2285.

31. *Murel v. Baltimore City Criminal Court*, 407 U.S. 355 (1972).

32. Md. Ann. Code art. 31B.

33. 407 U.S. at 358; quoting Md. Ann. Code art. 31B, § 5 (1971).

34. Id. at 794.

35. Id. at 359, 364–65.

36. *Addington v. Texas*, 46 Law Week 3671, filed 1/6/78, prob. juris. noted 4/6/78.

37. Reisner, *University of Illinois Law Forum*, supra.

38. See, Mental Health Codes in Cal., Col., Ill., Kan., N.M., N.C., Ohio, Pa.; from Civil commitment of the mentally ill, *Harvard Law Review*, supra at 1250.

39. *Lake v. Cameron*, 364 F.2d 657 (D.C. Cir. 1966), cert. denied, 382 U.S. 863 (1966).
40. Id. at 659.
41. D.C. Code Encyl. § 21–545(b) (Supp. V. 1966).
42. Id. at 663.
43. Stone, Recent mental health litigation, *American Journal of Psychiatry*, supra at 277–78.
44. *In the Matter of Jones*, 336 F. Supp. 428 (D.C., 1972); *Covington v. Harris*, 136 U.S. App. D.C. 35, 419 F.2d 617 (D.C. Cir. 1969).
45. *Covington v. Harris*, id. at 623–24.
46. *In the Matter of Jones*, supra at 430.
47. *Eubanks v. Clarke*, 434 F.Supp. 1022 (D.C. Pa. 1977).
48. *Dixon v. Attorney General*, 325 F. Supp. 966 (M.D. Pa., 1971).
49. *In the Matter of Patterson*, 148 N.J. Super. 515, 372 A.2d 1173 (1977); *Dixon v. Attorney General*, id.

CHAPTER 6

Criminal Justice System

In the criminal justice system, the state's source of power to commit individuals lies in the police power granted in the United States Constitution. Under this power, the state has the authority to pass laws to protect its citizens from each other and from themselves. Thus, legislatures pass laws regulating speed limits; requiring motorcyclists to wear helmets; and prohibiting robbery, murder, assault and battery, and the carrying of concealed weapons. States have the power to enforce such legislation by imposing such sanctions as fines and prison sentences. It is fairly easy to justify committing a criminal defendant to a mental hospital in lieu of a prison sentence after he has been found guilty of a crime but has also been found to have a mental disorder that negates the "scienter" or intent to commit the crime.

A more difficult situation arises where a court-ordered psychiatric examination reveals that the defendant is unfit to stand trial. This means that he is unable to understand the charges against him and is unable to communicate with his lawyer to prepare a defense.

Many rather appalling cases have exposed some of the gross inequities of commitments in this area. Persons unfit to stand trial have spent years in mental institutions; periods longer than if they had, in fact, been found guilty and given prison sentences. In most of these cases, the mental institutions were, in reality, prisons where little or no treatment was made available to these persons.

One case involved a 48-year-old man, arrested and indicted in New York City for second-degree assault. He had allegedly been involved in a stabbing incident and had pleaded not guilty to the charge. After having appeared 18 times before a court on the charge, he finally agreed to plead guilty to a lesser charge, claiming he could no longer afford a lawyer and would lose his job if he had to keep appearing in court. He pleaded guilty and was placed on probation.

He was taken into custody four months later for a violation of probation. The judge ordered a psychiatric examination, which revealed that he was "in such a state of insanity that he was incapable of understanding the charges, or making his defense." He was a chronic alcoholic. The judge ordered him committed to Matteawan State Hospital, where he remained for 12 years and four months.

If he had been sentenced for the original crime or for violation of probation, he would have received a three-year sentence at most. For four years of his "commitment," he was locked in a cell in the maximum-security ward, with time out of his cell for exercise and toilet requirements only. He was awarded $300 thousand by a jury as compensation for the moral and mental degradation, and pain and suffering. He had been the subject of many attacks and beatings from other patients and from the guards—a heavy price to pay for being "unfit to stand trial."[1]

The United States Supreme Court, in an attempt to remedy such unfortunate situations, held in *Jackson v. Indiana* that the indefinite commitment of a criminal defendant found incompetent to stand trial until certified "sane" is a violation of the equal protection and due process clauses of the Constitution when there is no substantial probability that the person would ever be able to participate fully in a trial.[2]

The equal protection count of the appeal alleged that a criminal defendant is subjected to a more lenient commitment standard than others exposed to involuntary civil commitments and more stringent standards for release. The petitioner in this case was a 27-year-old, mentally defective deaf-mute who could not read, write, or communicate. Under the Indiana statute he could be committed until sane enough to stand trial. Since Indiana had no facilities available to train him in even minimal communication skills, his ability to ever stand trial was more than highly unlikely. Thus, he was in fact given a "life sentence" for two offenses involving the theft of $9.00 worth of property, offenses of which he was never even found guilty.

The Supreme Court reversed the commitment. The Court was not willing to go so far as to order his release but remanded the case to the Indiana Supreme Court and ordered that court to determine if there was a substantial probability that the defendant would attain competency in the foreseeable future. If the court were to find that he would not obtain competency, the state would have to release him or institute civil-commitment proceedings, using the same statutory standards and burden of proof used for those not charged with a crime.[3]

One disgruntled federal judge ordered the release of a criminal defendant who had been subjected to custody and confinement for almost three years after having been indicted under the Bank Robbery

Act.[4] He was found unfit to stand trial after having been arrested and indicted for his involvement in the bombing and robbery of a bank, a crime in which 26 persons had been injured. The judge lamented his position in being "confronted with the following painful alternatives: either to authorize the continued incarceration of a defendant in violation of his constitutional rights, or to release him into the community where he may be a danger to himself and to the public."[5] The problem was that there were no federal facilities available to offer the psychiatric services needed to treat this person so that he would eventually be able to stand trial, and there were no state psychiatric facilities with adequate security in which to keep such a person.

This case demonstrates the balance that must be struck between protection of society and individual rights. One can appreciate the frustration of the Federal Bureau of Investigation, which spent so much time and manpower investigating this incident, finally gathering enough evidence to arrest the person. On the other hand, here is a person who was never given his constitutional right to a fair trial, in which the government had to prove his guilt beyond a reasonable doubt. Instead, he was subjected to a series of sanity hearings and confinement in seven different correctional institutions.[6] This case also demonstrates the problem of dealing with the lag between the court's ordering reform and the legislature's implementing the reform by allocating funds to develop treatment facilities.

The Appellate Court of Illinois was faced recently with the uncomfortable situation of dealing with a criminal defendant in a robbery trial who was found unfit to stand trial. When the state attempted to have him civilly committed he was found not "in need of mental treatment" under the Mental Health Code.[7] Under the *Jackson v. Indiana* (supra) dictate, the Illinois court had to determine whether the defendant would be competent to stand trial in the foreseeable future. He would not be. There was some discrepancy in the psychiatric testimony as to whether he was "dangerous" by code standards to warrant a civil commitment.

The judge refused to order his release and ordered him hospitalized pending appeal. The judge believed he had "to safeguard the six million people in the surrounding community."[8] This court found a loophole in *Jackson v. Indiana* and the subsequent Illinois Supreme Court decision in *People ex rel. Martin v. Strayhorn*, which ordered the release of a defendant in such a situation.[9]

The court determined that a release on bail was appropriate under such conditions as the court deemed necessary, including the requirement that the defendant submit to or secure treatment for his mental condition on his own. The court ordered him discharged from the custody of the department of mental health and remanded the case for a new hearing to set an appropriate bail. Thus, this court fashioned a new remedy to keep the defendant under the supervision of the court without ordering a formal commitment to an institution, an action which would have been constitutionally and statutorily impermissible.

These cases suggest the important delicate balance that courts must strive to maintain between individual rights, which the Constitution protects and which the courts must uphold, and the state's interest in the protection of its citizens. It should be clear that this is not an easy balance to maintain.

Aside from commitment for unfitness to stand trial, another category has been developed. It deals with a criminal act, but the actual commitment for mental care is civil. Under a Sex Crimes Act or a Sexual Psychopathic Act, which many states have enacted, where a person is found guilty of a crime that the judge determines to be motivated by some sexual deviancy, the judge has the option to order either civil commitment to a mental hospital or an indefinite period of incarceration in a prison with hospital facilities. One can imagine the potential for gross abuse in a system in which the judge alone makes this determination. A few examples of different state procedures follow.

The Supreme Court dealt with a commitment under the Wisconsin Sex Crime Act in *Humphrey v. Cady.*[10] The petitioner was convicted of contributing to the delinquency of a minor, a misdemeanor carrying a maximum sentence of one year. Under that statute, if the court finds that crime was "probably motivated by a desire for sexual excitement," it can commit the defendant for treatment for a period up to the maximum sentence authorized; but every five years the court can renew the commitment indefinitely after notice and a hearing. The petitioner was ordered recommitted after his initial one-year commitment. He appealed to the Supreme Court on the grounds that he had to serve a second punishment for the same crime, *i.e.* "double jeopardy." The petitioner also argued that a commitment for compulsory treatment is equivalent to a civil commitment under the Wisconsin Mental Health Act, which provides for trial by jury on the issue of need for mental treatment. In this case the issue would be whether he was a sexual deviate. Thus, he claimed that he was denied equal protection under the law.

The Supreme Court reversed and remanded the case back to the Wisconsin court to hold an evidentiary hearing. The Supreme Court found the petitioner's claims persuasive and indicated in the opinion that the renewal proceeding every five years under the Sex Crimes Act seemed to warrant the same due process requirements as an independent civil-commitment hearing. Also, Justice Thurgood Marshall indicated that the Mental Health Act and the Sex Crimes Act were not mutually exclusive.

Another case, *Sarzen v. Gaughan,* exemplifies the rather grim consequences of such a commitment.[11] The petitioner was convicted in 1961 of rape, assault and battery and was sentenced to four-to-seven years. He spent 11½ years at the Massachusetts Correctional Institute at Bridgewater, after the district attorney had petitioned the court in 1962 to have petitioner committed as a sexually dangerous person.[12] Under the applicable statute, the court can commit a defendant for a 60-day observation period, during which time he would be examined by two psychiatrists who would report to the court if, in their opinion, the person was sexually dangerous. If he was, the judge could order that he be committed for an indeterminate period.

In 1964, more than two years after the psychiatrists reported that the petitioner was a sexually dangerous person, he was given a hearing with an attorney who had been appointed to him on that day. Of the two psychiatrists who had testified, one had examined him once, two days before the hearing. The other had had six interviews with the petitioner, four of which were held in the initial 60-day commitment period, three years prior to this hearing. Evidence revealed that this psychiatrist had been influenced by certain mistakes in the petitioner's record.

The court remanded the case for a determination of due process violations in the late appointment of an attorney and the unannounced original psychiatric examination. In the meantime, the petitioner was released after a successful habeas corpus petition. This case demonstrates the problems and injustice that can result with such commitments.

Recently, several states have updated their acts to incorporate more due process protections. In Illinois, the statute requires that a charge of mental disorder that has existed for not less than one year, coupled with "criminal propensities toward acts of sexual assault or acts of sexual molestation of children," be proved at a civil proceeding. The state, however, bears the burden of proof of beyond a reasonable doubt that the defendant fits this definition of a sexually dangerous person.[13]

The defendant has the right to a trial by jury and to be represented by counsel. If the defendant is found sexually dangerous, the director of corrections, not the department of mental health, becomes his guardian as in civil commitments. This guardianship is indefinite, as the code establishes its existence until the person "recover(s)." Thus, such a commitment could be for life. Discharge would occur upon a successful application by the person committed, filed before the committing court, showing recovery. Such a release can be conditional if the director is uncertain as to whether full recovery has occurred.

The constitutionality of this act was attacked but upheld in *Stachulak v. Coughlin*, in which a person confined under the act brought a civil rights and habeas corpus action.[14] One of the claims was that the Illinois Sexually Dangerous Persons Act violated the equal protection clause in that treatment was worse than afforded criminal defendants or those civilly committed. The court upheld the constitutionality of the act and ordered discovery to see if any treatment is afforded defendants under this commitment process.

In *People v. Pembrock*, an Illinois court held that there was no denial of equal protection because of the substantial differences between commitments under this act and under the Mental Health Code.[15] The court determined that justification for any disparity in treatment lies in the fact that the requirements of "criminal propensity toward sex offenses or acts of sexual molestation of children" set this group apart from others that fall within the Mental Health Code.

Alabama's Criminal Sexual Psychopath Statute was declared unconstitutional in *Davy v. Sullivan.*[16,17] The court interpreted the statute as allowing the possibility of two criminal sentences for the same crime, which could include the "crime" of having a mental disorder. The Alabama statute has a definition for sexual psychopath similar to that of the Illinois Code, in that it requires a finding of a mental disorder and some evidence of criminal propensities to the commission of sex offenses. A psychiatric examination and a hearing are required but with no right to a jury. Confinement continues until full and permanent recovery, with no provision for conditional release as in Illinois.

The court analyzed the statute and determined that, even if a person committed under the Alabama statute is confined to a mental hospital, he could be transferred administratively into the prison system. Upon discharge, he must be placed on probation for a reasonable time, and, if probation is violated, he can be recommitted or sentenced for the initial conviction. Commitment under the statute is not in lieu of sentencing or limited in duration to the maximum-permissible sentence for the criminal act. Thus, it potentially imposes double jeopardy on the defendant and is unconstitutional as a crime statute.

Likewise, this court held that the statute was unconstitutional as a civil-commitment statute in that the remedial aspects of the statute did not have foundation in fact, since confinement in "appropriate state institutions" does not limit incarceration to a hospital but provides for transfer to a prison.[18]

Thus, the superintendent of the state hospital had the authority to judge whether the committed sexual psychopath could not or would not benefit from further treatment, without any due process safeguards afforded the individual.[19] The court went on to consider the statutory standard of release, that of "full and permanent recovery." Applying the holding in *Jackson v. Indiana*, the court concluded that once it can be determined that the adjudged sexual psychopath cannot or will not benefit from further treatment, his release cannot be conditioned on "full and permanent recovery" unless further incarceration is justified by a finding of dangerousness to self or others or by the civil-commitment standard. Dangerousness must be grounded on the "likelihood of conduct which has a serious effect on the person incarcerated or others, rather than being merely repulsive or repugnant."[20]

Thus, this court upheld confinement of a sexual psychopath under different standards from a criminal or civil commitment, but the confinement was to be only to a hospital and only as long as treatment was being rendered and there was some positive response to treatment. When the confined person no longer benefitted from treatment, then civil-commitment standards and procedural due process requirements would have to be met for further commitment. This decision may propose the best solution to insure that persons with such criminal propensities can be removed from society without the relatively easy release under our parole system, while preserving the individual rights to due process and treatment and preventing the inevitable abuses that can occur when the judgment of individuals, such as the superintendent of a hospital, subject to their own concepts and prejudices, have such a permanent and far reaching effect on other persons' lives.

The main argument for withholding certain rights has been the "benign" rather than "punitive" nature of the commitment. Judges have been hesitant to turn a civil-commitment hearing into an adversary proceeding under *parens patriae* or police power. Such commitments are not for punishment but for treatment, and the argument progresses to distinguish the type of hearing and rights necessarily afforded anyone who is subject to civil commitment.

The emphasis on treatment as justification for the loss of liberty involved in a civil commitment without the full set of procedural, due process safeguards sparked a new wave of litigation, which surfaced during the 1960s. The wave began with an article by Morton Birnbaum, M.D., proposing a right to treatment for the mentally ill involuntarily committed by the state.[21] If the purpose of the commitment is treatment, then there must be some kind of protected interest or right to receive such treatment.

Notes and References

1. *Whitree v. State*, 56 Misc. 2d 693, 290 N.Y.S. 2d 486 (1968).
2. *Jackson v. Indiana*, 406 U.S. 715 (1972).
3. Id. at 451.
4. *United States v. Pardue*, 354 F. Supp. 1377 (U.S. D.C., D. Conn. 1973).
5. Id. at 1382.
6. See also, *United States v. Geelan*, 520 F.2d 585 (9th Cir. 1975).
7. *People v. Ealy*, 49 Ill. App. 3d 922, 365 N.E. 2d 149 (1977).
8. Id. at 153.
9. *People ex rel. Martin v. Strayhorn*, 62 Ill. 2d 296, 342 N.E.2d 5 (1976).
10. *Humphrey v. Cady*, 405 U.S. 504 (1972).
11. *Sarzen v. Gaughan*, 489 F.2d 1076 (1st Cir., 1973).
12. Mass. Gen. Laws ch. 123A.
13. Ill. Rev. Stat. ch. 38 § 105–1.01 (1975).
14. *Stachulak v. Coughlin*, 364 F. Supp. 687 (N.D. Ill. 1973), aff'd 520 F.2d 931, cert. denied 424 U.S. 947.
15. *People v. Pembroke*, 62 Ill. 2d 317, 342 N.E.2d 28 (1976).
16. Ala. Criminal Sexual Psychopath Stat. tit. 15 § 433–442 (1971 Supp).

17. *Davy v. Sullivan*, 354 F. Supp. 1320 (M.D.Ala. 1973).
18. In accord with, *Commonwealth v. Page*, 339 Mass. 313, 159 N.E.2d 82 (1959); *In the Matter of Maddox*, 351 Mich. 358, 88 N.W.2d 470 (1958).
19. *In the Matter of Maddox*, id. at 1329.
20. Id. at 1330.
21. Birnbaum, Morton, The right to treatment, *The American Bar Association Journal*, 46: 499 (1960).

CHAPTER 7

The Right to Treatment

The first major case arose in 1966 in a federal Court of Appeals in the District of Columbia Circuit. It involved a mental patient involuntarily hospitalized after having been acquitted, by reason of insanity, of the charge of carrying a dangerous weapon, a misdemeanor carrying a maximum sentence of one year. The patient brought a habeas corpus petition for release, arguing that in the four years he had spent in the hospital he had received no treatment for his "mental illness."

The court found a statutory right to treatment under the District of Columbia Mental Health Code and remanded the case to the district court to determine if the petitioner had received adequate treatment or whether the state had an "overwhelming or compelling reason" for the failure to provide adequate treatment.[1] In dictum, Judge Bazelon outlined a constitutional right to treatment under the due process and equal protection clauses of the Fourteenth Amendment and the Eighth Amendment, which ban cruel and unusual punishment. Thus, *Rouse* outlined two possible sources for the right of mentally ill patients to receive treatment for their mental illness: a statutory right and a constitutional right.

The civil-commitment statutes of at least 24 states make broad promises to provide treatment to their involuntarily committed mentally ill. These promises range from being implicit to explicit in their language. Some statutes imply the guarantee of treatment by providing that those who meet the standards of the mental health code for civil commitment should be admitted to a hospital.[2] A Minnesota Federal District Court examined such a statute in *Welsch v. Likins*, which defined a mentally disabled person as one requiring "treatment or supervision" and ordering such a person to be placed in a "home, hospital, or institution."[3] Such language was held to serve as a statutory basis for the right to treatment for the mentally ill in Minnesota.[4]

Other statutes more directly included the right to treatment in the section on patients' rights, without being explicit as to what this right entailed or without defining "treatment." Language such as that of the District of Columbia Code, interpreted in *Rouse* v. *Cameron*, exemplifies this group: "A person hospitalized in a public hospital for a mental illness shall, during his hospitalization, be entitled to medical and psychiatric care and treatment."[5] Judge Bazelon interpreted such "treatment" to mean contacts with both psychiatrists and hospital staff that are "designed to cure or improve the patient."[6]

The Florida Public Health Code states that "the policy of the state is that the department shall not deny treatment for mental illness to any person," but does not define what that treatment entails.[7] Kansas statutes provide that "every patient shall receive humane treatment consistent with accepted ethics and practices."[8] The statute defines treatment as "such necessary services as are in the best interests of the physical and mental health of the patient and rendered by or under the supervision of a physician."[9] Connecticut law provides that mental patients admitted under both voluntary involuntary proceedings "may receive medication or treatment," while New Jersey takes the position that the mentally ill are "entitled to fundamental civil rights and to medical care and other professional services in accordance with accepted standards."[10,11] It is clear that where these statutes say treatment must be provided, no specific or clear guidelines are given. The courts in at least two jurisdictions, however, the District of Columbia and Minnesota, have based a rather broad statutory right to treatment on such language.[12]

There is another group of states that have rather explicit mental health statutes emphasizing this right to treatment and more clearly defining what this right includes. The *Rouse* court opened the door to court examination of mental-hospital structure and policy and dictates for treatment plans. Examination of the *Rouse* opinion reflects how far a court would go to define "treatment" where the legislature did not. Many states updated their mental health codes in response to this trend, possibly in an effort to limit court interference as much as possible.

These new codes define treatment as clearly as possible to avoid the necessity of having a court do so to the financial disadvantage of the state. Judge Bazelon in *Rouse* dictated that, although hospital authorities need not prove that the treatment will actually cure or improve the patient's condition, they must make a bona fide effort in that direction by recording initial and periodic inquiries into the needs and conditions of each patient and by providing suitable treatment through individual treatment plans.[13]

In Ohio, mental hospitals' staffs are required by statute to evaluate the status, diagnosis, and probable prognosis of each patient, develop a treatment plan, and record this information on the patient's chart within 20 days of admission.[14] Treatment must be consistent with the treatment plan under standards set by the Ohio Department of Mental Health and Mental Retardation. Treatment must be evaluated at least every 90 days. The right to receive humane care and treatment includes the least restrictive environment, the necessary facilities and personnel to effect the treatment plan, the opportunity to learn skills needed to return to the community, and the right to be free of restraints, isolation, and unnecessary and excessive medication.[15]

Under North Carolina law, "Each patient shall have the right to treatment including medical care and habilitation, regardless of age, degree of retardation or mental illness. Each patient has the right to an individualized written treatment or habilitation plan, setting forth a program which will develop or restore his capabilities.[16]

The code provides that such treatment plan be implemented no later than 14 days after admission. Also, each institutionalized patient shall have a postinstitutional plan including vocational counseling and outpatient care. Each patient has the right to be free from unnecessary or excessive medication. Electroshock therapy, treatment with experimental drugs or experimental surgery shall not be given without the consent of the patient or, if the patient is incompetent, the patient's guardian.

New Hampshire defines the treatment guaranteed the mentally ill patient as including "such psychological, medical, vocational, social, educational or rehabilitative services as his condition requires to bring about an improvement in condition within the limits of modern knowledge."[17] This section of the code allows only 30 days per year of maintenance care alone with notice to the patient's representative of the reason for such passive treatment along with an entry in the person's clinical record. The Public Health Code also provides for an individualized treatment plan "specifically tailored to the patient's own needs."

Several states, fearful of a court's revamping the entire program for the mentally ill as was the case in the *Wyatt v. Aderholt* decision (infra) have included limiting language in their right-to-treatment sections. The phrase, "to the extent that facilities, equipment and personnel are available," has been included to reduce potential liability for claims against the state for lack of treatment.[18] Dealing with a statute omitting such language, the *Rouse* decision determined that the lack of sufficient staff or facilities is no justification for failure to provide treatment. Other states that have deleted this limiting language include Colorado, Illinois, Indiana, Nevada, Texas, Washington, Idaho, and California.[19]

As noted previously, aside from statutory grounds for the right to treatment, the *Rouse* court suggested that there might also be a constitutional right to treatment based on the due process and equal protection clauses and the ban against cruel and unusual punishment of the Fourteenth and Eighth Amendments. The due process argument takes several turns in its application to the right-to-treatment issue. The first case holding that mental patients have a constitutional right to treatment was *Wyatt v. Stickney*, now *Wyatt v. Aderholt*.[20] The court held that mental patients have a constitutional right "to receive such individual treatment as would give them a realistic opportunity to be cured or to improve his or her mental condition."[21]

This case involved the Bryce State School for the mentally retarded in Alabama. At the time the suit was brought, the school was operating with five thousand residents, three medical doctors (with *some* psychiatric training), two social workers, one psychologist, and a food allotment of fifty cents per patient per day. The court reasoned that "to deprive any citizen of his or her liberty upon the altruistic theory that the confinement is for humane therapeutic reasons and then fail to provide adequate treatment violates the very fundamentals of due process."[22]

The treatment necessary for the mentally retarded was defined as "care provided by mental health professionals and others that is adequate and appropriate for the needs of the mentally impaired inmate...[and] also encompasses a humane physical and psychological environment."[23] If rehabilitation is impossible, then "minimally adequate habilitation and care" must be provided that is "beyond the subsistence level custodial care that would be provided in a penitentiary."[24] The court of appeals upheld both the constitutional right-to-treatment issue and the implementation through judicially manageable standards, which the district court promulgated. These included the following:

- *minimal acceptable staffing patterns*
- *protection to insure a humane psychological environment*
- *a human-rights committee at each state institution*
- *detailed physical standards*
- *minimal acceptable nutritional requirements*
- *individual evaluations of residents*
- *treatment plans and programs*
- *the least restrictive setting for treatment.*

This court took the theoretical leap from the *Rouse* court's dicta to find a constitutional right-to-treatment based on due process and took an even bigger step to supply a remedy, going far beyond ordering the patient's discharge. The *Wyatt* court actually promulgated its own standards of change within the institution to satisfy the right to treatment.

This due process argument was also raised in *O'Connor v. Donaldson*, where the Fifth Circuit Court of Appeals reasoned that where a commitment is under the *parens patriae* rationale and the person is in need of treatment, due process requires that treatment be provided.[25]

The treatment required was adopted from the Wyatt decision: the person has "the right to receive such individual treatment as will give him a reasonable opportunity to be cured or improve his mental condition."[26]

Donaldson had been committed involuntarily by his parents and had spent 15 years in the Florida State Hospital. He repeatedly had demanded his release claiming that he was dangerous to no one, was not mentally ill, and was not receiving any treatment.

Both the district court and the Fifth Circuit Court of Appeals awarded him release and $38 thousand in compensatory and punitive damages against the hospital superintendent and the attending physician for the intentional and malicious deprivation of Donaldson's right to liberty.

The United States Supreme Court vacated the judgment and remanded the case, holding that (1) a state cannot constitutionally confine without more a nondangerous person who is capable of surviving safely in freedom by himself or with the help of willing and responsible family members and friends, and (2) the court of appeals must reconsider the scope of qualified immunity of state officials (thus questioning the superintendent's liability for damages). The Supreme Court refused to deal with the right-to-treatment issue and dealt only with the constitutional right to liberty. But this case does demonstrate another due process rationale and another type of action taken by a patient to protest his treatment in a mental hospital, that of an action for damages under the Civil Rights Act.[27]

Another form of the due process argument for the right to treatment is the quid pro quo rationale that the state must provide treatment in exchange for the relative ease with which persons can be committed under civil-commitment statutes, that is, without the full procedural safeguards of the criminal system. In other words, society must "pay" for ridding itself of dangerous or incompetent members, with the subsequent great loss of liberty to these individuals, by providing adequate and proper treatment.

Such an argument was posed in the Welsch v. Likins case involving the mentally retarded in Minnesota.[28] The quid pro quo argument was taken a step further by the counsel for the plaintiffs in this case; counsel proposed that where a person is not guilty of a criminal offense against society, treatment is the only purpose of confinement that is constitutionally permissible regardless of procedural protections offered in the commitment process.

The district court accepted this argument and held that "due process requires that civil commitment for reasons of mental retardation be accomplished by minimally adequate treatment designed to give each committed person a realistic opportunity to be cured or to improve his or her mental condition."[29] This holding was affirmed on appeal.[30] The district court ordered extensive reforms, as did the Wyatt court, including improvements in the physical plant; limits and restrictions on the use of seclusion, restraining devices, and drugs; and upgraded staffing ratios and requirements.

Several other cases have held that confinement without treatment is a due process violation. One such decision involved a man found incompetent to stand trial for murder, *Nason v. Superintendent of Bridgewater*.[31] He was confined at a maximum security facility in the Massachusetts Department of Corrections.

Another court has held that the right to treatment is so important or basic that it can only be terminated with due process safeguards. That case involved a mentally ill prisoner who was about to be transferred from the state hospital where he was being treated to the penitentiary without a pretermination hearing.[32]

Aside from due process grounds, several cases have revolved around equal protection analysis. A relatively simple statement of the typical equal protection argument follows:

> ... because commitment trenches upon fundamental liberties and is based upon the suspect classification of mental illness, only a compelling state interest can sustain the identification of the mentally ill as special objects of state benevolence or intervention.... [T]he only compelling justification for commitment is treatment and failure to provide treatment vitiates the constitutionality of a commitment.[33]

Such an analysis can be applied to police-power commitments, where the category for the dangerously mentally ill is overly broad. The due process analysis, however, is used much more frequently.

Finally, a constitutional right to treatment has been predicated on the Eighth Amendment prohibition against cruel and unusual punishment. The famous Supreme Court case of *Robinson v. California* has been used as a basis for several court decisions that confinement for mental disability without providing treatment is unconstitutional.[34]

In *Robinson*, the Supreme Court held that the Eighth Amendment prohibits conviction for a criminal offense and incarceration solely for the "status" of being a narcotics addict. The Court in *Welsch* was willing to broadly construe *Robinson* to include those subject to detention for mental illness where there was no curative program being offered to them.[35] The argument is that commitment without treatment is punishment for the status of being mentally ill, a condition over which the person has virtually no control, in violation of the Eighth Amendment. This court goes on to say, however, that the right to treatment essentially comes from the due process clause of the Fourteenth Amendment.

Much criticism from the medical community, especially the psychiatric community, has been leveled against this new wave of right-to-treatment litigation. One noted author, Alan A. Stone, M.D., comments on several issues involved in this area.[36] He notes that this right has been one of judicial action without financial backing from the

Congress and state legislatures to carry out the minimum standards promulgated by such courts as *Wyatt*. Courts have given little guidance to psychiatrists or legislatures as to the general standards of treatment required of mental hospitals and staffs. One of the results of such fast-pased litigation ahead of the dollars to implement such programs is the effects on such groups as the chronically ill but incurable patients. One case cited by Stone was *Lynch v. Baxley*, where a judge of a federal district court held that one of the findings necessary for a valid involuntary commitment order was that treatment be available for the diagnosed illness.[37] The only exception to this rule was for a seriously dangerous person whose confinement was necessary for both the patient himself and the community's safety.[38] As a result of such a holding, there is a potential for a dangerous situation where mentally ill patients who have chronic, incurable conditions may be discharged into a community with few community-based alternatives (other than the institution for care).

Stone discusses the situation in New York, where the civil-commitment statutes require a finding of dangerousness before a person can be involuntarily committed. According to this author's statistics, in 1975, 25 thousand former mental patients were living in rundown inner-city hotels on welfare, with no supervision, medication, or care. Stone raises the question, "Will we choose in the name of freedom to move from warehousing to abandonment?"[39] He suggests that mental health treatment be provided that is as similar as possible to medical health care, with the same alternatives and with some financial support for programs for the mentally ill from a national health insurance plan.

The courts face serious dilemmas in promulgating higher standards of treatment for the mentally ill. There is the possibility that the states will simply close mental institutions rather than try to conform to these judicial standards. This happened in Texas, where a decision dictating standards for juvenile detention homes resulted in the closure of the majority of boys' homes in that state.[40] Unless state legislatures agree to release the needed money, or until a court can successfully pressure them to do so and still stay within its authority, these newfound rights might be slow in being implemented.

The attorney for the plantiffs in the *Wyatt* case from Alabama searched the legislative records to find data on other state expenditures, including the Miss Alabama Pageant, a football hall of fame, and a livestock coliseum, and "observed that more money was spent on individual animals at the local zoo than on his clients." He quipped wryly that his clients would be better cared for in Alabama if they were "athletic or photogenic cows of Confederate ancestry."[41] As in all cases, state expenditures are on a priority basis. Mental health advocates will have to continue to work with the legislatures toward establishing a priority for mentally ill patients.

One hopes that our courts will continue to play an important role in the implementation of the right to treatment through pressure on the legislature. One judge expresses the sentiments that

> Courts cannot force legislatures to provide adequate resources for treatment. But neither should they play handmaiden to the social hypocrisy which rationalizes confinement by a false promise of treatment. Quite the contrary, courts should and must reveal to society the reality that often festers behind the euphemism of "hospitalization."
>
> •
>
> When the legislature justifies confinement by a promise of treatment, it thereby commits the community to provide the resources necessary to fulfill the promise. In the rarefied world of orthodox legal reasoning, infinitely more elegant statutory and constitutional arguments are possible and perhaps necessary. But whether the right to treatment is rooted in statutory provisions or in concepts of due process of law, equal protection, or cruel and unusual punishment, the duty that society assumes, to fulfill the promise of treatment employed to justify involuntary hospitalization, is clear.[42]

Notes & References

1. *Rouse v. Cameron*, 373 F.2d 451, 458–59 (D.C. Cir. 1966).
2. See, McKinney's Consol. Laws of N.Y. vol. 34A § 9.03.
3. *Welsch v. Likins*, 373 F. Supp. 487 (D. Minn 1974).
4. Minn. Stat. Ann. § 253 A.02 (5) and .07 (18).
5. D.C. Code Encycl. 1965 § 21–562.
6. Id. at 456.
7. Fla. Public Health Code § 394.459.
8. Kan. Stat. Ann. 1976 § 59–2927.
9. Kan. Stat. Ann. 59–2902 (10).
10. Conn. Gen. Stat. § Ann. 1976 § 17–206 d.
11. N.J. Stat. Ann. 1975 tit. 30 § 4–24.1.
12. *Rouse v. Cameron* and *Welsch v. Likins*, supra.
13. *Rouse v. Cameron*, id. at 456.
14. Page's Ohio Rev. Code § 5122.27(a); other rules cited from the Ohio Code are from § 5122.27 (C) (D) and (F) 1–7.
15. See also, Wis. Stat. Ann., State Mental Health Act § 51.61 1 (f)—(r); Code of Ga. Ann. 1978 § 88–501 (g) and (w).
16. Gen. Stat. of N.C. 1973 ch. 122 § 122–55.5; other N.C. rules cited are from § 122–55.6
17. N.H. Rev. Stat. Ann. 1973 § 135–B:43 and 135–B:44.
18. See, N.J. Stat. Ann. 1965 tit. 30 § 4–24.1 before words deleted by laws of 1975, ch. 85 § 1, effective May 7, 1975.
19. Civil commitment of the mentally ill, *Harvard Law Review* 87:1320, n. 16, Apr. 1974.

20. *Wyatt v. Stickney*, now *Wyatt v. Aderholt*, 325 F. Supp. 781 (M.D. Ala. 1971), 344 F. Supp. 373 (M.D. Ala. 1971), 334 F. Supp. 1341 (M.D. Ala. 1972), aff'd in part, modified in part, 503 F.2d 1305 (5th Cir. 1974).
21. *Wyatt v. Aderholt*, 344 F. Supp. at 387.
22. *Wyatt v. Aderholt*, 325 F. Supp. at 785.
23. *Wyatt v. Aderholt*, 503 F.2d at 1306, n. 1.
24. *Wyatt v. Aderholt*, id. at 1306.
25. *O'Connor v. Donaldson*, 493 F.2d 507, 521 (5th Cir. 1974).
26. Id. at 520.
27. Civil Rights Act § 1983.
28. *Welsch v. Likins*, supra at 487.
29. Id. at 499, citing *Wyatt v. Aderholt*.
30. *Welsch v. Likins*, 550 F.2d 1120 (8th Cir. 1977).
31. *Nason v. Superintendent of Bridgewater*, 233 N.E.2d 908 (1968); see also, *Negron v. Preiser*, 382 F. Supp. 535 (S.D. N.Y. 1974).
32. *Burchett v. Bower*, 355 F. Supp 1278 (D. Ariz. 1973).
33. Civil commitment of the mentally ill, *Harvard Law Review*, supra at 1329–30.
34. *Robinson v. California*, 370 U.S. 660 (1962); *Welsch v. Likins*, supra; see also, *Martarella v. Kelley*, applying to juvenile delinquents, 349 F. Supp. 575 (D.C. N.Y. 1972).
35. *Welsch v. Likins*, 373 F. Supp., id. at 496.
36. Stone, Alan A., Overview: the right to treatment—comments on the law and its impact, *American Journal of Psychiatry* 132(11):1125–34, Nov. 1975.
37. *Lynch v. Baxley*, 368 F. Supp. 378 (M.D. Ala. 1974), cited in Stone, id.
38. *Lynch v. Baxley*, id. at 391.
39. Stone, Overview: the right to treatment, *American Journal of Psychiatry*, supra at 1133.
40. *Morales v. Turman*, 364 F. Supp. 166 (E.D. Tex. 1973).
41. Friedman, Paul, Behind the institutional wall, *Trial* 11 (6): 30, Nov.-Dec. 1975.
42. Bazelon, David L., Implementing the right to treatment, *University of Chicago Law Review* 36:742, 749, Summer 1969.

CHAPTER 8

Informed Consent and the Right to Refuse Treatment

The mentally ill, involuntarily committed to an institution for treatment, face even more serious problems than have previously been discussed. Many "therapeutic techniques," imposed upon them in the name of "treatment," represent a grave physical assault on their persons, often without their consent or in spite of their refusal. Informed consent treatment by the mentally ill patient is not a uniform requirement from state to state. Just as civil-commitment statutes differ, so do the statutes regarding consent required for certain new and more intrusive forms of therapy, such as electroconvulsive therapy (ECT), psychosurgery, drug therapy, and behavior modification.

In many states, patients involuntarily committed through civil proceedings must accept the treatment their doctor prescribes. Other states allow patients to demand a review by other members of the hospital staff if they object to the prescribed therapy. Many states do require the consent of the patient; but if the patient withholds consent or if a court has determined him to be incompetent, the court allows consent from a guardian or by a court order. Only a few states absolutely respect the right of a mental patient to consent or refuse to consent to the psychiatric treatment recommended by the physician in charge of the case.

INFORMED CONSENT

Theoretically, since those civilly committed are confined in hospitals for treatment, they can quite simply be considered patients in a therapeutic relationship with the attending physician or psychiatrist.

This relationship should be governed by the common-law notions of informed consent, as all other such therapeutic relationships are and have been for decades. The three elements of informed consent are competency, voluntariness, and knowledge. The physician is required to disclose all risks arising from and alternatives to the treatment plan he proposes to a competent patient, who must then have an atmosphere free from coercion or stress in which to decide on consent. Exceptions to the personal consent of the patient include minors and incompetents, for whom the law permits the third-party consent of the parents or legal guardian.

The most important issues involving the mentally ill in this area are (1) whether they are competent to consent to treatment in the first place and (2) whether their consent can be voluntary when they are being involuntarily committed to an institution. If, in fact, the mentally ill who are involuntarily committed are capable of giving informed consent to treatment, then the question becomes whether such consent should be obtained for all treatments or at least for all those that are more intrusive.

The National Commission for the Protection of Human Subjects of Biomedical and Behavioral Research studied research on the institutionalized mentally infirm and published their findings and recommendations. In a rather extensive survey of state status, they compared similarities and differences in standards for commitment and for adjudication of legal incompetency. Their findings are summarized as follows:

> The effect in law of a hospitalization order on the competency status of a patient varies from state to state. In a few states the hospitalization order is also an adjudication of incompetency; in others, it results in at least presumptive incapacity; and in still others, there is a complete separation of hospitalization and incompetency... the trend in legislation has been toward the complete separation of hospitalization and incompetency.[1]

Although the modern trend is to separate the question of competency from commitability, and although competency is not a medical decision but one to be determined by a court, in practice, institutional psychiatrists often control the treatment decision. Psychiatrists argue that the very fact that a person is involuntarily civilly committed implies his incompetence voluntarily to seek and consent to treatment.[2] At least one court has used this rationale to refuse to award damages for a nonconsensual administration of electroshock therapy.[3]

As far as voluntariness goes, another problem arises for the institutionalized mental patient. It is arguable whether a voluntary consent is possible in such an atmosphere of separation from society; dependence on treatment personnel; and vulnerability to force, duress, or coercion. Nevertheless, several courts have balanced the factors and found that voluntary informed consent can be given in prison settings, which may be even more coercive environments than mental hospitals.[4]

Although lawyers have argued that both the competency and voluntary elements are lacking in the institutional setting, courts have held that mental patients have the right to give or withhold consent to treatment.[5]

THE RIGHT TO REFUSE TREATMENT

The treatment afforded the mentally ill has a rather interesting and alarming history. In the early eighteenth century, such outrageous cures as bloodletting and the "well cure" were commonly used. The latter procedure involved chaining the patient to the bottom of a well into which water was slowly poured to create the terror of being close to death.[6]

The psychiatric profession developed more humane, conventional forms of treatment, getting away from the physical to a more verbal approach to treatment, requiring the patient's active and voluntary participation. These types of therapy include psychoanalysis, group therapy, and environmental or mileau therapy. In psychoanalysis, the doctor and patient conduct dialogues, in which unconscious and preconscious material is brought to the patient's consciousness and analyzed. Group therapy involves two or more patients and a therapist who verbally and emotionally interact as a group to discover and treat mental disorders. The final mode of therapy, mileau therapy, has been criticized as "simple custodial hospitalization" in disguise.[7] This form of therapy controls the emotional climate surrounding the patient to accomplish a therapeutic goal.[8]

In recent years, such conventional modes of therapy are being replaced by or supplemented with more radical methods. The new methods of treatment do not require the patient's cooperation (aside from his initial consent to the procedure where state statute or hospital policy requires such consent), and the treatments can often be administered against the patient's will. These more intrusive methods of treating mental disorders include psychosurgery, electroconvulsive therapy, psychopharmacology, and behavior-modification programs.

Psychosurgery

The most radical procedure for treating the mentally ill is psychosurgery, a term referring to the modification of a patient's behavior through surgery on the brain. This term is often used incorrectly as synonymous with lobotomy. Lobotomy is one form of psychosurgery. Lobotomy technically means an "incision into a lobe [of the brain] for any purpose" or a "division of one or more nerve tracts in a lobe of the cerebrum."[9] Lobotomy has also been described as the "amputation of the prefrontal, bimedial or transcortical portions of the brain."[10]

The first lobotomy performed in the United States occurred circa 1936 when two surgeons implemented the research techniques of a Portugese team of physicians who had successfullly performed bilateral, prefrontal lobotomies on human subjects.[11]

This technique can be considered highly controversial, since the purpose, effectiveness, adverse effects, and ethics of psychosurgery are highly debated. Also, the National Commission for the Protection of Human Subjects of Bethesda, Maryland, labeled it "an experimental procedure to be regulated by stringent safeguards."[12] Nevertheless, it was widely used until, in 1977, a moratorium was declared on its use pending investigation by the United States Department of Health, Education, and Welfare (DHEW). This moratorium was lifted in 1978 and the Commission published their recommendations. The National Commission on the Protection of Human Subjects, under the auspices of DHEW, conducted extensive research on and investigation of psychosurgery and recommended that this technique be performed only after review by an institutional review board to determine such issues as consent, medical necessity, and lack of alternative forms of treatment.[13]

Psychosurgery is a unique form of treatment in that the change is irreversible. While in many cases those previously considered hopelessly ill were eventually rehabilitated and released by this radical procedure, the risks and untoward effects are tremendous and have been the source of debate over the effectiveness and ethics of such treatment. For example, many lobotomized patients experience a profound reduction in frontal-lobe functions, which include insight, empathy, sensitivity, self-awareness, judgment and emotional response.

Psychosurgery has been used "to modify such behavior as homosexuality, frigidity, hyperactivity, schizophrenia, acute depression, criminal activity, compulsive gambling, alcoholism and drug addiction."[14] Studies indicate more favorable results in combating depression, neurosis, and phobias and less favorable results in schizophrenia.[15]

A "sizeable and vocal minority" led by Peter Breggin, M.D., is pushing for abolition of this controversial technique. They take the position that mutilation of the brain can never be justified by an "improvement in function."[16]

Despite the lack of agreement surrounding this controversial technique, psychosurgery is legal and may be performed on mental patients, subject to state regulation, since the Department of Health, Education, and Welfare's appointed commission refused to recommend a ban. Currently, Texas has banned all frontal lobotomies, and several states let the patients determine whether psychosurgery may be performed, a decision which cannot be overriden by the hospital, a relative, or a court order.[17]

Most states require the patient's consent before psychosurgery can be performed but allow a substituted consent of the guardian or a court order to override the patient's wishes. Several states give the mental patient the right to have the recommendation for surgery reviewed by the medical staff prior to use, which, in effect, gives the hospital a final say in the matter; although, under the commission recommendations adopted by DHEW, such a review board must take into account the medical necessity and the alternative forms of treatment along with the patient's competency to consent.[18]

One case that may have an impact on both these consent statutes and the use of psychosurgery in state institutions is *Kaimowitz v. Michigan Department of Mental Health* (supra). A Michigan Circuit Court held that neither an involuntarily committed patient nor his legal guardian could give legally adequate consent to experimental brain surgery.

The court determined that there were two constitutional rights at stake: the First Amendment right of free expression and the right to privacy. A rather innovative interpretation of the First Amendment was used in this case: "To the extent that the First Amendment protects dissemination of ideas and expression of thoughts, it equally must protect the individual's right to generate ideas."[19] The court found the right to privacy based on a recent decision of the Ninth Circuit Court of Appeals in *Mackey v. Procunier*.[20] The forcible injection of an experimental drug was found to be "impermissible tinkering with the mental processes," in violation of the right to privacy.[21] Since psychosurgery is far more intrusive than the injection of a drug, it must fall within the scope of the right to privacy.[22]

Because there are constitutional rights at stake, the court determined that the three elements of competency, knowledge, and voluntariness must be present for a person effectively to waive these rights. The patient had a diminished capacity for evaluation and judgment due to his "prolonged incarceration in [a] mental facility"; so he did not possess the sufficient competency required to wave his constitutional rights to free expression and privacy. "Despite outward manifestations of competency and lucidity, the court reasoned that a *priori*, a patient whose every decision has been superimposed by administrative order cannot independently decide to consent to experimental psychosurgery."[23]

The court likewise dispensed of the possibility of the patient's having "knowledge," since psychosurgery has such uncertain risks and effects.[24] Because the atmosphere of the institution was inherently coercive and because Smith (the patient) was obviously motivated by his desire to be released, the court found that the element of voluntariness likewise was missing. The patient lacked the means to consent; so the court held that the patient's parents could not consent for him.

Thus far, the *Kaimowitz* decision has not been widely followed. It utilizes an unprecedented First Amendment approach and a restrictive informed-consent analysis in the institutional setting. Yet, it may represent a future trend in prohibiting psychosurgery.

Electroconvulsive (Shock) Therapy (ECT)

ECT is a technique commonly used to treat psychotic depression "whereby 70-130 volts of electricity is permitted to flow through the patient's brain causing a convulsion equivalent to an epileptic seizure."[25] This form of treatment, along with psychosurgery, is often labeled "intrusive." The theory behind this radical treatment is that a series of severe shocks to the brain can reverse behavioral patterns and stimulate a previously unresponsive patient out of depression, mania, or schizophrenia. The adverse side effects produced by this treatment include disorientation, confusion, and some memory impairment (long term more often than short term). Also, there is the possibility of bone fractures due to the severity of the convulsions produced; and, in rare cases, death has occurred.[26] The permanency and extent of these effects is difficult if not impossible to predict and subjects this treatment to some controversy.

Most states have enacted legislation in regard to the necessity of the patient's consent to use ECT. No states have outlawed its use thus far, but several states require the patient's consent before such treatment is given, thus acknowledging the right to refuse this form of treatment.[27] A few states require an additional consent from the guardian, along with a review by some regulatory board.[28] As with psychosurgery, most states permit a substitute consent from a parent or guardian or a court order that may override the patient's consent or refusal to consent.

Several states, Idaho for one, allow the doctor or the hospital authorities to make the ultimate decision to use ECT. Several add other requirements.[29]

- Authorities must submit to the district court a statement of good cause explaining why the treatment should be given over the patient's objections (Indiana, Massachusetts, and Nebraska).
- The consent of the patient's guardian or nearest relative as well as the physician's decision is needed (Oregon, Texas).
- A court order is needed to proceed with treating a minor over a parent's objections (Vermont).

Thus, the patient's right to refuse this intrusive form of treatment varies widely from state to state.

Several courts have ruled on ECT, reflecting a trend toward guaranteeing a right to refuse hazardous or experimental therapies including ECT. In *Wyatt v. Stickney*, the court held that the mentally ill in Alabama have the right to not be subjected to lobotomy, ECT, adversive reinforcement conditioning, or other unusual or hazardous conditioning without their express and informed consent and even then only after consultation with counsel or another interested party.[30]

In the companion decision concerning the mentally retarded, the court added the additional requirements of review by a human-rights committee and personal or third-party consent before ECT could be administered. The court went on to say that ECT could be administered only "in extraordinary circumstances to prevent self-mutilation lead-ing to repeated and possibly permanent physical damage... and only after alternative techniques have failed."[31] Alabama statutes are silent about the extent to which a patient can withhold consent for ECT or psychosurgery.

In *New York City Health and Hospitals Corporation v. Stein* (supra), the judge was asked to interpret the new New York Mental Hygiene Law, which provided that "subject to the regulations of the commis-sioner [of the department of mental hygiene], the director of a facility shall require... consent for... shock treatment."[32] Despite the failure of the statute to dicate whose consent is required, the court interpreted the statute to mean that "consent of the patient himself" is required "provided that he possess the mental capacity to knowingly consent or withhold his consent, or, in the absence of such mental capacity, the consent of the closest relative or guardian of the person, if there be any, or, when necessary, of the Court."[33]

The court was dealing with a petition from the hospital requesting an order authorizing the psychiatric staff to administer ECT over the objections of an adult patient. The patient in question had been involuntarily committed for care and treatment under a commitment statute. Her mother had given her consent to the treatment.

Although evidence was produced to show that the respondent was a chronic schizophrenic, was not responding to "conventional psycho-pharmaceutical treatment," and showed marked improvement after two prior ECT treatments, and in spite of testimony from the doctors in charge that she was incapable of making a rational decision about treatment, the court denied the petition.

Two court-appointed psychiatrists determined that this women had the mental capacity to "know and understand whether she wishes to consent to electoshock therapy."[34] The court relied on their testimony to uphold the patient's refusal of ECT. Thus, in New York, if it is determined that a mental patient has the mental capacity to consent to treatment, her decision will be upheld.

A more recent Minnesota case took a somewhat different approach in finding that the state could override the express wishes of a patient's guardian and administer ECT treatments to a minor. In *Price v. Sheppard*, a mother brought an action for damages under the Civil Rights Act (§ 1983), when her son was subjected, without her consent, to a series of 20 ECT treatments over a six-to-seven-week span of time.[35]

The court determined that the use of ECT in this case was not "punishment" for purposes of the Eighth Amendment ban on cruel and unusual punishment. The constitutional right that was found to be at stake here was the right to privacy, which can be intruded upon only where there is "a legitimate and important state interest." Since the state's interest is sufficient to deprive this person of his physical liberty, the court held that this interest is likewise "sufficiently important for the state to assume the treatment decision."[36] After the importance of the state's interest is established, under constitutional analysis, the next step is to determine whether the action taken was necessary and reasonable under the facts in the case. This court chose not to proceed with this step, instead relying on the qualified immunity of state officials acting in their official capacity.

In order for the mother to succeed under the Civil Rights Act and to overcome the medical director's qualified immunity, she would have to prove that the individual acted with the malicious intention of causing a deprivation of a constitutional right.[37] The court determined that the right of privacy is so vague that the defendant could not reasonably have known that administering ECT would violate this right, and that the defendant acted in good faith, having used a less intrusive form of treatment, psychopharmacology, for three months prior to using ECT. The doctors in charge determined that administering ECT would benefit the patient much more than keeping him confined to his room, which had been necessary owing to his assaultive behavior.

The Minnesota Court set a more stringent standard for the use of ECT. Where both the patient and his guardian refuse to consent to ECT, hospital authorities must secure a court order. The action is similar to the procedure used in *New York City Health and Hospitals Corporation v. Stein* (supra). The court laid the following guidelines for balancing the need for treatment against the intrusiveness of the prescribed treatment:

> *Factors which should be considered are 1) the extent and duration of changes in behavior patterns and mental activity effected by the treatment, 2) the risks of adverse side effects, 3) the experimental nature of the treatment, 4) its acceptance by the medical community of this state, 5) the extent of intrusion into the patient's body and the pain connected with the treatment, and 6) the patient's ability to competently determine for himself whether the treatment is desirable.*[38]

The Minnesota legislature has not yet acted to uphold these guidelines by statute, but this case is still the law in Minnesota.

Psychopharmacology

Most statutes exclude drug therapy with antidepressants, antipsychotics, tranquilizers, hormones, and neuroleptics to treat mental disorders from the more intrusive therapies. Many legal commentators, however, consider psychopharmacology in a class with ECT and psychosurgery. Many critics argue that drugs are used primarily for control purposes rather than treatment. This form of treatment is used throughout mental hospitals and does not require the voluntary cooperation of the patient to be effective, just as ECT and psychosurgery do not. According to one author, research is inadequate to demonstrate the effectiveness of many of the drugs being used, and medical students are not being properly trained in the use of these drugs.[39] Some of the adverse effects of these routinely used drugs included muscle spasms, restlessness, agitation, drooling, tremors, drowsiness, weakness, dizziness, apathy, and depression. Death has occurred in rare instances.[40]

Statutory restrictions on the use of drugs in mental hospitals are much less prevalent than for either ECT or psychosurgery. Only three states give patients the ultimate decision on accepting drug therapy, but they may decide only in certain circumstances. In Michigan, the patient can refuse drugs unless they are necessary to prevent physical injury to the patient or another.[41] In New York, a mental patient has the absolute right to refuse experimental drugs.[42] Arguably, all these drugs are experimental, considering the adverse side effects and the inadequacy of research. In Washington, a patient may refuse any medication for up to 24 hours prior to his probable-cause-commitment hearing.[43] Illinois's new Mental Health Code (effective January 1, 1979), gives the patient the right to refuse medication except where, in the opinion of the medical staff, "substantial harm" would occur to himself or others.

Most states are silent as to the consent required for drug therapy. Several states including Florida, Montana, New Jersey, North Dakota, Iowa, and Wisconsin simply provide that the mental patient has the right to be "free from unnecessary and excessive medication." Such a phrase, however, gives patients of the kind to whom drugs are usually considered necessary little armor to fight against a medical staff that uses these drugs as standard procedure.

A few states limit the use of drugs as a restraining device (for control of the patient only) to emergency situations,[44] or where "medical needs require."[45] Kansas places a blanket restriction on all experimental medication.[46]

The cases that have been brought to court protesting institutional drug use have involved mental patients, prisoners, and juvenile delinquents. The cases all involve violations of constitutional rights including the right to privacy, the Eighth Amendment ban against cruel and unusual punishment, the First Amendment freedom of religion, the right to be free of "impermissible tinkering with mental processes," and Fourteenth Amendment due process.

The administration of drugs to control or punish behavior has been held to be a violation of the Eighth Amendment. In *Knecht v. Gillman*, the Eighth Circuit Court enjoined the use of the drug apomorphine at the Iowa Security Medical Facility, a state mental institution.[47] The drug was being injected intramuscularly as part of a behavioral modification program, which inmates "voluntarily" joined. Patients received the drug after violations of hospital rules, such as not getting up on time, lying, swearing, or talking at inappropriate times. The drug causes vomiting that persists for 15 minutes to one hour.

The hospital authorities defended the use of apomorphine as "aversion therapy," used only after obtaining the patient's initial written consent. There was no evidence, however, that consent could be withdrawn at any time, which the court believed was necessary to uphold the ethics of such a program. The court held that the use of this drug was cruel and unusual punishment prohibited by the Eighth Amendment and enjoined its use unless the written and demonstrated informed consent of a competent inmate was secured but could be revoked at will.

The court ruled that the drug must be authorized individually by a doctor, administered by either a doctor or a nurse, and used only after a member of the professional staff personally observed the conduct requiring such behavior modification. The hospital staff had been administering the drug on occasion where another patient reported the offender, without the personal observation of a staff member.

A mental patient involuntarily committed after having been found not guilty of murder by reason of insanity claimed his First and Eighth Amendment rights were violated when he was treated with several drugs without his consent. The drugs chlorpromazine (Thorazine) and prochlorperazine (Compazine), which produced a "dazed condition, engendering apathy and slowing the thought processes," were administered to this patient.[48]

The court held in *Scott v. Plante* that the district court's summary dismissal of the plaintiff's claim was improper, since there were "at least three constitutional violations that may accompany the involuntary administration of such substances by state officers under color of state law to inmates confined in a state institution."[49] The court discussed a possible deprivation of First Amendment rights where drugs are administered "which affect mental processes," a possible violation of Fourteenth Amendment due process for treating a person without notice or the opportunity to be heard as to his competency to consent to the treatment, and a possible Eighth Amendment violation for cruel and unusual punishment.

A state prisoner brought a civil-rights action against a prison official of California state when he was administered succinylcholine, a "fright drug" that causes breath stoppage and temporary paralysis.[50] This prisoner, without his consent, was part of an experiment that used aversive treatment on criminal offenders in the form of ECT and drug injections. The court remanded the case with instructions to proceed on the merits, finding that "serious constitutional questions respecting cruel and unusual punishment or impermissible tinkering with the mental processes" had been raised.

Authorities in a medium-security correctional institution for boys were administering the tranquilizing drugs, promazine (Sparine) and chlorpromazine (Thorazine) intramuscularly to control the boys' "excited behavior." One boy testified he had been given an injection after he yelled for help following a fight in which his nose was bloodied.

Another was drugged to prevent his running away after an attempt to escape failed. The court found the practice to constitute cruel and unusual punishment.[51]

Evidence showed that nurses made the case-by-case determinations on administering the drugs and then administered them "upon recommendation of the custodial staff and under standing orders of the physician." This meant that the doctor did not prescribe the drug on a case-by-case basis. Medication milder than the intramuscularly injected tranquilizers was not used. The juveniles were never examined before or after the injections to determine their tolerance for the drugs. The district court order enjoining such practice was upheld by the court of appeals. The court ordered that the drugs be administered only when authorized and directed by a physician in each case and only after oral medication was first tried.[52]

In *Winters v. Miller*, a woman involuntarily admitted to a hospital under the New York Emergency Commitment Statute brought a civil-rights action against the mental hygiene commissioner.[53] She claimed her First Amendment right to freedom of religion was violated when she was forced to take medication contrary to her beliefs as a Christian Scientist. The medication consisted of "heavy doses of tranquilizers [administered] both orally and intramuscularly" over a period of approximately six weeks.[54] The court held that the plaintiff had successfully stated a claim for damages based on a violation of her First Amendment rights, since she was never adjudged mentally incompetent and since the doctor and hospital had been notified of her religious beliefs.

These cases clearly demonstrate that a mental patient's consent is necessary before the administration of any type of experimental drug that has serious physical repercussions. Drugs used strictly for control purposes may be banned as cruel and unusual punishment unless other and less drastic alternatives are first attempted. Finally, a patient's religious beliefs must be respected where consent is withheld. Possible limitations on this rule may occur where drugs may be necessary to save the life of the patient. Violation of such rights may result in damages being assessed against the hospital or mental health department (unless qualified immunity applies). If qualified immunity applies, the result may be an injunction prohibiting the use of the drugs.

Behavior Modification

Behavior-modification techniques (behavior therapy) also are used to treat mental disorders. "Behavior modification rests on the assumption that people can be influenced by the consequences of their behavior, and that through controlling these consequences by a number of diverse techniques, their behavior can be changed."[55] There are several types of behavior therapy including desensitization, aversion therapy, and operant conditioning.[56] Desensitization combats phobias by gradually exposing the patient to unpleasant experiences. Aversion therapy, the most controversial treatment in this category, involves punishment for inappropriate behavior. Often drugs or electric shock are administered as the aversive devices.[57] Aversion therapy has been used to treat homosexual fixations, alcoholism, drug addiction, and sexual deviances.[58] Operant conditioning is the opposite of aversion therapy, in that the desired behavior is reinforced, or approval is withheld after unwanted behavior.

Behavior modification has become the subject of substantial criticism for several reasons. Since there is no "clear and universally recognized norm for acceptable behavior," the behavior therapist himself becomes the "ultimate arbitrater of social acceptability."[59]

The patient often has no real choice in planning the therapeutic goals and methods to be used in a behavior-modification program, but simply is "plugged-in" to a program the hospital staff have developed. The *Knecht* and *Mackey* cases (the cases involving apomorphine and succinylcholine) are two good examples of how physically intrusive and dangerous such programs can be. It is arguable how voluntary and informed the consent can ever be to such programs, given the institutional setting and the experimental nature of the drugs in behavior therapy. According to the ethics of the psychiatric profession, DHEW regulations, and case law in this area, programs involving noxious stimuli must have the express and informed consent of the patient, meaning as follows:

> The rights and welfare of subjects must be adequately protected, the risks to an individual must be outweighed by the potential benefits to him... and informed consent should be obtained by methods that are adequate and appropriate... risks are defined to include not only potential physical harm, but also adverse psychological reactions or social injury.[60]

Not many state statutes deal directly with behavior modification in the Mental Health Code. One state, Florida, bans the use of "aversive stimuli"; several statutes have general language that implies the right to refuse behavior therapy, and Montana statutes restrict behavior modification and unusual or hazardous treatment programs.[61] At least two state statutes require informed consent for aversive stimuli: Ohio and California.[62]

Although few cases deal specifically with behavior modification programs, one author states, "Judicial rulings are not necessary to emphasize that aversive techniques are neither legally nor ethically acceptable when they are used solely for oppressive purposes or *without the consent* of the person on whom they are used, or his guardian."[63] [Emphasis added]

In *Wyatt v. Stickney* (supra), the Federal District Court in Alabama held that the mentally ill were not to be subjected to aversive reinforcement conditioning without their express and informed consent and then only "after consultation with counsel or interested party of the patient's choice."[64] In a companion decision, the court added requirements for review by the human-rights committee before such therapy could be used on the mentally retarded.[65]

There is definitely a judicial and legislative trend toward guaranteeing the mental patient's right to refuse any hazardous or experimental therapy. The use of aversive stimuli such as drugs or electric shocks definitely would fall within the class of "hazardous" therapies.

Courts have also looked at behavior modification programs that use positive reinforcement. Many mental hospitals have a "token" economy, whereby patients can earn money or tokens by working in the hospital on various jobs. The program gives them an opportunity to learn skills and reinforces acceptable behavior, along with increasing their self-respect. Two cases, *Wyatt v. Stickney* (supra) and *Jobson v. Henne,* bar all involuntary work by patients on hospital operations and maintenance and disallow a system in which patients must work for certain privileges.[66] *Wyatt* also held that mental patients must earn the minimum wage for any hospital work, except for therapeutic work unrelated to hospital maintenance and operations or personal housekeeping chores.[67] Several states have codified these holdings in mental health statutes.[68]

Many of the "privileges" ordinarily paid for by tokens in such programs have now been determined to be constitutional rights.

> *According to recent legal developments, patients may have a constitutional right to a residence unit with screens or curtains to insure privacy, a comfortable bed, a closet or locker for personal belongings, a chair, a bedside table, nutritionally adequate meals, visitors, attendance at religious services, their own clothes or a selection of suitable clothing, regular physical exercise including access to the outdoors, interaction with members of the opposite sex, and a television in the day room.*

> •

> *[T]he result of the rulings is to permit the restriction in availability of these items and activities only with the consent of the patients or representatives of the patients.*[69]

Several state statutes list many of these rights in their "patients' rights" section. The extent to which these rights may be limited or restricted is strictly defined. In North Carolina, for example, a mental patient has the following statutory rights:

> *[E]ach treatment facility shall insure to each patient the right to live as normally as possible while receiving care and treatment.*

> **(a)** *Each patient of a treatment facility shall at all times retain the right to:*

1) Send and receive sealed mail, and have access to writing material, postage, and staff assistance when necessary;
2) Contact and consult with legal counsel and private physicians of his choice at his expense.

• •

(b)
1) Make and receive confidential telephone calls. . . .
2) Receive visitors between the hours of 8:00 A.M. and 9:00 P.M. for a period of at least six hours daily. . . .
3) Make visits outside the institution unless such patient was committed under Article 11, Ch. 122 (criminal code)
4) Be out of doors daily and have access to facilities and equipment for physical exercise several times a week;
5) Keep and use his own clothing and personal possessions;
6) Communicate and meet under appropriate supervision with persons of his own choice, upon the consent of such persons;
7) Participate in religious worship;
8) Keep and spend a reasonable sum of his own money;
9) Retain a motor vehicle driver's license. . . .
10) Have access to individual storage space.[70]

Similar statutory schemes may be found in New Jersey, Washington, California, and Wisconsin.[71]

Since the preceding rights are now considered constitutional or are statutorily guaranteed in many states, mental health workers and hospitals can restrict these rights only under circumstances that constitute a valid waiver of these rights. Where a constitutional right exists, a patient can waive this right only where three elements are present: voluntariness, competency, and knowledge. In other words, the patient must be informed that he has the rights in question, he must be competent to relinquish his rights, and the atmosphere in which he makes this decision must be free of any coercion or duress.

Where these rights are guaranteed by statute, the hospital and therapists must comply with the provision regarding the prohibition or restriction of the rights. For example, in North Carolina, only the second set of rights (those listed under **b** in the statute just quoted) can be limited or restricted by the hospital and only when a written statement of reasons is made by the professional in mental health or mental retardation who is responsible for that patient's treatment plan.[72] Notice of the restrictions, which cannot exceed 30 days, along with the detailed reasons must be given to the patient, his next of kin or guardian, and the secretary of human resources.[73]

New Jersey has a similar provision, the only difference being that the patient's attorney must also be notified of any denial of the patient's rights.[74] In Wisconsin, patients' rights are separated into two categories as far as denial or restriction goes. Rights such as those previously mentioned under North Carolina law can be denied, but the patient has the opportunity to refute the grounds for denial.[75] The more basic or fundamental rights such as the right to treatment, the right to be free of unnecessary or excessive medication, and the right to the least restrictive conditions, however, may not be denied without an administrative hearing, subject to court review.[76] Unlike the New Jersey and North Carolina statutes, the Wisconsin legislation considers the right to receive wages or allowance for work, the right to send sealed mail and have access to letter-writing materials, and the right to religious worship in the facility to be in this category of rights that cannot be denied without an administrative hearing.

LEGAL TRENDS AND THE PSYCHIATRIC PROFESSION

The emerging legal trend granting mental patients, including those involuntarily committed, the right to refuse treatment has caused some consternation in the psychiatric community. One author discusses a case in which a psychiatric treatment team was faced with a dilemma involving the right to treatment and the patient's right to refuse ECT treatment.[77]

The case involved a 43-year-old woman hospitalized for severe depression, weight loss, and insomnia. The woman expressed the desire to kill herself and mentioned a "plan." She had responded favorably to ECT in the past but refused to consent to treatment during this hospitalization, saying that she was incapable of being helped and wanted to die. The team, with the cooperation of the patient's family, initiated a 48-hour emergency commitment and petitioned the court for an indeterminate commitment, which would require a hearing. Scheduling the hearing would take two to three weeks.

In the meantime, the attending physician determined that this woman had the right to treatment, which imposed on him and on the hospital the legal duty to begin a treatment plan. Considering her condition and her response to treatment in the past, the obvious treatment, in his opinion, was ECT. Eight treatments were administered in the three-week period prior to the commitment hearing, in spite of the patient's protests but with her husband's consent.

The treatments produced marked improvements, such that, at the beginning of the hearing, the woman was no longer a danger to herself or to others. She was not formally committed. The court pointed out, however, that since the woman had initially rejected this treatment, her civil rights had been violated. Although the court took no action against the psychiatrists, they put them on notice that such action was illegal under these circumstances.

This author, William D. Weitzel, goes on to lament the plight of psychiatrists in such cases:

> Psychiatrists, as physicians, are trained to render treatment for mental illness. Patients rightfully expect it. Hospital utilization review committees, PSROs, and insurance carriers all contribute

to the proper expectations that each patient should be treated without delay in a fashion consistent with sound professional judgment. Recent legal decisions indicate that individual psychiatrists will be held responsible in the future for inadequate treatment that their patients may receive in public institutions.

•••

It seem[s] self-evident that there [is] something logically inconsistent in allowing a person so incapacitated by illness to make an antitherapeutic decision with respect to treatment.... Psychiatrists may no longer presume to know what is best and to implement a treatment plan forthwith unless the patient or a legally designated guardian has been informed and has participated in an affirmative decision.[78]

Another noted psychiatrist and professor, Alan A. Stone, discusses the results in a mental hospital after a federal district judge in Massachusetts issued a temporary restraining order allowing patients the right to refuse treatment and preventing the use of seclusion except in extreme emergencies.[79] The Massachusetts Psychiatric Society submitted an amicus curiae brief to the court summarizing the results of the order:

Tensions seem to fill the air at the Austin Unit twenty-four hours a day. One wing has been destroyed by fire, set by a patient. One female patient attempted to burn a staff member, to choke a patient, and to strangle herself with a ripped dress.... A[n]other patient became so threatening that the night staff sent a letter to Dr. G. signed by all informing him that they could not and would not work under these circumstances.

Another female Austin Unit patient punched a social worker and several patients, cut herself with fliptops, and "gouged her face with her fingernails until she bled; this continued almost daily throughout the month of June."

•••

Patients in the May Unit have experience similar problems. One woman, while refusing medication, became psychotic and left the hospital in anger, lived on a doorstep without changing her clothes for two weeks, was twice returned to the hospital by police, and twice set fire to herself in her room.[80]

Stone goes on to argue that an unqualified right to refuse medication will result in serious harm to both patients and staff, especially where patients are committed for dangerousness. "As one reads this description, one can only conclude that the courts are unwittingly reversing 200 years of progress and transforming the twentieth century dream of the mental health center into the eighteenth century nightmare of Bedlam."[81]

Another group of authors, Roth et al., suggest that competency should be an important criterion in the right to consent to or refuse treatment and that varying degrees of competency should be required, depending on the degree of intrusiveness of the treatment.[82] The authors outline several tests reflecting, in order, the lowest to the highest levels of competency. The tests are "1) evidencing a choice, 2) 'reasonable' outcome of choice, 3) choice based on 'rational' reasons, 4) ability to understand, and 5) actual understanding."[83]

The level or test of competency applied in each case depends on two factors: (1) the interplay between the risks and benefits to the patient, and (2) the patient's decision to either consent or refuse. Figure 8-1 represents this interplay.

Where the "risk/benefit ratio is unfavorable or questionable and the patient refuses treatment, a test employing a low threshold of competency may be selected so that the patient will be found competent and his or her refusal honored."[84] On the other hand, where the risk-benefit ratio is unfavorable and the patient consents to the treatment, a higher threshold of competency should be applied. The *Kaimowitz* case serves as an example of a high test of competency applied to test the consent for a highly intrusive treatment, psychosurgery.

Fig. 8–1. Weighing Mental Patients' Competence to Consent to Treatment*

Low Test of Competence Acceptable when	High Test of Competence Called for when
—a patient consents to a treatment with a high benefit-to-risk ratio. For example, uncomprehending patients may sign themselves into a mental hospital for treatment.	—a patient refuses a treatment with a high-benefit, low-risk ratio. The physician may try to have a fairly comprehending patient declared incompetent, so someone else can sign the consent.
—a patient refuses a treatment with an unfavorable or questionable risk-benefit ratio. Our society feels growing reluctance to let patients undergo extremely risky treatments.	—a patient consents to a treatment with an unfavorable or questionable risk-benefit ratio, for example, psychosurgery.

*Adapted from Roth, et al., "Tests of Competency to Consent to Treatment," ref. 82, p. 283.

In theory, a patient's competence is a question to decide independently. In practice, physicians and judges weigh the patient's comprehension and decision against the value and risks of the treatment.

Roth et al. say that this model could be applied to psychosurgery as follows: Since the side effects of psychosurgery can be extremely adverse (death or loss of frontal lobe functions), in light of a questionable benefit to the patient, a refusal must be honored if he meets a low test of competency, such as "evidencing a choice," or "reasonable outcome of choice." Under the former criterion, "the competent patient is one who evidences a preference for or against treatment," focusing not on the *quality* but the "presence or absence of a decision."[85] The latter test considers whether the patient can make a decision that is "roughly congruent with the decision that a 'reasonable' person in like circumstances would make." If the patient does consent, the highest test of competency should be applied, that of "actual understanding."

Kaimowitz (supra) indicates that mental patients may never be competent for purposes of consenting to psychosurgery after having been institutionalized for any length of time. DHEW regulations and several state statutes indicate that a high level of competency must be met. Under this test, the patient must provide a "knowledgeable consent to treatment" after having been educated by the physician as to the risks and benefits of the treatment. The physician must then "directly ascertain whether he or she has *in fact* understood" these risks and benefits.[86] [Emphasis added]

Alternatively, the hospital may require the next lower level of competency, that of "the ability to understand," which is the test most consistent with the doctrine of informed consent. Here, the patient must have sufficient mental ability to comprehend the elements that are part of the treatment decisions, but the decision-making process itself need not be rational. In other words, as long as the patient can understand the risks and the benefits, how he actually weighs or values these elements is not important.

The Roth-Meisel-Lidz model is an interesting one, attempting to protect the patient's right to treatment and right to refuse treatment. In light of recent developments in the law separating civil commitment from an adjudication of incompetence, it follows that, at least in those jurisdictions with statutes reflecting this trend, the hospital must seek an adjudication of incompetency for each patient who refuses treatment. Where a patient obviously cannot meet even the lowest test for competency, such as "evidencing a choice," use of such a plan would allow necessary treatment to be administered, at least temporarily, without long court delays. The application of different levels of competency, depending on the circumstances in the individual case, seems to combine the most favorable elements of informed consent without crippling the ability of the psychiatrist to practice professionally to the benefit of patients.

The cases that have come down in this area paint a rather bleak picture of institutional treatment of the mentally ill, something which may leave mental health advocates reluctant to leave such discretion in the hands of the treatment staffs. Yet, until a happy medium is reached where the seemingly conflicting right to treatment and right to refuse treatment are protected, it is the mental patient who will suffer. Either extreme appears intolerable; either the patient is given total control over his treatment plan without consideration of mental competence, or the right to treatment somehow translates into the "therapeutic orgy" Plotnick described.

It is obvious that patients will receive little benefit where members of the treatment staff—which usually includes few qualified physicians and psychiatrists—spend most of their time in the courtroom defending the executed treatment plan or the withholding of treatment, or appearing at hearings on the issue of competency.

For the right to treatment and the right to refuse treatment to operate in patients' best interests, a merger of legal principles with good psychiatry must be effected. As long as the two are at odds remaining on separate sides of the courtroom, one questions remains: "Is it really the patients who have had their day in court?"[87]

Notes and References

1. U.S., National Commission for the Protection of Human Subjects of Biomedical and Behavioral Research, *Research Involving Those Institutionalized as Mentally Infirm*, DHEW Publ. No. (OS) 78-0006-7, 1977, quoting Allen, R., Ferster, E., and Weihofen, H., *Mental Impairment and Legal Incompetency* (Englewood Cliffs, N.J.: Prentice-Hall 1968), p. 70.
2. Plotnick, Richard, Limiting the therapeutic orgy: mental patients' right to refuse treatment, *Northwestern Law Review* 72:461, 465, 1978.
3. *Price v. Sheppard*, 239 N.W.2d 905 (Minn. 1976).
4. *Knecht v. Gillman*, 488 F.2d 1136 (8th Cir. 1973); *Henry v. Ciccone*, 315 F. Supp. 889 (W.D. Mo. 1970); Plotnick, supra at 487–88.
5. *Kaimowitz v. Michigan Department of Mental Health*, No. 73-19434-AW (Cir. Ct. Wayne Co. Mich. July 10, 1973).
6. Plotnick, Limiting the therapeutic orgy, *Northwestern U. Law Review*, supra at 46, referring to Deutsch, A., *The Mentally Ill in America*, 1949.
7. Id. at 466.
8. Fabri, Candace J., Constitutional law—an involuntarily detained mental patient's informed consent is invalid for experimental psychosurgery, *Chicago-Kent Law Review* 50:526, Winter 1973.
9. *Stedman's Medical Dictionary*, 22d ed. s.v. "lobotomy."
10. Fabri, Constitutional law, *Chicago-Kent Law Review*, supra at 527.
11. Plotnick, Limiting the therapeutic orgy, *Northwestern U. Law Review*, supra at 467.
12. National Commission for The Protection of Human Subjects of Biomedical and Behavioral Research, March 1978, Bulletin.
13. 42 *Federal Register* 26,318; 26,329 (1977).
14. Fabri, Constitutional law, *Chicago-Kent Review*, supra at 527.
15. Plotnick, Limiting the therapeutic orgy, *Northwestern Law Review*, supra at 470.
16. Plotnick, id. at 470, quoting Breggin, P., "The Return of the Lobotomy and Psychosurgery" 1972, unpublished, reprinted in 118 *Congressional*

Record 5567, 5575, (1972).

17. Tex. Rev. Civ. Stat. Ann. art. 3174b(2); Cal. Welfare and Institutions Code § 5325(f)-(g) (West Supp. 1977); N.Y. Mental Hygiene Law § 15.03(b)(4) (1976); Wash. Rev. Code Ann. § 71.05.370(7) (1975); Wis. Stat. § 51.61(k); S.C. Codes § 44-23-1010; Ky. Rev. Stat. § 202A.180; Mont. Rev. Codes Ann. § 38-1322; N.J. Rev. Stat (if patient also competent) § 30:4-24.2(d)(3).
18. Ind. Code § 16-14-1.5-3(g); see also, Mass. Gen. Laws ch. 123 § 23; Ore. Rev. Stat. § 426.385(2); 426.705; 426.720.
19. *Kaimowitz v. Michigan Department of Mental Health,* supra at 32.
20. *Mackey v. Procunier,* 477 F.2d 877 (9th Cir. 1973).
21. Id. at 878.
22. Fabri, Constitutional Law, *Chicago-Kent Law Review,* supra at 533.
23. Id. at 534.
24. *Kaimowitz v. Michigan Department of Mental Health,* supra at 25.
25. *New York City Health and Hospitals Corporation v. Stein,* 355 N.Y.S. 2d 461 (1972).
26. See, Plotnick, Limiting the therapeutic orgy, *Northwestern Law Review,* at 472–73; id. at 464.
27. See, Mental Health Codes of Cal., Ky., Mont., N.J., N.Y., and Wis.
28. Mont. Rev. Codes Ann. § 38-1228; Cal. Welfare and Institutions Code § 5326.7.
29. Idaho Code § 66-346(c); Ind. Code § 16-14-1.5-3(f); Mass. Gen. Laws Ann. ch. 123 § 23; and Neb. Rev. Stat. § 28-840(4); Ore. Rev. Stat. § 426.385(2); Tex. Stat. Ann. art. 3174b(2); Vt. Stat. Ann. tit. 18 § 7304, 7502.
30. *Wyatt v. Stickney,* 344 F. Supp. 373 (M.D. Ala. 1972), 344 F. Supp. 387 (M.D. Ala. 1973); aff'd sub nom. *Wyatt v. Aderholt,* 503 F.2d 1305 (5th Cir. 1974); id. at 380.
31. *Wyatt v. Stickney,* 344 F. Supp. at 401 (1972).
32. N.Y. Mental Hygiene Law § 15.03, effective Jan. 1, 1973.
33. *New York City Health and Hospitals Corporation v. Stein,* supra at 463.
34. Id. at 465.
35. *Price v. Sheppard,* supra at 905.
36. Id. at 911.
37. *Wood v. Stickland,* 420 U.S. 308 (1974).
38. *New York City Health and Hospitals Corporation v. Stein,* supra at 913.
39. Plotnick, Limiting the therapeutic orgy, *Northwestern U. Law Review,* supra at 477–78.
40. Id. at 475–76.
41. Mich. Comp. Laws § 14.800 (718).
42. N.Y. Mental Hygiene Law § 15.03(b).
43. Wash. Rev. Code § 71.05.200 (1) (e).
44. See, Mass. Gen. Laws ch. 123 § 21; Mich. Comp. Laws § 14.800 (718).
45. Utah Code Ann. § 64-7-47; S.C. Code § 44-23-1020.
46. Kan. Stat. Ann. § 59-2929 (6).
47. *Knecht v. Gillman,* 488 F.2d 1136 (8th Cir. 1973).
48. *Scott v. Plante,* 532 F.2d 939, 945 (3rd Cir. 1976).
49. Id. at 946.
50. *Mackey v. Procunier,* supra.
51. *Nelson v. Heyne,* 491 F.2d 352 (7th Cir. 1974) cert. denied 417 U.S. 976 (1974).
52. Id. at 356–57.
53. *Winters v. Miller,* 446 F.2d (2d Cir. 1971), rev'd on other grounds, 446 F.2d

65 (2d Cir. 1971), cert. denied 404 U.S. 985 (1971); N.Y. Mental Hygiene Law § 78(1).

54. *Winters v. Miller*, id. at 68.

55. Brown, Bertram S., Behavior modification in the right hands, *Trial* 11(6):32, Nov. 12, 1975.

56. Plotnick, Limiting the therapeutic orgy, *Northwestern U. Law Review*, supra at 478–79.

57. *Knecht v. Gillman* and *Mackay v. Procunier*, supra.

58. Plotnick, Limiting the therapeutic orgy, *Northwestern U. Law Review*, supra at 479.

59. Id. at 480.

60. Brown, Behavior modification, *Trial*, supra at 33.

61. Mental Health Codes: Fla. Stat. § 393.13 (4) (j) (1); Ore. § 426.070(6); Idaho § 66-346(a) (4);(c); Wis. § 51-61-(k); R.I. § 23-26-19.1(4) (can be denied by director for good cause); Mont. Rev. Codes Ann. § 38)1227 (4) 1227(5), 1322.

62. Ohio Rev. Code § 5122.271(E); Cal. Welfare and Institution Code § 2670.5 (a), (c) (3).

63. Brown, Behavior modification, *Trial*, supra at 33.

64. *Wyatt v. Stickney*, 344 F. Supp. (1972), supra at 380.

65. Id. at 387.

66. *Wyatt v. Stickney*, supra; *Jobson v. Henne*, 355 F.2d 129 (2d Cir. 1966).

67. See also, *Souder v. Brennan*, 367 F. Supp. 808 (D.C. D.C. 1973).

68. See, Wis. Stat. Ann. § 51.61(b).

69. Brown, Behavior modification, *Trial*, supra at 33, 36.

70. N.C. General Stat. § 122–55–1 and (a) (1)(2); (b) (1)-(10).

71. N.J. Stat. Ann. tit. 30 § 30:4-24.2; Wash. Rev. Code § 71.05.370; Cal. W & I Code § 5325; Wis. Stat. Ann. § 51.61(1); see, new Ill. Mental Health Code, effective 1-1-79 at Ill. Rev. Stat. Ch. 95½, § 1-101 et seq.

72. N.C General Stat. § 122-55.2 (b).

73. N.C. Gen Stat. § 122-55.2 (d).

74. N.J. Stat. Ann. § 30:4-24.2 (g).

75. Wis. Stat. Ann. § 51.61 (2).

76. Wis. Stat. Ann. § 51.61 (3).

77. Weitzel, William D., Changing law and clinical dilemmas, *American Journal of Psychiatry* 134:293-295 Mar. 1977.

78. Id. at 294.

79. Stone, Alan A., Recent mental health litigation; a critical perspective, *American Journal of Psychiatry*, 134(3): 273–79, Mar. 1977.

80. Id. at 278.

81. Id.

82. Roth, Loren H., Meisel, Alan, and Lidz, Charles W., Tests of competency to consent to treatment, *American Journal of Psychiatry* 134:279–83, Mar. 1977.

83. Id. at 280.

84. Id. at 283.

85. Id. at 280.

86. Id. at 282.

87. Stone, Recent mental health litigation, *American Journal of Psychiatry*, supra at 278.

Part THREE

THE MINOR PATIENT

Introduction

Traditionally, minors have been protected under the law from
their lack of experience and understanding. The law treats them
as lacking the capacity to conduct their own affairs. Thus, their
ability to form contracts is limited, and they may escape liability for
breach of contract under certain circumstances. In the sphere of
medical treatment, minors cannot, in general, consent for their own
treatment. A parent's or guardian's consent is required. If a physician
treats a minor without such third-party consent the parent may hold
him liable for battery.[1] Even when the unauthorized act did not lead
to any injury of the child, nominal damages may be awarded.[2]

The tradition of parental consent for treatment of minors dates
back to the English common law, where minority persisted until the
age of 21 years. Parents' right to control their children was considered in the nature of a property right. In exchange for the duty to
support, parents were entitled to the custody, services, and earnings
of their children. The requirement of parental consent was thought to
promote family harmony, discipline, and authority.[3] Originally,
treatment of children separately from adults was considered humane,
because of the conditions in prisons, mental hospitals, and factories.
In modern times, the separate treatment of children has resulted in a
deprivation of legal rights rather than conferring any advantages.
Courts and legislatures are gradually beginning to remedy this
situation by insuring that certain due process rights, previously
available only to adults, are extended to minors as well.

American courts have generally upheld the English common-law
tradition of almost absolute parental control over their children's
health, education, and welfare. The United States Supreme Court
has decided in a number of cases that parents have a fundamental
right to make child-rearing decisions free from governmental
interference, provided they exercise their duty to care for and
support their children.[4]

In recent years, the Supreme Court has dealt with minors' rights in
certain areas, displaying a trend toward defining minors' legal status

as "persons" protected by the constitution, and away from regarding children as property. In a recent decision upholding the right of a "mature minor" to obtain an abortion without her parent's consent, the court noted that "minors, as well as adults, are protected by the constitution and possess constitutional rights."[5]

Not all constitutional rights afforded adults, however, are available to minors. "[T]he power of the state to control the conduct of children reaches beyond the scope of its authority over adults," even where there is an invasion of constitutionally protected freedoms.[6] In *Prince v. Commonwealth of Massachusetts*, the Supreme Court sustained the conviction of the guardian of a nine-year-old girl (both were Jehovah's Witnesses) for violating the Massachusetts child-labor law by permitting the child to sell religious magazines on the street. The court held that the child's right to practice her religion could be limited by a state statute regulating the hours, times, and places children could work.

In another decision, the Supreme Court held that the state has an independent interest in the well-being of its minor citizens and can regulate First Amendment freedoms, such as the availability of pornography to children.[7] Likewise, the state as *parens patriae* has the authority to provide for compulsory education, detention and rehabilitation of juvenile delinquents, and vaccination programs and can limit the minor's right to purchase alcohol and cigarettes and drive an automobile.[8]

Almost every state today has departed from the common law and by statute has lowered the age of majority to 18 or 19 years.[9] Thus, the general rule that parents must consent to medical treatment for their minor children includes, in most states, only children under the age of 18 or 19.

Several exceptions originated at common law and subsequently were codified by statutes. The exceptions include (1) emergency medical care; (2) the emancipated minor (in general, one who is economically independent); (3) the mature minor (the focus is on understanding rather than external circumstances); (4) drug-abuse, alcohol-abuse, and venereal-disease treatment; and (5) the obtaining of contraceptives, sterilization, and abortion.

A few of the exceptions have their source in state legislation; the last two are the product of constitutional interpretation by the United States Supreme Court.

Notes and References

1. *Bonner v. Moran*, 126 F.2d 121 (D.C. Cir. 1941); *Lacey v. Laird*, 166 Ohio St. 12, 139 N.E.2d 25 (1956).
2. *Reddington v. Clayman*, 134 N.E.2d 923 (Mass. 1956).
3. Comment, Minor's consent to medical care: the constitutional issue in Oklahoma, *Tulsa Law Journal* 12:512-13, 1977.

4. See, *Pierce v. Society of Sisters*, 268 U.S. 510 (1925); *Meyer v. Nebraska*, 262 U.S. 390 (1923); *Prince v. Commonwealth of Massachusetts*, 321 U.S. 158 (1944); *Wisconsin v. Yoder*, 406 U.S. 205 (1972); see also, Jenkins, Rights of children, *Fordham Law Review* 46: 669, 671, 1978.

5. *Planned Parenthood v. Danforth*, 428 U.S. 52 (1976); see also, *Tinker v. Des Moines Independent Community School District*, 393 U.S. 503 (1969) (recognizing a minor's First Amendment right to freedom of speech); *In re Gault*, 387 U.S. 1 (1967) (recognizing a juvenile's right to some but not all adult due process safeguards when charged with a crime and subject to a delinquency adjudication).

6. *Prince v. Commonwealth of Massachusetts*, supra.

7. *Ginsberg v. State*, 390 U.S. 629 (1968).

8. Comment, The minor's right to privacy: limitations on state action after *Danforth* and *Carey*, *Columbia Law Review* 77:1216, 1221, 1977.

9. See, for example, the following statutes, all of which make 18 the age of majority: Okla. Public Health and Safety Code ch. 54 § 2601 (a); McKinney's Consol. Laws of N.Y., Public Health Law § 2504 (1); Pa. Codes ch. 50 § 10101; Ill. Rev. Stat. 1976 ch. 91 § 18.1.

CHAPTER 9

Exceptions to the Requirement of Parental Consent

MEDICAL EMERGENCIES

In an emergency, where a delay in treatment will jeopardize an adult patient's life, the physician may begin treatment without obtaining the patient's consent. With regard to obtaining parental consent, the same is true for a minor patient. This exception was created at common law to remedy the increased injury or suffering that could occur if the parent or guardian could not be located to give the requisite consent. Most states have codified this common-law exception. Under Massachusetts law, for example, the wording limits physician liability:

> No physician, dentist, or hospital shall be held liable for failure to obtain consent of a parent, legal guardian, or other person having custody or control of a minor child, or of the spouse of the patient, to emergency examination and treatment, including blood transfusions, when delay in treatment will endanger the life, limb, or mental well-being of the patient.[1]

Other states focus on the consent element and provide that medical services may be rendered without a parent's or a guardian's consent "when in the physician's judgment, an attempt to secure consent would result in delay of treatment which would increase the risk to the minor's life or health."[2] In Illinois, the statute reads even more liberally. There, the consent of the parent or guardian is unnecessary, "if in the sole opinion of the physician, dentist, or hospital, the obtaining of consent is not reasonably feasible under the circumstances without adversely affecting the condition of such minor's health."[3]

Most of that states that have codified this common-law exception require the physician or hospital authorities to make every attempt to notify the child's parents or guardian before treatment if at all possible. If prior notification is not possible, every attempt must be made after treatment. If the minor patient is conscious, some statutes provide that he may legally consent to treatment.[4]

EMANCIPATED MINORS

The emancipation of a child is the parents' relinquishment of control and authority over their child, terminating their legal duty of support and conferring on the child the exclusive right to his own earnings. At common law, an emancipated minor could consent to his own medical treatment and that of his children and be held liable for the subsequent medical bills. At least 20 states have codified this common-law exception both as to the ability to legally consent and the unavailability of the defense of minority to avoid contractual liability for health care.[5]

The emancipation exception developed at common law for reasons similar to those of the medical-emergency exception. A potential for harsh results existed where the minor who was an economically independent unit, living separate and apart from his parents, had to notify them and secure consent for treatment.

Aside from current statutory provisions, case law defines the concept of emancipation. In general, emancipation results when a child leaves home and becomes economically independent from his parents. The most common way emancipation is effectuated is through marriage (with or without parental consent),[6] or by military service.[7] Emancipation can occur by parental consent or by an express or implied agreement between the parent and child.[8] In *Crosby v. Crosby*, a New York court noted that a 19-year-old woman (minority persisted until 21 at the time) who lived at home and paid room and board could be considered emancipated for purposes of tort negligence. Likewise, where a child is abandoned or forced to leave home, emancipation can be effected.[9]

In *Roe v. Doe*, a 20-year-old woman was held emancipated for purposes of liability to pay college tuition when she chose to live contrary to the expressed wishes of her father. The court determined that the daughter forfeited her claim for support by voluntarily abandoning her parents' home and by avoiding parental discipline and restraint.[10]

In some states, current statutory law restricts the definition of emancipation for purposes of consenting to medical and health care.[11] In Texas, the minor must be at least 16 years old, reside separate and apart from his parents, and manage his own financial affairs. The statute allows parents to remain a source of income, however. The California statute uses similar wording but lowers the age to 15. New

York restricts the concept of emancipation to a minor who has married or to a girl who has borne a child. Massachusetts has a more liberal definition of emancipation than at common law, including not only the previously mentioned categories, but also minors who are pregnant or believe themselves to be pregnant. Pennsylvania adds high school graduates to the list of emancipated minors for purposes of consenting to medical treatment.

THE MATURE MINOR

The mature-minor exception focuses on mental capacity and understanding rather than on external physical circumstances. A *mature minor* is "one who is sufficiently intelligent and mature to understand the nature and consequences of the medical treatment being sought."[12] One court has expressed the relevant factors to be considered in determining whether the minor is mature enough to give valid consent. They are "age, intelligence, maturity, training, experience, economic independence or lack thereof, general conduct as an adult and freedom from the control of parents."[13]

This exception began to develop in cases dealing with tort actions for assault and battery brought against physicians who had treated minors with their consent but without the consent of their parents or guardian. In order for the court (or the jury) to determine if the minor effectively consented to what otherwise would constitute an assault, the capacity of the patient to understand or appreciate the consequences of the "invasion" of his or her person was examined.[14]

Where the jury made such a finding of fact, the necessary consent was present, and the physician could not be held liable for assault and battery. In several cases, the minor's consent was successfully argued by the defendant-physician in support of an assumption-of-risk defense to the tort action.[15]

In *Bonner v. Moran*, the District of Columbia Court of Appeals had to determine whether damages for assault and battery should be awarded against a surgeon who had taken a skin graft from a 15-year-old donor for the benefit of his cousin. The District of Columbia court considered three main factors: (1) whether the minor was himself capable of appreciating and did appreciate the nature and consequences of the operation, (2) whether he actually consented or implied consent by his conduct, and (3) whether the operation was for the benefit of the child and was done with the purpose of saving his life or limb. The court held the surgeon liable since "the operation was entirely for the benefit of another and involved the sacrifice on the part of the infant [i.e., minor] of fully two months of schooling, in addition to serious physical pain and possible results affecting his future life."[16]

The court also found it significant that the procedure was technical and that the physician had failed to explain to the boy the nature or extent of the operation. In other cases, where the surgical treatment is both an approved one and in the best interest of the minor patient, the third criterion mentioned by the *Bonner* court, that of benefit to the child, would be satisfied.[17]

Recently, the Supreme Court recognized and applied the mature-minor exception in recognizing that a minor had a right to privacy, which encompassed her decision whether to bear a child or terminate her pregnancy. In the *Danforth* case, the court held that under certain circumstances a minor could choose to have an abortion without parental consent. The court, however, emphasized that "our holding does not suggest that every minor, regardless of age or maturity, may give effective consent for termination of her pregnancy."[18] Implicit in this passage is the recognition that only "mature minors" can exercise this constitutional right of privacy.

A few state statutes have codified this exception. In Mississippi, for example, "any unemancipated minor of sufficient intelligence to understand and appreciate the consequences of the proposed surgical or medical treatment" may consent to treatment.[19] A few statutes absolve a physician or hospital from any civil or criminal liability for treating a minor if the minor represented that he was legally able to consent to treatment and if the physician or hospital relied in good faith upon such representation.[20]

DRUGS, ALCOHOL, AND COMMUNICABLE DISEASE

In light of the growing adolescent involvement with drugs, alcohol, and sexual activity, and the subsequent medical and social problems relating to drug addiction and venereal disease, many legislatures have passed statutes allowing minors to obtain medical care without parental consent. Often, teenagers living at home and subject to parental care and discipline are hesitant to inform parents of their medical needs in these areas. Rather than face a serious disruption in the family or cause a further breakdown in communications with parents, these adolescents often choose to go untreated rather than have physicians or hospital or clinic authorities inform their parents of the problem in order to obtain consent for treatment. To remedy, in part, this enormous social problem, statutes have been passed in virtually every state allowing minors to obtain treatment and counseling for drug and alcohol addiction and for the diagnosis and treatment of venereal diseases and other communicable diseases.

Statutes generally fall into three categories: (1) those allowing minors of any age to consent to treatment, (2) those allowing minors of certain ages to consent to treatment, and (3) those leaving it to the discretion of the physician to determine whether to notify the parents of the treatment rendered and whether to first obtain their consent for treatment.

These categories may overlap in some instances. For example, under Oklahoma law, a minor of any age may consent to drug- or alcohol-abuse treatment and venereal-disease diagnosis and treatment, but the law also provides as follows:

> [T]he health professional may, but shall not be required to inform the spouse, parent or legal guardian of the minor of any treatment needed or provided. The judgment of the health professional as to notification shall be final, and his disclosures shall not constitute libel, slander, the breach of the right of privacy, the breach of the rule of privileged communication.[21]

Parents, spouse, or guardian, however, are not to be notified without the minor's consent if the minor is not suffering from a communicable disease or drug or alcohol addiction. Likewise, the minor's consent is necessary to disseminate information to any other person, agency, or official, except through specific legal requirements or where health needs permit.

Massachusetts and Pennsylvania permit a minor of any age to consent to treatment for venereal disease without any provision for parental notification; and a Wisconsin statute provides that "a physician may treat a minor afflicted with v.d. [venereal disease] or examine and diagnose a minor for the presence of such disease without obtaining the consent of such minor's parents or guardian."[22] The word may can be interpreted as giving the physician the discretion whether to obtain parental consent.

California and Illinois laws provide that minors 12 years of age or older may consent to treatment for drug abuse and venereal disease.[23] California provides for treating alcohol abuse as well. Both states provide for parental notification. In Illinois, the statute leaves it to the treating physician's or counselor's discretion whether to notify the parents or guardian of "the treatment given or needed." California law provides for such notification only for treating drug or alcohol abuse where the cooperation of the parents is needed in the counseling portion of the treatment plan.

These statutes do not give the minor patient an absolute right to receive treatment without parental consent but merely provide physicians and hospitals with the leeway to treat such a patient without obtaining consent if warranted. If a minor patient would withdraw from treatment or would not pursue it without assurance that the relationship would be kept in confidence, the physician or hospital authorities should not notify the parent. On the other hand, under most of these statutes, where the physician believes that the presence of the parents and their active cooperation would benefit both the patient and the treatment plan, he is free to notify them.

Case law in this area mainly involves testing the validity of state statutes requiring physicians to report names and other information about drug-dependent persons to the state commissioner of health. A psychiatrist brought a class-action suit on behalf of himself and all physicians in Connecticut for declaratory and injunctive relief from enforcement of a Connecticut statute that required him to report to the health commissioner the full name, address, and date of birth of every drug-dependent person (i.e., dependent on "controlled drugs") that he had treated.[24]

His basic contention was that the enforcement of the statute violated the psychotherapist-patient privilege to not disclose his patient's confidential communications. The court rejected the claim, reasoning that the statute in question required this information to be kept confidential even in criminal proceedings, and thus the privilege was left intact.

ABORTION, CONTRACEPTIVES, AND STERILIZATION

Three recent Supreme Court decisions, *Planned Parenthood v. Danforth, Bellotti v. Baird*, and *Carey v. Population Services International*, extended the right of privacy to include a minor's right to make childbearing decisions free from parental and state interference.[25] The freedom to make such decisions is more limited than that granted to adults in the major contraception and abortion decisions of the 1960s and early 1970s.

Griswold v. Connecticut held that the state statute prohibiting use of contraceptives for married adults violated the constitutional right to privacy and the decision was extended to unmarried adults in *Eisenstadt v. Baird* and *Roe v. Wade*.[26] The right of privacy was broad enough to encompass a woman's decision to terminate her pregnancy during the first trimester. The Supreme Court in *Roe* declined to decide the issue of whether a minor's right of privacy was similar to that of an adult.[27] This reluctance reflects a "traditional judicial caution in extending adult constitutional protections to juveniles."[28]

The interplay of interests in this area includes the state as *parens patriae* protecting the child's best interests, the broad discretion granted parents in the upbringing of their children, and the concept of legal incapacity of minors at common law (id.). After the *Roe* decision, many state legislatures drafted statutes limiting or restricting the minor's decision to abort. These statutes generally fall into three main categories: (1) those requiring parental consent before an abortion can be obtained, (2) those requiring that the parent be notified of the minor's decision to have an abortion, and (3) those providing for judicial sanctioning of the decision to abort absent parental approval where the minor demonstrates the capacity to give an informed consent (i.e., "mature minor") or if an abortion has been determined to be in her best interests.[29]

The Supreme Court in *Danforth* examined a Missouri statute requiring a woman, if married, to obtain the consent of her spouse, or if unmarried and a minor, the approval of her parents. *Danforth* held that during the first trimester of pregnancy, the state lacked the authority "to give a third party an absolute, and possibly arbitrary, veto over the decision of the physician and his patient to terminate the patient's pregnancy."[30] The court went on to suggest, however, that there may be a significant state interest in conditioning an abortion on parental consent, although in the present case "the safeguarding of the family unit and parental authority" were held insufficient. In the words of the court:

It is difficult, however, to conclude that providing a parent with absolute power to overrule a determination, made by the physician and his minor patient, to terminate the patient's pregnancy will serve to strengthen the family unit. Neither is it likely that such veto power will enhance parental authority or control where the minor and the nonconsenting parent are so fundamentally in conflict and the very existence of the pregnancy already has fractured the family structure. Any independent interest the parent may have in the termination of the minor daughter's pregnancy is no more weighty than the right of privacy of the competent minor mature enough to have become pregnant.[31]

The lower court, which had heard the case prior to the Supreme Court, found that the state had a compelling interest "in improving the quality of the minor's decision," but the Supreme Court failed to consider this.[32] The majority opinion did note that the decision did not suggest that "every minor, regardless of age or maturity, may give effective consent for termination of her pregnancy." The opinion did not furnish any guidelines for states on circumstances that would justify their restricting a minor's right to obtain an abortion.[33]

The criteria announced in Danforth were further amplifed in Bellotti vs. Baird.[34] The Bellotti case concerned the constitutionality of a Massachusetts statute providing for conditions that would permit a minor to obtain an abortion. In an earlier decision concerning the same statute, Bellotti vs. Baird, the Supreme Court reversed the decision of a three-judge district court holding the statute to be unconstitutional.[35]

The majority opinion delivered by Justice Powell, and concurred in by Chief Justice Burger, Justice Stewart, and Justice Renquist, held the statute to be unconstitutional, because it allowed the state court to substitute its judgment and required in every instance parental consultation and notification.

The Court remanded the case with directions that certain questions should be certified to the Supreme Judicial Court of Massachusetts concerning the meaning of the statute, since its construction was susceptible to several interpretations, which could have impact on its constitutionality.

The Massachusetts Supreme Court, dealing with the construction of the statute, answered nine questions which had been considered by the Supreme Court in holding the Massachusetts statute to be unconstitutional.

The significant portions of the statute permitted a minor to obtain an abortion on her own decision if she satisfied a court that she had attained sufficient maturity to make a fully informed decision. Even in such instances, however, the court had the power to substitute its own judgment as to whether such an abortion was in the best interests of the child. The statute also required parental consultation and notification in every instance, without affording the pregnant minor an opportunity to receive an independent judicial determination that she is mature enough to consent or that an abortion would be in her best interests.

Thus, the opinion in *Bellotti* suggests that a state statute can provide for the prohibition of an abortion if a minor desires one only on the finding of a court that the minor does not possess sufficient maturity and competency to make an independent decision of her own in that regard.

While *Bellotti* expands on the criteria set forth in *Danforth*, the Supreme Court will most likely be soon called upon to provide additional and specific guidelines for state judges in their determination of whether the minor has sufficient maturity and capacity to decide for an abortion.[36]

Hunerwadel v. Baird presented this question for review: Is the Massachusetts statute prohibiting physicians from performing abortions on unmarried, minor girls under the age of 18 without parental consent or consent of a judge of the superior court unconstitutional on its face under the due process and equal protection clause of the Fourteenth Amendment? The district court answered in the affirmative.[37]

A seventh-circuit district court struck as unconstitutional certain provisions of the Illinois Abortion Act of 1975, including the requirement that an unmarried minor must attempt to obtain parental consent before she has an abortion.[38]

The Supreme Court has dealt with the issue of a minor's access to contraceptives in *Carey v. Population Services International*.[39] At issue was the New York statute prohibiting any person from selling or distributing any contraceptive aid to a minor. The Supreme Court found the statute unconstitutional after rejecting, under a "significant state interest" test, the state's assertion that the legislation was necessary to deter juvenile sexual activity. The court expressed doubt that barring contraceptives would effectuate the state's objectives. The court reasoned that the result instead would be greater risk of unwanted pregnancy and venereal disease.[40] As with *Danforth*, however, the court left open the possibility that the state might have a constitutionally valid interest in limiting access to contraceptives as long as access was not totally restricted.[41]

The trend in most states is toward removing all restrictions on minors' access to contraceptives, reflecting a growing awareness that teenage sexual activity is unrelated to the availability of contraceptives and that pregnancies and venereal disease present considerable problems in this age group.[42]

The only other time the Supreme Court addressed the issue of contraceptives for minors was in another 1976 decision, *Jones v. T-H.*[43] Utah regulations required parental consent before minor members of families receiving federal aid could obtain contraceptives. The Court held this to be inconsistent with the Social Security Act.[44] The Act requires states to provide family planning services for individual members of such families, including minor members who are sexually active.

Sterilization of minors, on the other hand, is more stringently regulated or prohibited in most states even with parental consent or under state authority. Courts are extremely hesitant to allow a minor, regardless of maturity and capabilities, to make such a permanent and far-reaching decision.

Several states allow sterilization of minors under certain circumstances. Tennessee has a statute providing that a person under 18 years of age can consent to sterilization if legally married and the physician or surgeon has given a "full and reasonable medical explanation... as to the meaning and consequences of such an operation." Massachusetts permits a minor who is married, widowed, or divorced to consent to sterilization.[45]

The most controversial area of sterilization is the parents' right to have their mentally deficient minor children sterilized. With only one reported exception, courts will permit sterilization of minor mentally deficient children only where expressly authorized by statute. Today, 27 states authorize, in certain circumstances, compulsory sterilization of the mentally deficient.[46]

The rationale behind such legislation is twofold: the eugenics argument and protection against unfit parents. The former argument can be structured as follows: the state has a compelling interest in ordering sterilization of the mentally retarded who are likely to have mentally retarded children. Thus, eugenics is used to preserve the quality of society. Justice Oliver Wendell Holmes's famous quotation from the 1927 case of *Buck v. Bell* expresses the widely held sentiment that "three generations of imbeciles are enough."[47]

The latter argument about unfit parents reflects the state's concern that mentally ill and mentally retarded persons will be unable to properly care for their offspring, who will become neglected or dependent and, as a result, necessitate the state's becoming the guardian with responsibility for their care and support.

These statutes have been attacked on various constitutional grounds including due process, equal protection, and cruel and unusual punishment, but have been almost universally upheld.[48] In *North Carolina Association for Retarded Children v. State of North Carolina,* the North Carolina Supreme Court upheld the statute in spite of the Fourteenth Amendment due process and equal protection attack.

North Carolina restricts voluntary and involuntary sterilization of the mentally retarded to certain cases in which "the person would be likely, unless sterilized, to procreate a child or children," and the state requires that the judge make a finding that the person is likely to engage in sexual activity without the use of contraceptive devices.[49] In addition, a finding must be made that there is either a likelihood that a defective child would be the result of any pregnancy or that the child would be improperly cared for because of the degree of the parent's retardation.

In re Cavitt, the United States Supreme Court held that under the applicable Nebraska statute, a specific finding was not required that the offspring of a party to be sterilized would very likely be defective.[50] The court, however, did strike down that portion of the statute making it the duty of the director of an institution or of county social services to institute the sterilization petition at the request of the next of kin or the legal guardian of the retarded person. The court said that such a grant of authority was "the power of a tyrant" since "for any reason, or for no reason at all, he may require an otherwise responsible public servant to initiate the procedure. This he may do without regard to the public interest or the interest of the retarded person."[51]

The procedural due process rights in North Carolina are similar to those of the other states that authorize sterilizing the mentally retarded. The retarded person has the right to receive a notice of the petition, to give consent if capable or to register his objection, to have a hearing, to present evidence in his own behalf (including subpoena power), to cross-examine witnesses in support of the petition, to have counsel, to receive a transcript of the proceedings, and to appeal the decision to the North Carolina Court of Appeals and the Supreme Court. In re Sterilization of Moore, the Supreme Court of North Carolina held that the petitioner's burden of proof was "clear, strong and convincing evidence" of the statutory standards before a sterilization order could be entered.[52]

In Cook v. State, an Oregon Court of Appeals affirmed the sterilization order of a 17-year-old girl with a history of severe emotional disturbance, brain damage (rendering her unstable despite continuous medication), and indiscriminate and impulsive sexual activity in the state hospital.[53] The court reasoned in this way:

> The state's concern for the welfare of its citizenry extends to future generations and when there is overwhelming evidence, as there is here, that a potential parent will be unable to provide a proper environment for a child because of his mental illness or mental retardation, the state has a sufficient interest to order sterilization.[54]

In the vast majority of cases, the courts have refused to order sterilization where there is no express statutory provision authorizing it. In the past, courts have refused on grounds of lack of jurisdiction.[55] A recent U.S. Supreme Court decision in Stump v. Sparkman, however, held that although he is bound by statutory limits, a judge sitting in a court of general jurisdiction does have the power to act on a petition for sterilization.[56] If a petition does not fit the statutory criteria for sterilization (or by implication, there is no statute), then the petition should be dismissed on the merits rather than for lack of jurisdiction.[57] It should be noted that in most of the previously cited cases the courts petitioned were of limited or special jurisdiction.

In *A.L. v. G.R.H.*, the mother of a 15-year-old boy with an intelligence quotient seven points below the lower limits of the normal range (the category called "dull" or "borderline-retarded") sought to have him sterilized under the common-law attributes of the parent-child relationship.[58] Under Indiana's sterilization statutes, only institutionalized persons could be sterilized and only under special circumstances.[59]

The mother was concerned that her son might impregnate a retarded or handicapped classmate. The court considered, however, that the mental disability was not inheritable, that the boy had not displayed any propensity toward forcing his attention on others, and that he would be able to support himself in the future if he continued to show improvement in his special-education classes. The Indiana Court of Appeals affirmed the lower court's denial of the request. The court found that "the common law does not invest parents with such power over their children even though they sincerely believe the child's adulthood would benefit therefrom."[60]

In summary, then, parents have no right to have their mentally deficient minor children sterilized unless there is statutory authority for such a procedure, the statutory conditions exist, and the proper party (usually the director of the hospital or institution) brings the petition. If a parent does convince a judge to order a sterilization, however, even if statutory conditions are not complied with (for example, the child is not institutionalized or does not fall within the retarded range), the child may be unable to collect any damages.

In *Stump v. Sparkman*, the Supreme Court held that the judge who ordered the sterilization was not acting without "clear absence of jurisdiction" since he was sitting in a court of general jurisdiction and there was a sterilization statute in existence in Indiana. He was, therefore, immune from prosecution under the Civil Rights Act (section 1983). Likewise, the doctor or hospital that complies with the sterilization order would be immune, since they would act under court order.

CONCLUSIONS

The common-law tradition requiring parental consent to medical treatment, while generally still respected and followed, is gradually being eroded with exceptions, as courts and legislatures painstakingly and often begrudgingly empower minors to control their own welfare. In this day and age, adolescents mature much faster and are exposed to much more of life at a far earlier age than formerly. To reflect the times, courts and lawmaking bodies must respond to the young people of today in a realistic manner.

More than ever before, and at an earlier age, adolescents leave home to marry or pursue careers. Their economic independence and control and management of their own affairs are no longer the exception. Sexual activity and the use of drugs and alcohol are widespread. To protect the minor patient from the possible adverse results of such activity, consent provisions must be relaxed so that growing social problems can be checked. While parents, who are still legally responsible for the care and upbringing of their minor children, cannot be totally pushed out of the picture, the reality of the minors' needs in relation to access to medical care must be considered.

Notes and References

1. Mass. Gen. Laws ch. 112 § 12 F (1975).
2. Pa. Code ch. 50 § 10104 (1970); McKinney's Consol. Laws of N.Y. book 44 § 2504 (3).
3. Ill. Rev. Stat. ch. 91 § 18.3.
4. See, for example, Okla. Stat., Public Health and Safety Law ch. 63 § 2602 (A) (7).
5. Ariz. Rev. Stat. § 44-132 (1967 Supp.); Cal. Civil Code § 25.6, 34.6 (1967 Supp.); Del. Code tit. 13 § 707; Idaho Code § 32-101; Ill. Rev. Stat. ch. 91 § 18.1–18.2 (if married); Ind. Ann. Stat. § 35-4407 et seq.; Minn. S.F. No. 1496 ch. 544 § 144.341, 144.342; Miss. Code Ann. § 7129–81; Mont. Rev. Codes Ann. § 69-6101 (1970); Neb. Rev. Stat. § 38-101 (1969); Nev. Rev. Stat. § 129.030; N.J. Stat. Ann. § 9:17A-1; N.M. Stat. Ann. § 12-12-1, et. seq.; N.C. Gen. Stat. § 90-21.5; Okla. Stat. § 2601 (a) (Supp. 1976) (person under 18 in military is no longer considered a minor); Pa. Stat. tit. 35 § 10101; Va. Code Ann. § 32-137 (1970); Vernon's Ann. Civ. Stat. of Tex. ch. 35, § 35.03 (person in military or 16 years of age or older in addition to other criteria); Kan. Stat. Ann. § 38-122 (if minor is a parent).
6. *Smith v. Seibly*, 72 Wash. 2d 16, 431 P.2d 719 (1967); *Bach v. Long Island Jewish Hospital*, 49 Misc. 2d 207, 267 N.Y.S. 2d 289 (Sup. Ct. 1966).
7. *Swenson v. Swenson*, 241 Mo. App. 21, 227 S.W.2d 103 (1950).
8. *Crosby v. Crosby*, 230 App. Div. 651, 246 N.Y.S. 384 (Sup. Ct. 1930).
9. *Murphy v. Murphy*, 206 Misc. 228, 133 N.Y.S. 2d 796 (Sup. Ct. 1954); see also, *Gillikin v. Burbage*, 263 N.C. 317, 139 S.E.2d 753 (1965).
10. *Roe v. Doe*, 29 N.Y.2d 188, 272 N.E.2d 567 (1971), at 74.
11. Tex. Family Code ch. 35 § 35.03(a) (2), Cal. Civ. Code § 34.6; McKinney's Consol. Laws of N.Y. art. 25 § 2504 (1); Mass. Gen. Laws Ann. ch. 112 § 12F; see also, Ill. Rev. Stat. ch. 91 § 18.1-18.2; Pa. Stat. tit. 35 § 10101.
12. Paul, Legal rights of minors to sex-related medical care. *Colorado Human Rights Law Review* 6: 357 (1974–75).
13. *Smith v. Seibly*, supra at 723.
14. *Lacey v. Laird*, 166 Ohio St. 12, 139 N.E.2d 25 (1956) (concurring opinion); *Gulf and S.I.R. Company v. Sullivan*, 119 So. 501 (1929) (S. Ct. Miss); restatement of the Law of Torts § 59.

15. *Porter v. Toledo Terminal Road Company*, 152 Ohio St. 463, 90 N.E.2d 142 (1950); *Centrello v. Basky*, 164 Ohio St. 41, 128 N.E.2d 80 (1955).
16. *Bonner v. Moran*, 126 F.2d 123 (D.C. Cir. 1941).
17. *Younts v. Saint Francis Hospital*; 205 Kan. 292, 469 P.2d 330 (1970).
18. *Planned Parenthood v. Danforth*, 428 U.S. 52 (1976), at 75; see also, *Bellotti v. Baird*, 428 U.S. 132 (1976).
19. Miss. Code Ann. § 41-41-3 (h).
20. See, for example, Mass. Gen. Laws. Ann. § 12F; Okla. Public Health and Safety Code ch. 63 § 2602; Pa. Health and Safety Code § 10105; Vernon's Tex. Code Ann. § 35.03 (f).
21. Okla. Public Health and Safety Code § 2602 (A) (3) and (B); see also, Vernon's Tex. Code Ann. ch. 35 § 35.03 (a) (3) (6) and (d) (only for drug abuse and venereal disease).
22. Pa. Stat. tit. 35 § 521.14 (a) § 10103 (Purdon 1977); Mass. Gen. Laws Ann. ch. 112 § 12F; Wis. Public Health Code § 143.07 (1976).
23. Cal. Civ. Code § 34.7, 34.10; Ill. Rev. Stat. 1976 ch. 91 § 18.4, 18.5.
24. Gen. Stat. of Conn. § 19-48; *Felber v. Foote*, 321 F. Supp. 85 (D. Conn. 1970).
25. *Planned Parenthood v. Danforth*, supra; *Bellotti v. Baird*, 47 Law Week 4969–78 (July 2, 1979); *Carey v. Population Services International*, 431 U.S. 678 (1977).
26. *Griswold v. Connecticut*, 381 U.S. 479 (1965); *Eisenstadt v. Baird*, 405 U.S. 438 (1972); *Roe v. Wade*, 410 U.S. 113 (1973).
27. *Roe v. Wade*, id. at 165, n. 67.
28. Comment, The minor's right to privacy; limitations on state action after *Danforth* and *Carey*, *Columbia Law Review* 77:1220, 1979 [hereinafter called The minor's right to privacy].
29. Examples of each category follow. In category 1 are Alaska Stat. § 11.15.060 (a) (3) (1970); Col. Rev. Stat. § 18-6-101 (1973) (held unconstitutional in *People v. Norton*, 181 Col. 47, 507 P.2d 862 (1973), except that portion requiring parental or spousal consent for abortions for women under age 18); Fla. Stat. Ann. § 458.22 (3) (Cum. Supp. 1977); Idaho Code § 18-609 (Cum. Supp. 1977); Ind. Code Ann. § 35-1-58.5-2 (Burns Supp. 1976); see also, statutes in Ky., La., Mo., Neb., Ore., Pa., S.C., S.D., Va., and Wash. In category 2 are Mont. Rev. Codes Ann. § 94-5-16 (Supp. 1973); Okla. Public Health and Safety Code § 2602 (B) (up to discretion of physician). In category 3 are Mass. Gen. Laws Ann. ch. 112 § 12P (1976); Nev. Rev. Stat. § 442.250 (1977).
30. *Planned Parenthood v. Danforth*, supra at 74.
31. Id. at 75.
32. Minor's Right to Privacy, supra at 1227.
33. Id. at 1228.
34. *Bellotti v. Baird*, 47 Law Week, supra.
35. *Bellotti v. Baird*, 428 U.S. 132 (1976).
36. See also, Minor's Right to Privacy, supra at 1231; Comment, Minor's rights, *Tulsa Law Journal* 12: 391–92.
37. *Hunerwadel v. Baird*, U.S.D.C. Mass. 450 F. Supp 997, appeal filed 8/25/78 No. 78-330, probable juris. noted 47 *Law Week* 3301.
38. *Wynn v. Carey*, 449 F. Supp. 1302 (U.S.D.C., N. Ill. 1978), appeal dism'd on jurisdictional grounds, 47 Law Week 3264, now being appealed to the Seventh Circuit Court of Appeals.
39. *Carey v. Population Services International*, supra at 678.

40. See, Stevens's concurring opinion, id. at 715.
41. The Minor's Right to Privacy, supra at 1233.
42. Id. at 1231; see, Col. Rev. Stat. § 13-22-105 (1973); Ga. Code Ann. § 88-2904 (f) (Supp. 1976); Ill. Ann. Stat. ch. 91 § 18.7 (Smith-Hurd Supp. 1976); Md. Ann. Code art. 43 § 135 (a) (3) (Supp. 1975); Ore. Rev. Stat. § 109.640 (1971); Tenn. Health and Safety Code § 53-4607 (1971); Va. Code sec. 32-137 (7) (Supp. 1976).
43. *Jones v. T-H*, 425 U.S. 986 (1976).
44. Social Security Act., 42 U.S.C. § 602 (a) (15) Supp. IV 1974.
45. Tenn. Code Ann. § 53-4608 (1971); Mass. Gen. Laws Ann. ch. 112 § 12F (by implication).
46. See, statutes in Ala., Ariz., Ark., Cal., Conn., Del., Ga., Ind., Iowa., Me., Mich., Minn., Miss., N.H., N.C., N.D., Okla., Ore., S.C., S.D., Tex., Utah, Vt., Va., Wash., W.V., and Wis.
47. *Buck v. Bell*, 274 U.S. 200 (1927) (upheld constitutionality of the Virginia compulsory sterilization law for the feebleminded), quotation at 202.
48. *Buck v. Bell*, id.; *North Carolina Association for Retarded Children v. State of North Carolina*, 420 F. Supp. 451 (M.D. N.C. 1976).
49. N.C. Gen. Stat. § 35–36 through 35–50.
50. But see, *In re Cavitt*, 183 Neb. 243, 157 N.W.2d 171, 159 N.W.2d 566 (1968), appeal dismissed, 396 U.S. 996 (1970).
51. Id. at 455.
52. *In re Sterilization of Moore*, 289 N.C. 95, 221 S.E.2d 307 (1976).
53. *Cook v. State*, Or. App. 495 P.2d 768 (1972).
54. Id. at 771.
55. See, *Holmes v. Powers*, Ky., 439 S.W.2d 579 (1969); *Guardianship of Kemp*, Cal. App. 3d 758, 118 Cal. Rptr. 64 (1974); *In the Interest of M.K.R.*, *Mo. 515 S.W.2d 467 (1974)*; *Frazier v. Levi*, Tex. 440 S.W.2d 393 (1969).
56. *Stump v. Sparkman*, 435 U.S. 349 (1978).
57. Id. at 340.
58. *A.L. v. G.R.H.*, Ind. C. of A. 325 N.E.2d 501 (1975); 74 A.L.R.3d 1220, cert. denied 425 U.S. 936 (1976).
59. See, Ind. Code § 16-13-13-1 through -4 (1973).
60. *A.L. v. G.R.H.*, supra at 502.

CHAPTER 10

Parents' Right to Refuse Treatment for Minor Children

Although the law supports parents' natural interest in their children's care and custody including supervision of their physical well-being, courts do not grant them an absolute right to refuse medical treatment for their children. The state also has an interest in the health and welfare of its minor citizens and can intervene. Where parents refuse to consent to treatment because of religious beliefs or on other grounds, the state has the power, under the *parens patriae* doctrine, to insure that the child is given proper medical treatment to protect his life. Neglect statutes define conditions that permit the state to take custody of a child where his physical and emotional needs, including adequate medical care, are not being properly met.

Much of the case law in this area involves Jehovah's Witnesses, whose religious beliefs preclude them from having blood transfusions. These parents hesitate to authorize transfusions for their children. Although, in several cases, an adult Jehovah's Witness was allowed to maintain his position against such treatment, even where his life was endangered, courts have not allowed them such unbridled discretion with their own children, often expressing the view that "while adults may elect to become martyrs, it does not follow that they are free, in identical circumstances, to make martyrs of their children before they have reached the age of full legal discretion when they can make that choice for themselves."[1]

Where a child's life is in danger, courts have unanimously ordered blood transfusions.[2] This has been accomplished in one of several ways. First, the state may bring a neglect petition and ask the judge to order that the child can be made a ward of the court or that custody be given to the state department of children and family services (i.e. the child be adjudged "neglected" or "dependent"), and to order the emergency treatment.[3] Second, the state may ask that a specific guardian be appointed (guardian ad litem) for the sole purpose of authorizing the blood transfusion. In this way the child is adjudged "neglected" but the parents retain custody.[4] Third, the hospital can petition the court for an emergency writ ordering the necessary treatment, in which case the hospital administrator is appointed the guardian with authority to consent to treatment.[5]

Where a child's life is not in danger, courts have traditionally been more hesitant to involve themselves in the parent-child relationship and to order treatment over parental objections. In the Matter of Frank was a case in which the father of a child suffering from a speech impediment was allowed to retain custody of the child, although medical treatment was obtained to correct the impediment.[6]

Where the child's life is not endangered and the proposed treatment does require considerable risk, the parents are allowed considerable latitude. In a 1911 case, parents refused to consent to a common operation for rickets, although their child's condition was progressively worsening and use of the child's feet and legs would be seriously impaired if left untreated. The court considered the parents' fears that the operation would be fatal and that, since they had already lost seven children, the small chance of an adverse result from this operation was of little comfort to them. They were allowed to retain custody of the child.[7]

In the Matter of Hudson concerned the mother of a child who had been born with an abnormally large arm. She refused to consent to an arm amputation. She feared the operation would be fatal and wished to postpone a decision until the child attained majority and could make her own decision. The court chose not to intervene.[8]

Likewise, In the Matter of Green upheld a mother's refusal to consent to an operation on her minor son.[9] The child was a 17-year-old boy suffering from a spinal deformity. Correction required a dangerous operation, a spinal fusion. The mother, a Jehovah's Witness, objected to the necessary blood transfusions. The court held that the state's interest in insuring that the child lead a normal life was outweighed by the mother's constitutional right to freedom of religion, since the child's life was not immediately imperiled. The court remanded the case for an evidentiary proceeding in which the child would be given an opportunity to express his wishes in the matter.

Another series of decisions, however, reflects a different approach that results in overruling the parental refusal to consent, even where the child's life is not endangered. Under state statutes defining neglected and dependent children, courts have held that they have the authority to remove a child from parental custody or to appoint a guardian to consent to treatment even where the child's life is not endangered. These courts weighed the state's interest in protecting the lives and health of its children versus the desirability of religious freedom devoid of governmental intrusion. More often than not, they found in favor of the state, finding the parental refusal unreasonable.

In the Matter of Karwath was the case of a father of three children who were wards of the state social services department. He sought a reversal of an order for removal of the children's tonsils and adenoids after all three had suffered from serious middle-ear infections.[10] The father asked for a six-month delay in order to try chiropractic and medication as alternatives to the operations. The court upheld the order for the operations, based on evidence that they were necessary with reasonable medical certainty to restore and preserve the three children's health. The state agency had the statutory duty to provide ordinary medical care even in the absence of immediate risk to life or limb. Of course, where children are not wards of a state agency with such statutory duty, the result may differ.

A New York court determined it had statutory power under a neglect statute to order an operation to arrest and correct the progressive deformity from poliomyelitis of a child's foot. The father had objected to the operation for unstated reasons.[11] Likewise, In the Matter of Carstairs another New York court found the power to order a child's hospitalization for psychiatric study.[12] The child's mother had failed to obtain psychiatric advice or treatment after repeatedly being notified of her child's antisocial conduct.

In the Matter of Sampson ruled on a neglect petition.[13] The court authorized physicians to perform a very risky surgical procedure to improve the appearance of a 15-year-old boy with a massively disfigured face and neck. The disfigurement came from Von Reckling-hausen's disease, an inherited neurologic, neoplastic disorder. The mother, a Jehovah's Witness, consented to the operation itself but not the blood transfusions that would be needed to perform the operation. The deformity retarded the boy's educational and psychological development, since he was unable to attend school. The court more or less developed a new constitutional right "to live and grow up with a sound mind in a sound body" that must be protected by the state and held paramount to the parents' religious beliefs.[14] The court also concluded that it had wide discretion in ordering medical or surgical care or treatment of a minor even where there was no danger of death "if in the courts' judgment, the health, safety or welfare of the child requires it."[15]

A New York court ordered a medical examination of three children with hernias, dental cavities, and fractured teeth.[16] Their mother had protested, believing that God, without the assistance of doctors or dentists, would help her children.

Parents' refusal to have a child vaccinated to fulfill school-attendance requirements was held to be grounds for appointing a temporary guardian to consent to the vaccination. The state was found to have an overriding interest in protecting the community from communicable diseases.[17] Nevertheless, a statute requiring New York school children to be immunized against polio was held constitutional. The statute excepts those whose parents or guardians are bona fide members of recognized religious organizations whose teachings forbid such practices.[18]

In general, then, parents have the right to refuse treatment for their children where there is a strong religious conviction involved and the child's life is not endangered. The parental right to refuse is extremely limited or nonexistent where life or health is endangered and they have no reasonable or valid basis for the refusal.

Notes and References

1. *In the Matter of Brooks*, 32 Ill. 2d 361, 205 N.E.2d 435 (1965); *In the Matter of Osborne*, 294 A.2d 372 (1972); quotation from 52 ALR3d 1118, discussing *Prince v. Commonwealth of Massachusetts*, 321 U.S. 158 (1944).
2. *Jehovah's Witnesses in the State of Washington v. King County Hospital*, 278 F. Supp. 485 (N.D. Wash. 1967).
3. *Hoener v. Bertinato*, 67 N.J. Super. 517, 171 A.2d 140 (1961); *People ex rel. Wallace v. Labrenz*, 411 Ill. 618, 104 N.E.2d 769 (1952), cert. denied 344 U.S. 824.
4. *State v. Perricone*, 37 N.J. 463, 181 A.2d 751 (1962); *Muhlenberg Hospital v. Patterson*, 128 N.J. Super. 498, 320 A.2d 518 (1974).
5. *Application of Brooklyn Hospital*, 45 Misc. 2d 914, 258 N.Y.S. 2d 621 (1965); *In the Matter of Clark*, 21 Ohio Ops. 2d 86, 185 N.E.2d 128 (1962).
6. *In the Matter of Frank*, 41 Wash. 2d 294, 248 P.2d 553 (1952).
7. *In the Matter of Tuttendario*, 21 Pa. Dist. 561 (1911).
8. *In the Matter of Hudson*, 13 Wash. 2d 673, 126 P.2d 765 (1942); see also, *In the Matter of Seiferth*, 309 N.Y. 80, 127 N.E.2d 820 (1955).
9. *In the Matter of Green*, 448 Pa. 338, 292 A.2d 387 (1972).
10. *In the Matter of Karwath*, 199 N.W.2d 147 (Iowa 1972).
11. *In the Matter of Rotkowitz*, 175 Misc. 948, 25 N.Y.S. 624 (1941).
12. *In the Matter of Carstairs*, 115 N.Y.S. 2d 314 (1952).
13. *In the Matter of Sampson*, 328 N.Y.S. 2d 686, 278 N.E.2d 918 (1972).
14. Id. at 645.
15. Id. at 647.
16. *In the Matter of Gregory S.*, 85 Misc. 2d 846, 380 N.Y.S. 2d 620 (1976).
17. *Mannis v. State*, Ark. 398 S.W.2d 206 (1966), rehearing denied 2/14/66; see also, 42 Am. Jur. 2d Infants § 55.
18. *McCartney v. Austin*, 57 Misc. 2d 525, 293 N.Y.S. 2d 188 (1968), aff'd 31 App. Div. 2d 370, 298 N.Y.S. 2d 26 (1969).

CHAPTER 11

Parents' Right to Consent to Treatment That Does Not Directly Benefit Their Minor Children

"Parents may be free to make martyrs of themselves. But it does not follow that they are free, in identical circumstances, to make martyrs of their children."[1] This oft-quoted statement by Justice John Rutledge of the United States Supreme Court has been applied in the context of the parents' right to consent to nontherapeutic treatment for their minor and mentally incompetent children.

The major areas to which this doctrine applies are organ transplants and research on children. Older case law, while not directly dealing with this issue, indicated by implication that there is a parental right to consent to medical treatment that does not directly benefit the child. In *Bonner v. Moran*, a federal court faced the issue of whether a doctor who removed skin for a graft and let the blood of a 15-year-old boy for the benefit of his severely burned cousin could be held liable for assault and battery because the mother's consent was not secured.[2] The circuit court held that the lower court had made a reversible error, in that the jury had not been instructed that consent of both the boy and his mother must be obtained before such an operation could be performed legally.

In *Zaman v. Schultz*, a Pennsylvania court held that the jury had been properly instructed that parental consent should have been obtained before the minor daughter was subjected to blood taking for the benefit of her employer's wife.[3] In later cases, these decisions have been cited for the proposition that parents have the right to consent to nontherapeutic treatment for their children.

In another series of cases involving kidney transplants between twins, the rationale takes another turn, applying a "substituted judgment" theory. The theory is that if the minor or incompetent were legally capable of making a decision on his own, he would have chosen to consent to the organ transplant based on the emotional and psychological ties between twins.

The court of equity, empowered to order such a transplant, looks to the surrounding circumstances including the predictive success of the operation, the adverse effects on both twins if the operation is not performed, the alternatives to transplantation, and the psychological effect that the loss of one twin would have on the survivor.[4]

In Strunk v. Strunk, the doctrine of substituted judgment was taken a step further.[5] The Kentucky Court of Appeals held that the court of equity had sufficient power to order the removal and transplantation of the kidney of a 27-year-old, mentally incompetent man for the benefit of his older brother. His brother had a family and was dying of kidney disease. The court did add that the parents or guardian did not have the authority to consent on their own to such a transplant and that the county courts who had supervision over them also did not have such authority. With reasoning similar to that used in cases involving twins, the court determined that the incompetent brother would have consented if he were competent to do so, because of close ties with his brother.

More recent case law and statutory law demonstrate a reversal of this trend. In the Matter of Richardson involved parents of a 17-year-old, mentally retarded boy.[6] They petitioned the Louisiana court to have one of his kidney's removed and transplanted for his sister's benefit. The court denied the petition based on the rationale that a minor's right to be free from bodily intrusion to the extent of the loss of an organ must be afforded unqualified protection, just as his property rights are. Without a finding that the loss of the organ is in the best interest of the minor, the court would not order the transplant.

Legislation currently supports this reasoning in several states. In Oklahoma, under the Health Services to Minors Act, no research or experimentation may be performed on a minor "except where used in an attempt to preserve the life of that minor."[7] Thus, consent based on a indirect psychological benefit, as in the case of the survival of a twin, may no longer be legally effective.[8]

Experimentation and research on children has raised sufficient controversy so that a federal commission was appointed to study the problem under the auspices of the U.S. Department of Health, Education, and Welfare (DHEW). Thus was created, persuant to Public Law 93-348, the National Commission for the Protection of Human Subjects of Biomedical and Behavioral Research. Children became one of their subject areas. After several years of study and expert testimony, they made recommendations to DHEW as guidelines for federal support of research projects:[9]

1. Research involving children should continue with federal support.
2. An institutional review board should be set up in each institution to make the following determinations:
   a. the research is scientifically sound and significant;
   b. studies have been conducted first on animals and adult humans where possible and then on older children;
   c. the safest procedures are used to keep risk as low as possible;
   d. privacy and confidentiality are maintained;
   e. subjects will be selected equitably.
3. Research that does not involve greater than a minimal risk to children may be conducted provided that all of 2 is met and adequate provision has been made for the assent of the children and the permission of the parent or guardian.
4. If more than a minimal risk to the subject is anticipated, then some prospect of direct benefit to the individual subject or a monitoring procedure required for the well-being of the subject may be conducted provided that,
   a. the risk is justified by the anticipated benefit;
   b. all of 3 above is met.
5. If there is no direct benefit to the child and there is more than a minimal risk, then the research should be conducted only if,
   a. the risk is a minor increase over minimal risk;
   b. the information is likely to yield generalized knowledge relevant to the subject's disorder, and the experiences involved in the experiment are reasonably similar to those inherent in the subject's medical, psychological, or social situation;
   c. the knowledge is of vital importance, and all of the requirements of 4 are met.
6. Any other research that does not qualify under the above requirements can be conducted if,
   a. the research presents an opportunity to understand, prevent, or alleviate a serious problem affecting the health or welfare of children;
   b. the conduct of the research would not violate principles of respect for persons and beneficence and justice;
   c. the conditions of recommendation 2 are met, and adequate provisions for the assent of the child and permission of the parents are made.
7. To be included in any research, children who are wards of the state must have an advocate appointed with the opportunity to intercede on their behalf;
   a. the research must be related to their status as orphans or abandoned children, and so forth;
   b. or the research must be conducted in a school or similar

group setting in which the majority of the children are not wards of the state.

8. Children who reside in institutions for the mentally infirm or who are confined under a department of corrections can participate in research only after requirements for research on adults in the same kind of setting are complied with.

Researchers who seek federal funding must follow DHEW regulations and guidelines as well as state regulations. Where research and experimentation is not federally funded, it is subject to state regulation. For example, New York legislation authorizes experimental procedures involving children as long as both the child and parent or guardian give written informed consent and the child's consent is not deemed to release the doctor or hospital from liability. Oklahoma, on the other hand, no longer allows any research or experimentation on minors except those whose lives are endangered.[10]

Notes and References

1. *Prince v. Commonwealth of Massachusetts*, 321 U.S. 158, 170 (1944), rehearing denied 321 U.S. 804.
2. *Bonner v. Moran*, 126 F.2d 121 (D.C. Cir. 1941).
3. *Zaman v. Schultz*, 19 Pa. D & C 309 (1932), 35 A.L.R.3d 694.
4. See, *Hart v. Brown*, 29 Conn. Sup. 368, 289 A.2d 386 (1972); *Masden v. Harrison*, No. 68651, Eq. Mass. Sup. Jud. Ct. (June 12, 1957); *Hushey v. Harrison*, No. 68666, Eq. Mass. Sup. Jud. Ct. (Aug. 30, 1957); *Foster v. Harrison*, No. 68674, Eq. Mass. Sup. Jud. Ct. (Nov. 20, 1957).
5. *Strunk v. Strunk*, 445 S.W.2d 145 (Ky. App. 1969).
6. *In the Matter of Richardson*, La. App. 284 So. 2d 185 (1973) appeal dismissed 284 So. 2d 338.
7. 63 Okla Stat., Health Services to Minors Act § 2601 (c) Supp. 1976.
8. Note, Children: health services for minors in Oklahoma: capacity to give self-consent to medical care and treatment, *Oklahoma Law Review* 30:385, 395, 1977.
9. National Commission for the Protection of Human Subjects of Biomedical and Behavioral Research, *Research Involving Children: Report and Recommendations*, DHEW Publ. No. (OS) 77-0004, 1977, pp. 1–20.
10. N.Y. Public Law § 2440-46 (McKinney Supp. 1976); 63 Okla Stat. § 2601(c) (Supp. 1976).

CHAPTER 12

Parents' Right to Voluntarily Commit Their Minor Children for Mental Health Care

Parents have a great deal of authority over their children. Until recent years, this authority included having them admitted to mental institutions as "voluntary" patients, subject to release only upon the parents' express consent as long as they remained minors. As voluntary patients, minors do not have any of the procedural due process rights afforded those involuntarily committed. Nor do they have the rights afforded adults who voluntarily admit themselves for treatment. Thus, these minors do not have the benefit of a hearing and are without standing to petition for release.

The Supreme Court, after vacating the *Bartley* case (*infra*), finally consented to address this problem in *Parham v. J.L. and J.R., minors, etc.*[1]

The United States District Court for the Middle District of Georgia had held that the Georgia statute authorizing a parent or guardian to voluntarily commit persons under 18 years of age without affording those persons an opportunity to be heard violates the due process clause of the Fourteenth Amendment.

Chief Justice Burger, delivering the opinion of the Supreme Court, stated that the question presented in the appeal "is what process is constitutionally due a minor child whose parents or guardian seeks state administered institutional mental health care for the child and specifically whether an adversary proceeding is required prior to or after the commitment." The case was brought as a class-action suit against mental health officials of Georgia.

The majority opinion, in reversing the district court and in holding the statute constitutional, held that due process did not include the right to be heard before an impartial tribunal. This opinion was given considerable media attention and was characterized by the media as empowering parents to arbitrarily commit their children without adequate safeguards.

This certainly is not the case. The Georgia statute, while providing for the voluntary admission of children to state regional hospitals with an application for hospitalization signed by a parent or guardian also requires the superintendent of the hospital to observe the child and find "evidence of mental illness" and that the child is "suitable for treatment" in the hospital prior to admission. The hospital superintendent is further required to review periodically the child's condition and, as an affirmative duty after such reviews, to release any child "who has recovered from his mental illness or who has sufficiently improved that the superintendent determines that hospitalization of the patient is no longer desirable."

The majority opinion specifically noted that "a child has a protectable interest not only in being free of unnecessary bodily restraints, but also in not being labelled erroneously by some because of an improper decision by the state hospital superintendent."

The opinion, in concluding that the Georgia statute was consistent with the due process protection guaranteed the child by the Constitution, held that central to that issue was the kind of inquiry provided by a "neutral fact finder" for the ultimate determination as to whether the statutory requirements for admission had been satisfied. The Court noted that the statute provided for carefully probing the child's background and for an interview with the child and for giving the superintendent of the admitting hospital the authority to refuse to admit any child who did not satisfy the medical standards for such admission. The Court further noted that the Georgia statute provided for the continuing review of the need for commitment.

These procedures satisfied the Court that the statute protects the child from an erroneous-admission decision "in a way that neither unduly burdens the states nor inhibits parental decisions to seek state help."

Justice Brennan, joined by Justice Marshall and Justice Stevens, concurred in part and dissented in part. The dissent was concerned with a lack of a traditional commitment hearing. The dissent was not persuaded by the majority's reliance on the informal postadmission procedures provided by the Georgia statute. While agreeing that states may legitimately postpone formal commitment proceedings while parents seek in-patient psychiatric treatment, the minority held that such hearings cannot be foregone completely.

Justice Brennan concluded his dissent stating as follows:

> *Children incarcerated in public mental institutions are constitutionally entitled to fair opportunity to contest the legitimacy of their confinement. They are entitled to some*

*champion who can speak on their behalf and who stands ready to
oppose wrongful commitment. Georgia should not be permitted to
deny that opportunity and that champion simply because the
parents or guardians wish them to be confined without a hearing.
The risk of erroneous commitment is simply too great unless there
is some form of adversarial review. And fairness demands that
children abandoned by their supposed protectors to the rigors of
institutional confinement be given the help of some separate
voice.* [2]

Immediately following the decision in *Parham*, the Court decided
Secretary v. Institutionalized Juveniles, et al. [3] The issues concerned
the constitutionality of Pennsylvania statutory procedures for the
voluntary admission of mentally ill and mentally retarded children to a
state hospital. Justice Burger, once again delivering the majority
opinion, noted that the issues were similar to those decided in *Parham*,
namely: "as to what process is due when the parents or guardian of a
child seek state institutional mental health care."

Once again, the court was divided in affirming the constitutionality
of a statute providing for the commitment of minors without an
adversarial hearing. The majority opinion, in upholding the constitutionality of the Pennsylvania statute, as in *Parham*, was impressed with the statute's requirement of a preadmission screening and
constant review of each child's case. The majority concluded that the
criteria of its holding in *Parham* were met by the Pennsylvania statute.

Justice Brennan, along with Justice Marshall and Justice Stevens,
dissented on the grounds that Pennsylvania failed to provide representation or reasonably prompt postadmission hearings. The dissenting opinion noted that the burden of initiating contact with the
counsel and the burden of initiating proceedings to contest commitment are placed on the child. The dissent again emphasized that the
Fourteenth Amendment requires a fair hearing and that institutionalized children are not in a position to rationally waive these constitutional rights. The dissenting opinion would require the state to
"assign each institutionalized child a representative obliged to initiate
contact with the child and insure that the child's constitutional rights
are fully protected."

Thus, the *Parham* and *Secretary* decisions will permit involuntary
commitment of minors to state mental institutions without the traditional adversarial hearing, provided that sufficient safeguards against
error and abuse are provided in the applicable statute.

Considering the split in the court as to this issue, it is conceivable
that in the future some modifications of this principle are possible and
that greater safeguards for the child will be required.

Considering the most recent Supreme Court decisions (along with
other federal and state court decisions of late) involving juveniles and
those subject to civil commitment, one can safely predict that a change
in the law will occur assuring that minors will be provided more

procedural due process rights in this legal area of commitment.

In *Kent v. United States*, the Supreme Court held that certain minimum due process rights must be extended to juveniles who face delinquency proceedings.[4] In particular, a hearing must be provided that measures up to the essentials of due process and fundamental fairness.[5] In addition, several rights were extended to juveniles in *In Re Gault*: the right to notice of the charges and the proceeding to both the juvenile and his parents, the right to notice of the privilege against self-incrimination, and the right to counsel.[6] It can be argued that commitment for mental health treatment is no less a loss of liberty than detention for "treatment" of the juvenile delinquent. The *O'Connor v. Donaldson* and *Jackson v. Indiana* decisions, which reflect a concern with the rights of those subject to civil commitment, when read with *Gault* and *Kent*, supra, indicate that the minor mental patient likewise may be entitled to further procedural due process protection.[7]

The *Kremens v. Bartley* case, which unfortunately was vacated and remanded in 1977, presented the Supreme Court with precisely the same problem as the *Parham* case.[8] The plaintiff-appellees were five minors, aged 15 to 18 years, who had been committed by their parents under a 1966 Pennsylvania statute, which provided as follows:

> a) *Application for voluntary admissions to a facility for examination, treatment and care may be made by:... 2) A parent, guardian or individual standing in* loco parentis *to the person to be admitted, if such person is eighteen years of age or younger....*
>
> c) *Where application has been made under the provision of section 402(a) (2), only the applicant or his successor shall be free to withdraw the admitted person so long as the admitted person is eighteen years of age or younger.*[9]

This statute is similar to those of some 39 states, which provide for such admission of children by their parents.[10] After the original complaint was filed, and before the class certification and decision on the merits by the federal district court, a major change in the statutory scheme was effected in Pennsylvania. Under the Mental Health Procedures Act of 1976, any person 14 years of age or over may voluntarily admit himself for treatment, but his parents may not do this for him. The minor may withdraw himself from treatment at any time by giving written notice. Only those children 13 years or younger can be admitted by their parents, except for mentally retarded children, who are still subject to the old law permitting parental admission. Release of children 13 years of age or younger is by the parent's request, but the statute also provides that,

> *[A]ny responsible party [who] believes that it would be in the best interest of a person under 14 years of age in voluntary treatment to be withdrawn therefrom or afforded treatment constituting a less restrictive alternative, such party may file a petition on the Juvenile Division of the court of common pleas.*[11]

Since those aged 14 through 18, who were formerly committed by their parents, are now treated as adults under section 201 of the new Act and can withdraw from treatment at any time, the Supreme Court vacated and remanded the claims on the grounds of mootness, despite the fact that well over 80 percent on the plaintiff class were mentally retarded and not subject to the new Act's protections.[12]

Although the Supreme Court held the statute regarding commitment of juveniles in Pennsylvania to be constitutional in *Secretary v. Institutionalized Juveniles, et al.* (supra), as indicated earlier in this chapter, the lower court holding that the statute was unconstitutional is worth examining. In holding the statute unconstitutional, the Eastern District Court of Pennsylvania defined the essential components of due process regarding commitment of juveniles.[13] In the opinion of the district court, due process requires the following:

- A probable-cause hearing within 72 hours of the date of detention
- A postcommitment hearing within two weeks of the date of detention
- Written notice, including date, time, and place of the hearing, and a statement of the grounds for such commitment
- Counsel at all significant stages of commitment and, if the juvenile is indigent, the right to free counsel
- The right to be present at all hearings concerning the proposed commitment
- A finding by clear and convincing evidence of the need for institutionalization
- The right to confront and cross-examine witnesses, to offer evidence, and to offer testimony of witnesses.

In *Saville v. Treadway*, a federal district court in Tennessee struck down a voluntary-commitment statute for mentally retarded juveniles as violating due process rights under the Fourteenth Amendment.[14] Under the Tennessee Code, a parent or guardian could place a mentally retarded minor in a hospital or school without any restrictions, with release available only upon the consent of the superintendent of the institution or the commissioner of mental health, or a court proceeding.[15]

Two state court decisions have construed voluntary commitment statutes in a way favorable to the minor plaintiff. In *re Lee*, plaintiff wards of the juvenile court who had been adjudicated "neglected" challenged the Illinois voluntary-admission statute.[16] They had been "voluntarily" admitted to mental institutions by the state as their guardian. Under the applicable statute (since repealed), minors who were voluntarily committed had the right to seek and obtain their own release.[17] Although the court did not direct itself to the constitutional issue, it did interpret the statute to insure some fairness to the plaintiff class, a typical due process analysis.

In *Melville v. Sabbatino*, the Connecticut Superior Court held that the statute dealing with voluntary admissions must be read to apply equally to persons admitted on their own volition and those admitted by their parents.[18] Thus, where the statute provided that persons aged 16 to 18 could apply for hosptalization and release, those in the same age group, although signed in by their parents, could likewise sign themselves out.[19] The court went on to say that the due process requirements of *Gault* (supra) should apply to commitments of unemancipated minors by their parents.[20]

New legislation has been enacted in several states in accordance with such decisions, reflecting a trend toward protection of minors admitted by their parents. The Pennsylvania statute discussed in the *Bartley v. Kremens* case (supra) is one example of this trend. Another appears in the new Illinois Mental Health Legislation (effective January 1, 1979), which provides that minors 14 years of age and older can receive outpatient mental health care (up to five sessions of 45 minutes duration) on their own without parental consent. The new Act also provides that minors over 12 years of age can object to parents or a guardian having them admitted to mental hospitals. If they raise the objection, the admission is not deemed voluntary and the minor is given the right to an advocate and a court hearing. The hearing deals with a standard somewhat less than the involuntary commitment standard of "dangerous to self or others." The court must determine that either the minor is dangerous to himself or to others *or* the mental illness is of such severity that hospitalization is warranted and other alternatives have been explored.[21]

One author, Ellis, discusses the conflicts in this area. He believes that the parents of mentally ill and retarded youngsters are more often than not honestly trying to act in the best interests of the child and the family as a whole. With mildly retarded or mentally ill children who may be able to remain in the home and receive outpatient treatment, parents may nonetheless feel compelled to have them institutionalized because of the burden on other family members, the embarrassment of having an abnormal child who acts in a peculiar manner, or the need to alleviate the burden of caring for a helpless person in the home. Likewise, with older children, breakdown in communication may lead to conflicts that seem resolvable only by removing the child from the home. "The emergence of a counterculture lifestyle among young people in recent years, and the troubled reaction of some parents lends support to the suggestion that some parents have resorted to voluntary commitment proceedings in order to sanction behavior of which they disapproved."[22]

While laying blame on parents or psychologists who may encourage institutional care is pointless, it does seem that legislation increasing children's due process rights will serve to protect children's interests in remaining in their home settings wherever it is feasible, to prevent hasty decisions to institutionalize unnecessarily, and to educate parents to suitable alternatives to institutional care. Pressures on social agencies and state institutions may result in parents finding support in alternatives to institutionalization and becoming educated in the home care of the mentally ill and retarded.

Notes and References

1. *Parham v. J.L. and J.R., minors, etc.*, 47 Law Week 4740–54 (June 20, 1979).
2. Id. at 4754.
3. *Secretary v. Institutionalized Juveniles, et al.*, 47 Law Week 4754–57 (June 20, 1979).
4. *Kent v. United States*, 383 U.S. 541 (1966).
5. Id. at 562.
6. *In re Gault*, 387 U.S. 1 (1967).
7. *O'Connor v. Donaldson*, 493 F.2d 507, 521 (5th Cir. 1974); 422 U.S. 563 (1975); 45 L. Ed. 2d 396 (1975); *Jackson v. Indiana*, 406 U.S. 715 (1972); see Rights of the Mentally Ill.
8. *Kremens v. Bartley*, 431 U.S. 119 (1977); *Parham v. J.L. and J.R., supra.*
9. Pa. Stat. Ann. § 402 (1966).
10. See, voluntary commitment statutes in Ariz., Alaska, Ark., Cal., Colo., Conn., D.C., Fla., Ga., Hawaii, Idaho., Ill. (now repealed), Ind., Kan., Ky., Me., Md., N.D., Ohio, Okla., Ore., Pa., S.C., Tenn., Utah, Va., W.Va., Wis., and Wyo.
11. Pa. Mental Health Procedures Act § 201, 106(a) & (b) (1976).
12. See, Brennan's and Douglas's dissent, *Kremens v. Bartley*, supra at 141, 142.
13. *Secretary v. Institutionalized Juveniles, et al.*, U.S. D.C. E. Pa. (5/25/78).
14. *Saville v. Treadway*, 404 F. Supp. 430 (M.D. Tenn. 1974).
15. Tenn. Code Ann. § 33-501.
16. *In re Lee*, No 68 J.S. 1362 (Cook County Circuit Court, Juvenile Division, Illinois, February 29, 1972, cited in Ellis, Volunteering children: parental commitment of minors to mental institutions, *California Law Review* 62:840, 842, 1974.
17. Ill. Rev. Stat., 1969, Ch. 91½ § 5-1 through 5-3.
18. *Melville v. Sabbatino*, 30 Conn. Supp. 320 (1973), cited in Ellis, supra at 850.
19. Id., 30 Conn. Sup. at 325.
20. Id. at 322.
21. Ill. Mental Health Code.
22. Ellis, Volunteering Children, supra at 851.

Part FOUR

SPECIAL ISSUES REGARDING REPRODUCTION

CHAPTER 13

Abortion

Roe v. Wade was probably the most controversial case to come before the United States Supreme Court in this century.[1] In *Roe*, the court extended the right of privacy that had been defined and explained in two contraceptive cases, *Griswold v. Connecticut* and *Eisenstadt v. Baird*, to include a woman's decision whether or not to terminate her pregnancy.[2] At issue was the abortion statute of Texas that made it a crime to perform an abortion except to save the woman's life. Similar statutes existed in a majority of the states at the time, which was 1973.

Suddenly, abortion was legal in the United States, but not without sparking one of the hottest controversies in decades. For the women's movement, *Roe* represented a victory, liberating women from unsavory illegal abortions and unwanted children. For many in our society, *Roe* represented the death knell for the sanctity of human life and the potential for disregard of other helpless dependents of society, such as the elderly, the terminally ill, the defective newborns, and the mentally handicapped.

In sharp contrast, on February 25, 1975, the Federal Constitutional Court of West Germany announced that the statute that allowed unlimited abortions in the first trimester was unconstitutional. The court stated that the right to life expressly granted in the West German constitution "is guaranteed to everyone who lives; no distinction can be made here between various stages of the life developing itself before birth or between unborn and born life."[3]

The West German court was particularly sensitive to the "life unworthy of life" concept from the Weimar Constitution, which had been used as a legal and philosophical basis for the extermination of millions during World War II. "The security of human existence against encroachment by the State would be incomplete if it did not also embrace the prior step of 'completed' life, that is unborn life."[4]

Although recognizing the right of the woman to the "free develop-ment of her personality," the court found this right limited by the right of the fetus, the constitution, and moral law: "A compromise which guarantees the protection of the life of the one about to be born and permits the pregnant woman the freedom of abortion is not possible, since the termination of pregnancy always means the destruction of the unborn life."[5] In balancing the rights of both the mother and the fetus, "precedence must be given to the protection of the life of the child about to be born."[6] The court concluded by finding the statute unconstitutional in that the state has the duty to protect human life, a duty which cannot be abandoned to the decision of the mother. The statute that was ruled unconstitutional had allowed abortions to be performed by a physician with the consent of the woman within 12 weeks of conception. After 12 weeks, abortion had been legal only where performed by a physician with the woman's consent and when necessary to avert danger to her life or serious impairment of her health.

The United States Supreme Court could easily have taken a similar path. Its decision to go the other way has had a profound effect on this society, one which will be felt for some time. It, too, examined the two competing interests, the woman's right to privacy versus the state's interest in preserving maternal health. The Court found that the woman's right to privacy was paramount during the first trimester of pregnancy, since childbirth is far more dangerous to the woman's health than an abortion at this stage. The Court also took into account state interests in maternal health and the potential life of the fetus when the woman was in later stages of pregnancy.

In *Connecticut v. Menillo*, the Court ruled that during the first trimester of a woman's pregnancy, the only regulation the state may impose is that the abortion be performed by a licensed physician.[7] During the second trimester (approximately weeks 15 through 28), the state may regulate abortion only to protect maternal health. It is not until the fetus is determined to be "viable" (a medical decision made by a physician, usually around the twenty-eighth week) that the state may proscribe abortion.

Viability was defined in *Roe* as the "capacity of meaningful life outside the mother's womb."[8] At this point, the state's interest becomes compelling and, to effectuate its end, the state "may go so far as to proscribe abortion except when it is necessary to preserve the life or health or the mother."[9]

On the same day that the court decided *Roe v. Wade* it also handed down an opinion holding the Georgia statute, similar to those in effect in a minority of the states at the time, unconstitutional. The Georgia statute provided that abortions were legal only where the life or health of the pregnant woman was in danger; the fetus was likely to suffer grave, permanent, and irremedial mental or physical defect; or the pregnancy resulted from rape or incest. *Doe* established the right of a physician to challenge an abortion statute but excluded challenges by nurses, clergymen, and social workers.[10] The court deemed pregnant women and licensed physicians the appropriate parties, since they are the ones directly affected by such legislation.

After *Roe* and *Doe*, states begrudgingly implemented the right to abortion while imposing a variety of regulations to limit the availability of abortions. States relied on the following language from those opinions:

> [F]rom and after this point [the end of the first trimester], a State may regulate the abortion procedure to the extent that the regulation reasonably relates to the preservation and protection of maternal health. Examples of permissible state regulation in this area are requirements as to the qualifications of the person who is to perform the abortion; as to the licensure of that person; as to the facility in which the procedure is to be performed, that is, whether it must be a hospital or may be a clinic or some other place of less-than-hospital status; as to the licensing of the facility and the like.[11] [Emphasis added]

> This is not to say that Georgia may not or should not, from and after the end of the first trimester, adopt standards for licensing all facilites where abortions may be performed so long as those standards are legitimately related to the objective the State seeks to accomplish.[12]

Much of the new legislation enacted after *Roe* and *Doe*, or old legislation which states attempted to enforce was struck down by courts because the statutes included regulation of abortions during the first trimester of pregnancy. The language just quoted clearly gives the states some leeway in requiring licensure of physicians and hospitals and clinics, but, as this discussion will demonstrate, many municipalities went too far in their attempts to regulate the abortion procedure. Courts interpreted stringent regulations as limiting access in an unconstitutional manner.

REQUIREMENT OF SPOUSAL AND PARENTAL CONSENT

In 1976, the Supreme Court invalidated Missouri's statutory attempt to require the consent of the husband or parent before a woman (who was married or a single minor) could terminate her pregnancy, unless the abortion was necessary to preserve her life.[13] The case was *Planned Parenthood of Missouri v. Danforth*. The grounds for invalidation were predicated on *Roe's* prohibition of any state regulation proscribing or limiting abortion in the interests of maternal health during the first trimester. Such consent was deemed a third-party veto, which cannot be upheld constitutionally during the first trimester since the decision to terminate the pregnancy is medical and strictly between the woman and her physician. The woman's right to privacy is paramount at this stage and cannot be limited by the veto of a third party.

The *Danforth* decision reflected the reasoning of many lower federal and state court decisions, which invalidated similar requirements and, in some cases, prevented a plaintiff husband or potential father of the child from interfering with the abortion plans of the woman.[14]

ATTEMPTS TO REGULATE THE PLACE OF AND PROCEDURES FOR ABORTIONS

In *Doe v. Bolton.* the Supreme Court found that the Georgia requirement that all abortions be performed in a hospital approved by the Joint Commission on Accreditation of Hospitals could not withstand constitutional scrutiny. Although there is support in *Roe* and *Doe* for state regulation of the place where abortions are to be performed, the regulations must be "legitimately related to the objective the state seeks to accomplish."[15]

The court could find no reasonable relationship between state objectives and this requirement, since first-trimester abortions, which were included in the regulation, can be safely performed in other settings. Several lower federal courts have followed suit and invalidated state licensing requirements similar to the Georgia Abortion Act examined in *Doe.*[16]

Several municipalities including Chicago; Mobile, Alabama; Youngstown, Ohio; and St. Louis promulgated regulations that apply to both hospitals and clinics that perform abortions. Those adopted by the Chicago Board of Health serve as a representative sample of the group. These regulations address virtually every phase of operations in the hospital or clinic involved.

A Hospital Abortion Service (HAS) must be a licensed Chicago hospital. A clinic where abortions are performed, an Affiliated Abortion Service (AAS), must be within 15 minutes total traveling and admission time from an HAS. There must be a written affiliation agreement between an AAS and an HAS providing for both inpatient and outpatient support for clinic patients with complications.

Either a qualified obstetrician or a surgeon with specific enumerated specialities must be hired as supervisor. A registered professional nurse with postgraduate education or experience in obstetrics-gynecology must be on duty at all times when the clinic is in operation. The AAS must keep detailed records and send monthly reports to the Chicago Board of Health, reports that include the number of patients, their ages, periods of gestation, and abortion method used. The AAS must have extensive laboratory facilities on the premises, except that an AAS may share some with the HAS nearby; and drug and blood supplies specified must be on hand. Regulations describe in detail the instruments and equipment to be used.

In *Friendship Medical Center, Ltd., v. Chicago Board of Health*, a medical corporation and a physician who owned and operated an abortion clinic sought and won a declaratory judgment (a judgment that states rights of parties or answers legal questions) stating that these regulations unduly infringed upon the privacy of the patients involved and violated the equal protection clause of the Fourteenth Amendment.[17]

The court based its decision on *Roe's* limitation on state regulation of first-trimester abortions. These regulations were regarded as restrictions on the woman's and her doctor's decision to terminate the pregnancy and the manner of termination during the first trimester. "*Roe* and *Doe* compel us to conclude that the fundamental right of privacy includes, at least during the first trimester of pregnancy, the right to be free from governmental regulations that have an effect on the abortion decision."[18]

Since other complex and dangerous medical procedures also performed in hospitals and clinics were not subject to such regulations and were left up to the judgment of the physician, there was definitely an equal protection violation.[19]

In *Mahoning Women's Center v. Hunter*, an Ohio federal district court struck down the Youngstown ordinance extensively regulating its abortion clinics.[20] The court found that the termination methods (vacuum aspiration, and dilation and curettage) used in the involved clinic for first-trimester abortions were minor in complexity and risk, were low in complications, and did not require such extensive regulations. Reasoning similar to that of the Illinois federal court in *Friendship* was used to find an equal protection violation.

Aside from the regulation of medical personnel and procedures, city ordinances have attempted to restrict clinics from areas zoned for other medical and professional operations. A federal district court sitting in Ohio recently upheld Cleveland's zoning scheme in *West Side Women's Service v. City of Cleveland*.[21] The city of Cleveland had passed a municipal ordinance prohibiting abortion-service licenses in local retail districts of the city that were zoned to allow all other medical and professional services. Plaintiffs argued unsuccessfully that the ordinance was violative of due process and equal protection under the Fourteenth Amendment. The court found that the decision by the city to not allow abortion clinics in retail business districts was a permissible "value judgment," which did not "unduly burden" either the abortion decision or the physician-patient relationship.[22] Since the plaintiffs did not have a fundamental right to perform abortions, the state need show only a rational basis for the ordinance, an easy test to uphold.

On the other hand, where the effect of a zoning scheme was to effectively ban abortion clinics from an entire political subdivision, the scheme was not upheld. In 1976, Saint Paul's City Council (due to public pressure) passed an ordinance declaring a moratorium on the "construction, reconstruction, adaption, and modification of separate abortion facilities" within the city for six months pending a study to determine whether zoning restrictions should be imposed.

In *Planned Parenthood of Minnesota, Inc., v. Citizens for Community Action*, the Eighth Circuit Court of Appeals upheld a preliminary injunction against enforcement of the ordinance, since the likelihood of success on the merits was probable.[23] (A judgment on the merits is a final resolution after all evidence is heard.) The court reasoned that the city was not constitutionally entitled to control the composition and operation of facilities for first-trimester abortions.[24] The reasoning relied on the Supreme Court's summary affirmance in *Arnold v. Sendak*, which constitutes a disposition on the merits of the case. The city spokesmen argued, to no avail, that their zoning authority was broad enough to encompass such a scheme.

The court countered this argument as follows: "There is no judicial authority allowing a municipality, by imposing special restrictive zoning requirements on first trimester abortion clinics, to do indirectly that which it cannot do directly by medical regulation. . . . [T]he zoning ordinance in this case is only a disguised attempt to regulate medical practices in St. Paul."[25]

The Supreme Court dealt with restrictions on the method of abortion used in the *Danforth* case (supra). The Missouri legislature had attempted to prohibit use of saline amniocentesis during the second trimester, based on the state's interest in protecting maternal health. This rationale was countered by evidence that (1) the alternatives, hysterotomy and hysterectomy, were significantly more dangerous and critical than the saline technique; (2) the mortality rate for childbirth exceeded that where amniocentesis was used as the abortion technique; and (3) the safe alternative, prostaglandin, was not yet widely available in this country.

Thus, the ban on saline amniocentesis was not rationally related to the protection of maternal health. According to statistics presented to the court, 70 percent of all abortions performed after the first trimester were effected through this procedure. The court held that the statute was "an arbitrary regulation designed to inhibit, and having the effect of inhibiting, the vast majority of abortions after the first twelve weeks. As such, it does not withstand constitutional challenge."[26]

Other regulations that have fallen under constitutional scrutiny include the requirement of a two-physician concurrence before an abortion can be performed and the approval of each abortion by a hospital committee.[27]

ABORTION CONSCIENCE CLAUSES

The Congress and over 40 states have enacted statutes providing legal protection to individuals and institutions who, because of moral or religious objections, refuse to perform abortions.[28] The federal conscience clauses were enacted in response to the *Taylor v. St. Vincent's Hospital* decision, where a federal district court enjoined a private hospital with the town's only obstetrical facility from prohibiting sterilizations.[29] The court found that the hospital's receipt of Hill-Burton funds provided sufficient state action to support a civil rights claim.[30] The Hill-Burton Act authorizes federal-state aid for construction of public and private health care facilities. In exchange, recipients must provide a certain percentage of free health care to indigents.

Congress enacted the federal conscience clause to overrule the implication of *Taylor* that private hospitals receiving such funds could be compelled to perform abortions.[31] The act provides, in part, that the receipt of federal funds does not authorize any court or public official to require individuals or institutions "to perform or assist in the performance of any... abortion," when to do so would violate their "religious beliefs or moral convictions."

Most states have followed suit and now shield hospitals and physicians and medical and nursing personnel from civil liability and employment-discrimination claims for refusal to perform or participate in abortions.[32]

Such clauses have not stemmed the flood of litigation arguing that hospitals do, in fact, have a duty to provide abortion facilities. Federal courts in the first, sixth, and eight circuits have held that public hospitals that offer medical procedures indistinguishable from abortion could not forbid elective nontherapeutic abortions without violating the fundamental right of a woman to choose to terminate her pregnancy.[33]

The United States Supreme Court, in a widely criticized decision, reversed this line of cases in *Poelker v. Doe*. The court held that it was not a violation of the Fourteenth Amendment equal protection for a municipal hospital to "express a preference for normal childbirth."[34]

In a vociferous dissent, Justices Thurgood Marshall and Harry A. Blackmun expressed their affirmance of the Court of Appeals view that,

> *Stripped of all rhetoric, the city here, through its policy and staffing procedure, is simply telling indigent women like Doe that if they choose to carry their pregnancies to term, the city will provide physicians and medical facilities for full maternity care, but if they choose to exercise their constitutionally protected right to determine that they wish to terminate their pregnancy, the city will not provide physicians and facilities.*[35]

The dissenters argued that the state's preference for normal childbirth becomes compelling (under *Roe*) only after the first two trimesters, and, thus, a city hospital should be precluded from promulgating such a policy until the third trimester.[36]

A similar series of cases has considered the right of a private hospital that receives Hill-Burton funds to refuse to perform elective abortions. Based on *Poelker*, it is fairly easy to argue that their refusal will likewise be upheld, although, before *Poelker,* the Supreme Court had never granted certiorari to reconcile conflicting views between circuits.[37] (A certiorari is like an appeal, but one on which the court is not required to make a decision.)

Thus, abortion conscience clauses have effectively precluded hospitals and physicians from any liability for failure to perform or offer abortions, much to the chagrin of pro-abortion groups. Faced with a complicated mixture of philosophical-moral-religious convictions that are deeply imbedded, the Court could hardly have gone any other way. The liberal trend of the early 1970s, however, is most certainly being reversed as indigent women's access to abortions narrows considerably with decisions such as *Poelker.* Attempts to limit state and federal funding for abortions restricts access to abortions even further.

ATTEMPTS TO LIMIT STATE AND FEDERAL FUNDING

Despite a host of earlier decisions, to the contrary of lower federal courts, the Supreme Court in the companion cases of *Beal v. Doe* and *Maher v. Roe* upheld the right of a state to withhold Medicaid funds for nontherapeutic abortions.[38] In *Beal,* Pennsylvania limited use of state and federal Medicaid funds to those abortions considered "medically necessary," for which there was documented evidence that the pregnancy would endanger the health of the woman or where the infant was likely to be physically or mentally deformed or where the woman has been the victim of rape or incest. The court held that under Title XIX of the Social Security Act (Medicaid), there is no requirement that the state fund nontherapeutic abortions as a condition of participation in the joint federal-state program, although states are free to do so if they wish.[39]

In *Maher,* the court evaluated the Connecticut Medicaid program and found no violation of the equal protection clause of the Fourteenth Amendment, where the state paid for childbirth but excluded abortions not certified as "medically necessary." The court determined that indigent women did not constitute a suspect class and that there was no infringement on a fundamental right:

> There is no unduly burdensome interference with [the woman's] freedom to decide whether to terminate her pregnancy. [Roe] implies no limitation on the authority of a state to make a value judgment favoring childbirth over abortion, and to implement that judgment by the allocation of public funds.

• •

> An indigent woman who desires an abortion suffers no disadvantage as a consequence of Connecticut's decision to fund childbirth; she continues as before to be dependent on private sources for the service she desires. The state may have made

> *childbirth a more attractive alternative, thereby influencing the woman's decision, but it has imposed no restriction on access to abortions that was not already there.*[40] *[Emphasis added]*

The court considered the state's interest in encouraging normal childbirth to be legitimate and found the decision to subsidize childbirth to be related rationally to that interest. It is interesting to note the court's logic in this case. The fact that a woman is indigent certainly indicates her "private sources" are limited or nonexistent. In fact, if a woman on welfare is discovered to have such "private sources" of income, she can be assured that her welfare check will be reduced to that extent. That an indigent woman should be expected to find "private sources" of funding most definitely restricts her access to abortions. To conclude otherwise is incomprehensible.

Maher and *Beal* have been widely criticized and have been the subject of vigorous dissents from a minority of Supreme Court justices, including Harry A. Blackmun, William J. Brennan, Jr., and Thurgood Marshall, who joined in dissenting from the *Poelker v. Doe* opinion as well.[41]

> *[A] distressing insensitivity to the plight of impoverished pregnant women is inherent in the Court's analysis. The stark reality for too many, not just "some," indigent pregnant women is that indigency makes access to competent licensed physicians not merely "difficult" but "impossible." As a practical matter, many indigent women will feel that they have no choice but to carry their pregnancies to term because the State will pay for the associated medical services, even though they would have chosen to have abortions if the State had also provided funds for the procedure, or indeed if the State had provided funds for neither procedure. This disparity in funding by the State clearly operates to coerce indigent pregnant women to bear children they would not otherwise choose to have, and just as clearly, this coercion can only operate upon the poor, who are uniquely the victims of this form of financial pressure.*

> •

> *None can take seriously the Court's assurance that its "conclusion signals no retreat from Roe or the cases applying it."*[42]

The U.S. Department of Health, Education, and Welfare (DHEW) has promulgated rules and regulations governing the use of federal money to finance abortions through Medicaid. Federal financial participation is limited to where (1) a physician has found and so certified in writing that "on the basis of his or her professional judgment, the life of the mother would be endangered if the fetus were carried to term," (2) two other physicians find and certify that "severe and long-lasting physical health damages to the mother would result," or (3) the woman is the victim or rape or incest, certified by a signed document to that effect from a law-enforcement agency.[43]

Several states apply a more restrictive test than that of DHEW, providing funding only for situations in the first category, where the life of the mother is endangered. Two recent cases in lower federal courts have examined such limitations with different results: *Doe v. Kenley* in Virginia and *D.R. v. Mitchell* in Utah.[44] In *Doe v. Kenley*, the Fourth Circuit Court of Appeals held that the state of Virginia could not eliminate Medicaid funding for nontherapeutic abortions by using a policy standard that required a physician to certify that the life of the mother would be endangered if the fetus were carried to the full term of nine months.

The court examined the difference between "endangerment to health" and "endangerment to life" and found the latter too restrictive. This court effectively requires Virginia to regulate funding of abortions no more restrictively than the federal government. In other words, since DHEW will fund those abortions where two physicians agree that there is the possibility of "severe and long-lasting" endangerment of the mother's health, the state cannot further limit its funding to pregnancies causing "endangerment to the life of the woman."

The federal district court in Utah took a different stance on this issue. In *D.R. v. Mitchell*, Utah's Medicaid scheme, similar to the Virginia regulation in the *Kenley* case, was upheld. The court analyzed the case in a different manner relying on the reasoning in *Maher* that (1) the policy constitutes "*encouragement* of an alternative activity" and *not* "state interference with a protected right" and (2) under Title XIX the state has considerable latitude in appropriating Medicaid funds.[45] The court analyzed the Congressional objectives behind the Social Security Act and found that this scheme was not inconsistent with Congress's objectives. The plaintiff in this case argued that the former DHEW and *Maher* standard of "medically necessary" was too narrowly interpreted by Utah's requirement that abortion is permitted only where the life of the mother is endangered.

The Supreme Court has yet to iron out these differences in interpretation of the extent to which a state can eliminate funding under Medicaid. In any event, *Maher* and *Beal*, when taken to an extreme as in *D.R. v. Mitchell*, serve to severely limit indigent women's access to abortion.[46] The right to abortion secured for women in *Roe v. Wade* may prove to benefit only that class of women who have always had access to abortion because of wealth and ability to leave the country.

OTHER ATTEMPTS TO REGULATE ABORTION

The constitutionality of the Illinois Abortion Act was questioned recently in the companion cases, *Wynn v. Scott, Carey v. Wynn, Long v. Scott,* and *Diamond v. Wynn*.[47] The informed-consent provision of the Abortion Law of Illinois requires the woman to certify in writing that her consent is informed and freely given and that she has been informed of the following:

> a) *The physical competency of the fetus at the time the abortion is to be performed, such as, but not limited to, what the fetus looks like, the fetus' ability to move, swallow, and its physical characteristics;*
>
> b) *The general dangers of abortion, including, but not limited to, the possibility of subsequent sterility, premature birth, live-born fetus, and other dangers; and*
>
> c) *The particular dangers of the procedure to be used.*[48]

The Court upheld the requirement of the written certification of free and informed consent relying on *Danforth*,[49] but held that sections a and b (just quoted) were unconstitutionally vague and specific:

> *The physician does not have a fair warning of what is required. It is unclear whether the state could prosecute a physician for failure to warn the woman of a danger not included in the list. On the other hand, the very specificity of clauses (a) and (b) places the physicians in the "straight-jacket" condemned in Danforth. For example, a physician performing a first trimester abortion must tell the woman that there is a danger of a live-born fetus, when it is impossible that her abortion will result in a fetus born alive. And the physician must tell the woman that there is a danger of subsequent sterility despite the fact that studies have not shown that this danger actually exists.*[50]

The third requirement (section c) was upheld, since it was consistent with informed-consent requirements in general. While the court did not specifically address the plaintiff's claim that the clauses are aimed at thwarting and restricting (by employing psychological coercion) a woman's decision to have an abortion, it seems apparent that this is precisely what the Illinois legislature intended.

The circumstance where a fetus emerges alive from an abortion has prompted passage of a series of criminal statutes outlining the physician's and hospital's duty toward the fetus. The Supreme Court in *Danforth* struck down a provision pertaining to treatment of the fetus, since it included first-trimester abortions, which the state cannot regulate except for the the requirement that a licensed physician perform the operation.[51] The Illinois provision on point b, however, was upheld in *Wynn v. Scott* (supra). The statute reads,

> *No person who performs or induces an abortion after the fetus is viable shall fail to exercise that degree of professional skill, care and diligence to preserve the life and health of the fetus which such person would be required to exercise in order to preserve the life and health of any fetus intended to be born and not aborted. Any physician who shall intentionally fail to take such measures*

to encourage or to sustain the life of viable fetus or child, and the death of the viable fetus or child results, shall be deemed guilty of Class 2 felony.[52]

The court reasoned that the wording did not require the physician to increase the risk to the woman in order to save the fetus, but rather,

[W]here a physician has a choice of procedures, both of equal risk to the woman, the physician must choose the procedure which is least likely to kill the fetus. This choice would not interfere with the woman's right to terminate her pregnancy. It never could be argued that she has a constitutionally protected right to kill the fetus. She does not.[53]

The Supreme Court, in *Colautii v. Franklin*, examined the Pennsylvania Abortion Control Act, which requires every person who performs an abortion to first determine if the fetus is "viable."[54] If the fetus is viable, the physician is required to exercise the same care to preserve the life and health of the fetus as would be required in the case of a normal childbirth where the intent is that the fetus be born alive.

The court held the statute unconstitutional on several grounds. Since the statute imposes a duty to protect where the fetus is "viable" or "may be viable" and specifies criminal sanctions for breach of that duty without any requirement of scienter (knowledge), it is impermissibly vague. The statute leaves the physician uncertain as to whether his duty to the mother is to be paramount to the duty to the fetus, or whether a possible increased risk to the mother in selection of techniques would be justified to increase the chance of fetal survival. Such imprecision in drafting is unacceptable to the court.

The concept of viability was once again elaborated upon by the Supreme Court:

Viability is reached when, in the judgment of the attending physician on the particular facts of the case before him, there is a reasonable likelihood of the fetus' sustained survival outside the womb, with or without artificial support. Because this point may differ with each pregnancy, neither the legislature nor the courts may proclaim one of the elements entering into the ascertainment of viability—be it weeks of gestation or fetal weight or any other single factor—as the determinant of when the State has a compelling interest in the life or health of the fetus. Viability is the critical point. And we have recongized no attempt to stretch the point of viability one way or the other.[55]

The concepts of viability and a physician's and a hospital's duty toward the fetus will be an increasingly interesting topic in the future as scientific technology develops and premature infants have a greater chance for survival. An article in the *Southern California Law Review* advances the theory that the state may eventually require that abortions be nonfeticidal when possible and that the fetus must be kept alive in an artificial womb.[56] Doctors have discovered that premature babies who weigh less than two pounds and have attained at least 26 weeks gestation can be saved.[57] A story in the *Washington Post* indicated that development of an artificial lung may lower even more the age at which a fetus can survive.

As a pregnancy nears the end of the second trimester, closer to "viability," doctors who are to perform an abortion are met with a dilemma. The most frequently used method in the second trimester is saline amniocentesis, owing to its availability and relative safety for the mother. This procedure causes certain fetal death, however. It may become necessary, as viability approaches, to use other techniques that might not be as safe for the mother.

The Illinois Court, in *Wynn v. Scott* (supra), was unconvinced that this situation would impose added problems, adopting the dissent's view in *Doe v. Rampton*[58] that the physician's primary duty is to the woman, and that "it would be illogical to read the provision as requiring physicians to endanger the life of the woman at the same time as trying to save it by performing a therapeutic abortion."[59]

Criminal prosecution of physicians in the abortion context is a reality. Aside from the *Colautti* case (supra), another case is on appeal to the Supreme Court. In *Floyd v. Anders*, a physician was prosecuted for murder and illegal abortion where the fetus lived for 20 days outside the womb following an abortion on a woman in her twenty-fifth week of pregnancy.[60]

The district court found that the prosecutor acted in bad faith, since he was chargeable with knowledge of the decision in *Roe v. Wade* (supra), which invalidated the South Carolina abortion law on the books at that time. The question for review is whether any constitutional definition of viability "supports a conclusion that a child born as a result of abortion and lives for 20 days is not viable as a matter of the law."[61]

The Supreme Court decision in *Floyd v. Anders* will have a profound impact on abortion law in this country. Criminal prosecution of physicians based on a flexible and ever changing status of "viability" cannot help restricting access to abortion even further. The potential liability the physician faces, whether criminal or civil, may drastically reduce the number of physicians willing to perform this procedure.

CONCLUSION

It is apparent that states continue to erode the right to abortion by restricting access by every available avenue. Zoning; stringent regulations; unrestricted decisions to fund or not to fund, to open hospitals, or to choose not to offer abortions; and criminal prosecution of doctors who perform abortion all serve to limit availability indirectly. If the courts continue to uphold such legislation, a return to pre-*Roe* days of illegal and dangerous abortions might result.

Perhaps the Supreme Court was hasty in deciding the *Roe* case. Apparently, the court's reasoning did not reflect the philosophy concerning the sanctity of human life of the majority of American citizens. Although *Roe* continues to be challenged and upheld, our legislatures and courts continue to express their preference for the "right to life" in subtle and not-so-subtle ways.[62]

Notes and References

1. *Roe v. Wade*, 410 U.S. 113 (1973).
2. *Griswold v. Connecticut*, 381 U.S. 479 (1965).
3. See, Gorby, John, and Jonas, Robert E., West German abortion decision: a contrast to *Roe v. Wade, John Marshall Journal of Practice and Procedure* 9:551 at 638, 1976.
4. Id. at 638.
5. Id. at 641.
6. Id. at 643.
7. *Connecticut v. Menillo*, 423 U.S. 9 (1975).
8. *Roe v. Wade*, supra at 163.
9. Id. at 163–64.
10. *Doe v. Bolton*, 410 U.S. 194 (1973).
11. *Roe v. Wade*, supra at 163.
12. *Doe v. Bolton*, supra at 194–95.
13. *Planned Parenthood of Missouri v. Danforth*, 428 U.S. 52 (1976).
14. Id. at 340. See e.g., *Wolfe, v. Schroering*, 541 F.2d (6th Cir. 1976); *Planned Parenthood Association v. Fitzpatrick*, 401 F. Supp. 554 (D.C. Pa. 1975); *Doe v. Zimmerman*, 405 F. Supp. 534 (D.C. Pa. 1975); *Doe v. Doe*, 314 N.E.2d 128 (Mass. 1974); *Jones v. Smith*, 278 So.2d 339 (Fla. App. 1973); *Doe v. Rampton*, 366 F. Supp. 189 (D.C. Utah 1973); *Pound v. Pound*, Ill. Cir. C. 6th Jud. Dist. 1/31/74, 42 Law Week 2456.
15. *Doe v. Bolton*, supra at 195.
16. See e.g., *Arnold v. Sendak*, 416 F. Supp. 22 (S.D. Ind. 1976), aff'd 45 3398; 2068, *Emma G. v. Edwards*, 434 F. Supp. 1048 (D.C. La. 1977).
17. *Friendship Medical Center, Ltd., v. Chicago Board of Health*, 505 F.2d 1141 (1974), cert. denied 420 U.S. 997.
18. Id. at 1151.
19. See also, *Word v. Poelker*, 495 F.2d 1349 (8th Cir. 1974); Held: St. Louis ordinance requiring all abortion clinics to apply for a permit after disclosing extremely detailed information was unduly restrictive.
20. *Mahoning Women's Center v. Hunter*, 444 F. Supp. 12 (N.D. Ohio 1977).
21. *West Side Women's Service v. City of Cleveland*, 450 F. Supp. 796 (N.D. Ohio 1978), aff'd mem. 582 F.2d 1281 (6th Cir. 1978), cert. denied 47 Law Week 3368.
22. Id. at 798.
23. *Planned Parenthood of Minnesota, Inc., v. Citizens for Community Action*, 558 F.2d 861 (8th Cir. 1977).
24. Relying on the Supreme Court's summary affirmance in *Arnold v. Sendak* 416 Supp. 22 (S.D. Ind. 1976), aff'd 429 U.S. 968 (1976).
25. *Planned Parenthood of Minnesota, Inc., v. Citizens for Community*

Action, supra at 868; See, *Framingham Clinic, Inc., v. Board of Selectmen of Southborough,* 367 N.E.2d 606 (Mass. Super Jud. Ct. 1977) which struck down ordinance which, in effect, prohibited abortion clinics for entire town.

26. *Planned Parenthood of Missouri v. Danforth,* supra at 78; Accord, *Wolfe v. Schroering,* supra at 523.
27. See, *Doe v. Bolton,* supra.
28. See generally, Shapiro, Shelly C., Abortion and the patient's right to know, *Washington University Law Quarterly* 167:204 at 209, 1978.
29. *Taylor v. St. Vincent's Hospital,* 369 F. Supp. 948 (D. Mont. 1973), aff'd 523 F.2d 75 (9th Cir. 1975), cert. denied 424 U.S. 948 (1976).
30. Hill-Burton Act. 42 U.S.C. § 291, 1983 (1970).
31. See, Health Programs Extension Act of 1973, § 401 (b)-(c), 42 U.S.C. § 300 (a) (7) (Supp. V 1975).
32. See, *e.g.,* Ariz. Rev. Stat. Ann. § 36-2151 (1974); Cal. Health & Safety Code § 25955 (c) (Deering Supp. 1975); Ill. Rev. Stat. Ann. ch. 38 § 81-16, 81-33 (1977); Mich. Stat. Ann. § 14.57 (Supp. 1976); N.Y. Civil Rights Law § 79-i (McKinney Supp. 1976); Wis. Stat. Ann. § 448.06 (8) (West. Supp. 1974).
33. See, *e.g., Doe v. Hale,* 500 F.2d 144 (1st Cir. 1974), cert. denied 420 U.S. 907; *Nyberg v. City of Virginia,* 495 F.2d 1342 (8th Cir. 1974); *Wolfe v. Schroering,* supra.
34. *Poelker v. Doe,* 432 U.S. 519–20 (1977).
35. *Poelker v. Doe,* 515 F.2d 541, 544 (1975).
36. Id. at 525.
37. See, *Greco v. Orange Memorial Hospital Corporation,* 513 F.2d 873 (5th Cir. 1976), cert. denied U.S. (1977); *Doe v. Bellin Memorial Hospital,* 479 F.2d 756 (7th Cir. 1973).
38. See, *e.g., Doe v. Rose,* 499 F.2d 1112 (10th Cir. 1974); Held: denial of welfare funds for nontherapeutic abortions violated the Fourteenth Amendment and constituted invidious discrimination on the part of state officials; Accord, *Klein v. Nassau County Medical Center,* 409 F. Supp. 731 (E.D. N.Y. 1976), vacated and remanded in light of *Beal v. Doe* and *Maher v. Roe,* infra; *Roe v. Norton,* 408 F. Supp. 660 (1975); Held; state cannot deny Medicaid coverage for first-trimester elective abortions; *Beal v. Doe,* 432 U.S. 438 (1977); *Maher v. Roe,* 432 U.S. 464 (1977).
39. Social Security Act, 42 U.S.C. § 1396 et seq. tit. 19; *Maher v. Roe,* supra at 447.
40. *Maher v. Roe,* id. at 474.
41. *Poelker v. Doe,* supra at 519.
42. *Maher v. Roe,* supra at 483, dissenting opinion by Justice William J. Brennan, Jr.
43. DHEW Rules and Regulations, amended 7/14/78, 47 Law Week 2065.
44. *Doe v. Kenley,* 584 F.2d 1362 (4th Cir. 1978); *D.R. v. Mitchell,* 456 F. Supp. 609 (D. Utah 1978).
45. *D.R. v. Mitchell,* id. at 615.
46. See generally, DiStefano, Lenore, A meaningful right to abortion for indigent women? *Loyola Law Review* 24:301 Spring 1978.
47. *Wynn v. Scott,* 449 F. Supp. 1302 (N.D. Ill. 1978), appeal dism'd *sub. nom.; Carey v. Wynn,* 47 Law Week 3264; *Long v. Scott,* U.S.D.C. N. Ill (4/12/78), appeal dism'd *sub. nom.; Diamond v. Wynn,* 47 Law Week 3264 (1979).

48. Ill. Rev. Stat. ch. 38 § 81-23 (2) (a)-(c) (1976).
49. *Planned Parenthood of Missouri v. Danforth*, supra at 67.
50. *Wynn v. Scott*, supra at 1317.
51. *Connecticut V. Menillo*, supra.
52. Ill. Rev. Stat. ch. 38 § 81-26 (1) (1976).
53. *Wynn v. Scott*, supra at 1321.
54. *Colautii v. Franklin*, 47 Law Week 4094 (1/9/79); Pennsylvania Abortion Control Act. § 5 (a).
55. *Colautii v. Franklin*, id. at 4097.
56. See Note, Choice rights and abortion: the begetting choice right and state obstacles to choice in the light of artificial womb technology, *Southern California Law Review* 51:877–922, 1978.
57. Note, 26 weeks is two weeks earlier than noted in *Roe v. Wade*, supra at 63; Colen, B.D., Small premature babies' chances at life improve, *The Washington Post*, 12 Dec. 1976.
58. *Doe v. Rampton*, supra at 193.
59. *Wynn v. Scott*, supra at 1321.
60. *Floyd v. Anders*, 440 F. Supp. 535 (D. S.C. 1977), app'l pending No. 77-1255, sum. 47 Law Week 3045.
61. Id. at 3045.
62. See, e.g. *Gaetano v. Silbert* (C.A. D.C. 6/27/78), cert. denied 47 Law Week 3301; *Gaetano v. U.S. Court of Appeals for District for Columbia* (C.A. D.C. 6/27/78), mand. denied 47 Law Week 3302.

CHAPTER 14

Sterilization, Wrongful Life, Artificial Insemination

STERILIZATION

Sterilization is the ultimate birth control. Because of medical complications with a woman's past pregnancies or to avoid the imperfect methods available for temporary birth control, many women and men choose sterilization. For women, the most common technique is tubal litigation, where the fallopian tubes are tied off to prevent the ovum from being fertilized and from traveling to the uterus and being implanted there. For men, vasectomy is the usual sterilization procedure. A segment of the vas deferens is removed to prevent sperm from being ejaculated.

The case law in this area, similar to that of abortion, involves access and availability. Women face similar problems in seeking sterilizations where hospitals make it a policy not to offer this simple surgical procedure and husbands attempt to prohibit the operation. Malpractice claims have been brought against physicians because of negligent performance of the procedure where pregnancy has followed an operation for sterilization. These latter problems will be discussed in the next section, "Wrongful Life."

It seems fairly clear from case law concerning sterilization—and abortion by analogy—that women have the right to be sterilized without their husband's consent. Although it certainly would serve to keep a marriage harmonious for the parties to agree that they do not wish to have children, where there is conflict the woman can freely choose sterilization if she has the mental capacity to give informed consent for the operation. Several husbands have attempted to prevent their wives from being sterilized.

In *Murray v. Vandevander*, the plaintiff's wife was sterilized without her husband's consent.[1] He brought suit against the physician and the hospital; the case was based on the claim that the operation abridged his right of consortium and the right to reproduce another child. The court analyzed Oklahoma law and a woman's constitutional right of privacy based on *Roe v. Wade* and dismissed the case.[2] Under Oklahoma law, a woman has the "natural right to health," which includes the right to freely consent to surgical care to further her own interests.[3] Under *Roe*, a woman has the fundamental right to choose whether to bear children.[4] The Oklahoma court also noted that a husband has no right "to a child-bearing wife as an incident to their marriage."[5]

Another husband-plaintiff raised an interesting argument, based on *Skinner v. Oklahoma*, that he had a fundamental right to father children, which could not be extinguished by the voluntary sterilization of his wife without his consent.[6] *Skinner* involved an Oklahoma law where certain repeated felonious offenders were subject to mandatory sterilization to prevent their "criminal tendancies" from being passed on to their children. The court in *Doe* limited the application of *Skinner* in this situation, describing the right to procreate as one that "involved a shield for the private citizen against government action, not a sword of government assistance to enable [the potential father] to overturn the private decision of his [wife]."

In *Ponter v. Ponter*, the New Jersey court held that the woman-plaintiff had a constitutional right to be sterilized without her husband's consent.[7] The wife sought this declaratory judgment because of the policy of New Jersey physicians to require the husband's written consent before they would sterilize a married woman. The court found that case law supports the premise that a woman, regardless of her marital status, has the right to receive medical treatment and the right to the possession and control of her own person.[8] This right is paramount to her spouse's desires.[9]

"This court recognizes here... the sensible, logical and well-reasoned desirability of consultation between husband and wife regarding decisions in such matters. However, this is not to say that the spouse does or should have a power of veto."[10]

Subsequent to these cases, the Supreme Court held that the woman's right to an abortion in the first trimester could not be limited by the third-party veto of any other person, including her husband.[11] It seems apparent that this decision will apply universally to sterilization, since *Roe*, *Eisenstadt*, and *Griswold* all definitely set forth the right of a woman to determine whether or not to bear children; and sterilization fits neatly into this category.[12] A private hospital, however, may adopt and enforce a rule requiring the husband's consent if the hospital's only involvement with the government is receipt of Hill-Burton funds.[13]

Aside from the consent issue, several cases involve access to sterilization. Many hospitals, especially those with religious affiliations, refuse to perform sterilizations in certain situations. This presents a serious problem where the only hospital in an area follows such a procedure. While the Supreme Court has not specifically addressed this issue, the First Circuit Court of Appeals declared a city hospital's prohibition of sterilizations to be violative of equal protection.

In *Hathaway v. Worcester City Hospital*, the court held that under *Roe* and *Doe* "a complete ban on a surgical procedure relating to the fundamental interest in the pregnancy decision is far too broad when other comparable surgical procedures are performed."[14] In light of *Poelker v. Doe's* rejection of this argument as applied to abortion, however, it is fairly certain that *Hathaway* would not be followed today.[15]

As for private hospitals, the enactment by Congress of the Church Amendment of the Health Programs Extension Act of 1973, the "Federal Conscience Clause," specifically protects a private hospital that receives Hill-Burton funds from liability for failure to provide facilities for abortions or sterilization procedures when the action is based on religious beliefs or moral convictions.[16] The refusal to provide sterilizations on these grounds was upheld by the Ninth Circuit Court in *Chrisman v. Sisters of St. Joseph of Peace* and *Taylor v. St. Vincent's Hospital*.[17] Aside from the applicability of the Church Amendment, the court in *Chrisman* held that any infringement on the woman's privacy rights is "outweighed by the need to protect the freedom of denomination hospitals 'with religious or' moral scruples against sterilizations and abortions.'"[18]

Generally, sterilization is not as repugnant as abortion to physicians and hospital personnel and directors. Access to sterilization has not presented the same problem to women as access to an abortion. Likewise, no cases have challenged Medicaid-funding restrictions for sterilizatons.

WRONGFUL LIFE

Aside from the right to have access to abortion and sterilization, under tort law women have the right to have the procedure done correctly and effectively. Physicians today are facing a new form of medical malpractice claim: wrongful life. Simply stated, parents of children born subsequent to a negligently performed sterilization or abortion procedure have sought to bring an action in their name for malpractice and in their child's name for wrongful life.

This cause of action is not new. What is new is an increasing trend in the courts to award damages to parents to whom children are born after an abortion procedure or sterilization procedure that was characterized by some negligence or inadvertence on the part of their physician. The patient's having signed a consent form warning that the operation might not be successful has not protected physicians.[19]

Medical malpractice claims of this type have been brought for other reasons as well. In one case, the woman's physician failed to diagnose her pregnancy in time for her to procure a safe abortion. While the New York court that heard the case did not deal with a wrongful life claim per se, the court did recognize that "damages subsequently sustained... may be the natural consequences of defendant's malpractice for which recovery will lie."[20] Such damages could easily include the expense of raising the child, something that is generally asked for in wrongful-life claims.

The first case to introduce the term *wrongful life* into legal jargon was a 1963 Illinois case in which the child born of an adulterous relationship sued his father for the damages he had suffered from the stigma of being "an adulterine bastard."[21] In dismissing the complaint in *Zepeda v. Zepeda*, Judge Dempsey expressed a philosophy that has been recognized to this day by many courts when they decide similar cases:

> *His adulterine birth has placed him under a permanent disability. He protests not only the act which caused him to be born but birth itself. Love of life being what it is, one may conjecture whether, if he were older, he would feel the same way. As he grows from infancy to maturity the natural instinct to preserve life may cause him to cherish his existence as much as, through his next friend, he now deplores it.*
>
> *Recognition of the plaintiff's claim means creation of a new tort: a cause of action for wrongful life. The legal implications of such a tort are vast, the social impact could be staggering.*
>
> *Encouragment would extend to all others born into the world under conditions they might regard as adverse. One might seek damages for being born of a certain color, another because of race, one for being born with a hereditary disease....*
>
> *We have decided to affirm the dismissal of the complaint. We do this, despite our designation of the wrong committed herein as a tort, because of our belief that lawmaking, while inherent in the judicial process, should not be indulged in where the result could be as sweeping as here.*[22]

Judge Dempsey's predictions were fairly accurate. Since 1963 when this case was decided, parents in the name of themselves and their children have sought recovery for pain and suffering that stemmed not only from the child's birth defects, but also from the child's having been born healthy but unwanted. *Zepeda* remains the most oft-quoted opinion in this vast array of cases, but there is a decided trend toward finding a valid cause of action for having been born with and without defects.

The first case to actually recognize a cause of action for wrongful life was *Park v. Chessin*.[23] That was in 1977. The parents sued on behalf of themselves for their medical expenses, mental anguish, and emotional distress, and on behalf of their deceased daughter for wrongful life. Their daughter had been born with a fatal, hereditary kidney disease. The couple's first child had been born with the disease and died immediately.

Wishing to have another child but concerned that the situation might repeat itself, they sought the advice of an obsetrician, who assured them that the chances of having a future baby with the same kidney disease, were "practically nil."[24] Relying on this advice, the wife again conceived. The second child lived two-and-one-half years before dying of the fatal disease. After citing a string of cases, including *Zepeda*, where courts in New York, New Jersey, and Illinois had refused to find a cause of action on a wrongful-life theory, the court went on to reason that,

> Cases are not decided in a vacuum; rather, decisional law must keep pace with expanding technological, economical and social change. Inherent in the abolition of the statutory ban on abortion is a public policy consideration which gives potential parents the right, within certain statutory and case law limitations not to have a child. This right extends to instances in which it can be determined with reasonable medical certainty that the child would be born deformed. The breach of this right may also be said to be tortious to the fundamental right of a child to be born as a whole, functional human being. Under the circumstances presented, the portion of the complaint which seeks recovery on behalf of the infant for injuries and conscious pain and suffering caused by defendant's negligence, should be permitted to stand.[25]

It was somewhat easier for the court to find a cause of action in this instance, since the wrongful-life damage claim (the pain and suffering during the plaintiff's brief lifetime), was somewhat measurable. Pain and suffering is a common element in money damages, provable by testimony of the treating physician and submitted to the jury for evaluation.

A much tougher decision occurs where the baby is healthy. One of the main elements in finding tort liability is that of probable damages. Where it may be possible to prove the cost of medical care and institutionalization for a defective newborn, how does one measure damages for a healthy baby? A few recent decisions reflect a trend toward analyzing this factor in favor of the parents, while other courts persist in the *Zepeda* rationale that human life is a precious gift that can hardly be an assessable damage.

In *Stills v. Gratton*, a woman underwent an abortion attempt that failed.[26] Due to the negligence of the physician, so much time elapsed before the error was discovered that a second abortion procedure could not be performed. As a result, the woman delivered a healthy boy. She sued the physician for malpractice in her own name and wrongful life in the name of the child. In dismissing the latter claim, the court quoted the following language from *Gleitman:*

> *This court cannot weight the value of life with impairments against the nonexistence of life itself. By asserting that he should not have been born, the infant plaintiff makes it logically impossible for a court to measure his alleged damages because of the impossibility of making the comparison required by compensatory remedies.*[27]

The court, however, did allow the mother liberal damages for all the consequences of the physician's malpractice, as in the *Ziemba* case (supra). Even where the child was malformed following a negligent failure to perform a therapeutic abortion, the court refused the wrongful life claim of the infant because of the difficulty of measuring damages.[28] Nevertheless, the damages awarded the parents on the malpractice claim stood.[29]

New Jersey, reversing a decison that had represented the law for 12 years, permitted a claim for wrongful life while denying a claim for wrongful birth.[29A] In reversing the decision of the lower court, which had struck the plaintiff's complaint seeking damages for wrongful birth and wrongful life, the court did not have the same difficulty as the New York court with regard to the measure of damages for the wrongful claim. The court permitted the parents of a child suffering from Down's syndrome (mongolism) to maintain its action seeking damages for the emotional suffering resulting from the wrongful life of their defective child.

The action was predicated as a malpractice claim against the defendant doctors for their failure to inform the plaintiff mother of the existence of the procedure known as amniocentesis. The test would have enabled the physician to examine living fetal cells in the amniotic fluid to detect any gross chromosomal defects. This procedure can detect Downs syndrome in 95 percent of the cases in which it is performed.

The court, however, affirmed the dismissal of the wrongful life claim of the infant on the grounds that the child did not suffer any damage cognizable at law by being brought into existence. The court stated, as its basis for that conclusion, the deeply held belief of our society that life, whether experienced with or without major physical handicap, is more precious than nonlife.

The reader should appreciate, however, that courts only went so far as to state that the wrongful birth claim states a cause of action. It remains to be determined whether the plaintiffs could present sufficient and adequate evidence to convince a jury and reviewing courts that their claim is meritorious.

The type of tort damages awarded to the parents is often very liberal where the courts wish to both hold the physician liable and avoid the entanglements of assessing a wrongful-life claim in the infant's favor. While several courts have refused to award any damages to the parents where the child is healthy, others have granted varying degrees of relief.[30] Where an abortion or sterilization was determined to have been negligently performed resulting in the birth of a child or birth resulted through some other negligence, the parents were awarded their medical expenses for the unsuccessful operation,[31] damages for pain and suffering from pregnancy,[32] prenatal- and postnatal-care expenses,[33] costs of the delivery,[34] lost wages during the pregnancy and postpartum period,[35] and loss of consortium for the husband.[36]

The most recent addition to this list of damages awarded is the cost of raising and educating the child. Earlier decisons refused to award such extensive damages, relying on the premise that a child confers a benefit on the parents that offsets the pecuniary loss of raising the child.[37] This argument was first countered in *Troppi v. Scarf* in an action brought against a pharmacist who negligently filled a prescription for birth control pills, substituting tranquilizers.[38] The couple then conceived their eighth child. While recognizing that under tort law the dollar value of a benefit to the plaintiff should be subtracted from the dollar value of the injury, the court found the "benefit" of a healthy child to its parents to be a flexible concept that may vary from case to case.[39] The court described various situations:

> *Application of the benefits rule permits a trier of fact to find that the birth of a child has materially benefitted the newly wed couple, notwithstanding the inconvenience of an interrupted honeymoon, and to reduce the net damage award accordingly. Presumably, a trier of fact would find that the "family interests" of the unmarried coed has been enhanced very little.[40]*

The court went on to reject the pharmacist's claim that the benefit must necessarily wipe out the pecuniary loss to the parents, since it is up to the trier of fact to make that determination based on such factors as family size, family income, and the parents' age and marital status.[41] Three recent decisions either have awarded damages for anticipated costs of raising the unwanted child or have recognized the possibility that such damages could be awarded by a jury.

In *Rivera v. State* (supra), an unsuccessful tubal ligation was followed by the birth of a healthy child. The court recognized a cause of action in malpractice for the anticipated costs of raising the child. *Green v. Sudakin* (supra) was a case where a physician had negligently failed to perform tubal ligation after the delivery of a couple's third child and had failed to notify parents that the operation was not performed. The court upheld an award for damages for the expense of rearing the couple's fourth child. In the third case, *Becker v. Schwartz*, a physician had failed to inform a 37-year-old pregnant woman of the increased incidence of birth defects among offspring of women of this age and of tests available to determine if the fetus was defective.[42] A daughter with Down's syndrome was born, and the physician was held liable for the lifelong costs of caring for the child.

While none of these cases recognized a wrongful-life claim and all treated the case strictly as a medical-malpractice action under the tort principles, finding the physician liable for the costs of raising the child certainly leads one to conclude that the courts do in fact recognize that this life was wrongful. The court in *Rivera* addressed this concept as follows:

> We have noted the use of the term "wrongful life" in the decisions of other courts and in the media, mostly by those who oppose causes of action such as this one. The term is an unfortunate epithet, primarily because it is inaccurate as a description either of the wrong which has been committed or of the injury suffered.... On the other hand, wrongful life does seem to crystallize the fundamental idea underlying much of the opposition to such lawsuits—that idea being that birth or life, whether wanted or unwanted, perfect or deformed, is an ultimate good which can in no sense be regarded as a wrong.
>
> Nevertheless, the notion that individuals should be compensated for the negligence of a physician in facilitating the birth of an unwanted child, is no more offensive to such philosophical beliefs than is the concept of birth control itself.
>
> Substantial interference with the fundamental rights of the parents occurs, which may well have catastrophic financial consequences. To be realistic, one must acknowledge that there are both positive and negative aspects of childbearing. It is no answer to say that a result which claimant specifically sought to avoid, might be regarded as a blessing by someone else.[43]

While different courts take different views on wrongful-life cases, it is clear that physicians face extensive liability for negligent performance of sterilization or abortion procedures, for failure to diagnose genetic defects, or for failure to warn of the risks of pregnancy in time for an abortion to be performed. Such liability includes not only all the medical expenses of the pregnancy and delivery, loss of wages, and pain and suffering, but may well include footing the entire bill for feeding, clothing, and educating an unwanted child.

Many physicians have argued that the parents either should seek an abortion or put the unwanted child up for adoption to mitigate the damage claim. Courts responded by arguing that the abortion alternative is a right but never an obligation, which "would constitute an invasion of privacy of the grossest and most pernicious kind."[44] One commentator, Lutz, argues that this stance requires the defendant to "finance" the plaintiff's moral or religious beliefs against abortion.[45] Lutz argues that it is a contradiction to allow the parents to contend they have been damaged by the birth of an unwanted child while at the same time refusing to give up the child. He expresses the opinion of many wrongful-life critics that the courts must draw the line on damages, holding them to the lost wages, medical expenses, and pain and suffering that are related to the pregnancy and the delivery.

ARTIFICIAL INSEMINATION: UNFORESEEN PROBLEMS

The *Chicago Tribune* printed an article in its "Lifestyle" section entitled, "For Women Seeking Motherhood, There Is AID."[46] The story was about a small-town beautician in New Jersey who wanted to have a child while she was still young, yet she was not prepared to marry her man friend or have premarital sexual relations. The remedy: artificial insemination. The man produced the sperm in his apartment; and, on her own, the woman performed the insemination. The result: a male child.

After the couple's relationship ended, the courtroom became the forum for a discernment of rights and duties between the parties. In a case of first impression (a case that presents problems the answers to which have no judicial precedent), Judge Frank Testa of the Cumberland County Juvenile and Domestic Relations Court in New Jersey declared that the father-donor has both the right to visit the child and the duty to support him.

Artificial insemination has been used for decades but has become increasingly popular over the last 10 years. This is ascribed to both a gradual trend in state law toward giving these children the same rights as naturally conceived or adoptive children and a shortage of adoptable babies. Artificial insemination presents a practical solution for childlessness of married women with sterile mates and for single women who wish to have children without potential emotional and legal entanglements with the man; but legal problems are real enough, and many physicians are refusing to do artificial inseminations for unmarried women. Varied legal problems have arisen along with uncertainty and diversity of solutions from state to state.

Only 14 states, including New York and California, have passed legislation covering the legal consequences of artificial insemination. Oklahoma, for example, regards "Any child or children born as the result thereof [of artifician insemination] shall be considered at law in all respects the same as a naturally conceived legitimate child of the husband and wife so requesting and consenting to the use of such technique."[47]

To solve any consent problems, the statute goes on to require that both the husband and wife, along with the licensed physician and the judge who has jurisdiction over adoption, execute and acknowledge a consent form, which is to be filed with the court and released only to the parties, or one with both a legitimate interest and a court order.[48] Such clear and direct legislation solves many of the legal complications that artificial insemination has engendered, such as the legitimacy of the child and the duty to support. Oklahoma's scheme does not cover unmarried women and third-party anonymous donors. The statute may serve to preclude this class from using artificial insemination in Oklahoma.

Another legal problem, whether a wife's use of this technique constitutes adultery, has arisen in divorce and child-custody disputes. Several old cases have held that it does. *Doornbos v. Doornbos* held that artificial insemination by a third-part donor, with or without the husband's consent, constitutes adultery on the part of the wife.[49] *Orford v. Orford* held that a wife who underwent artificial insemination without her husband's consent committed adultery. A more recent decision in *People v. Sorenson* held that artificial insemination using semen from a third-party donor did not constitute adultery on the wife's part where the husband had consented.[50] Furthermore, the husband was obligated to support the child.

Aside from the question of adultery, many courts have faced the question of the child's status. Interestingly enough, almost all reported cases on this subject have come from New York, with an even split as to legitimacy. The most recent case has held, in accord with current legislation, that a child born of consensual artificial insemination is legitimate and entitled to the rights and privileges of a naturally conceived child of the same marriage.[51]

Generally, where the husband consents to the artifical insemination, he has the duty to support the child or children born as a consequence[52] even if the court considers the child illegitimate.[53] A man who is not the donor in consensual artificial insemination still has visitation rights after a divorce or separation[54] and must give consent before a later adoption by his former wife's new husband is possible.[55]

Several doctors refuse to perform artificial insemination fearing that a child born in such circumstances might bring wrongful-life action against the mother and the doctor. To date, no case law supports such misgivings, but in light of the growing number of wrongful-life cases and the increasingly broad scope of liability for medical malpractice, one certainly cannot blame a physician for being too cautious in these cases.

A research team at the University of Washington unearthed an interesting set of medical problems and concerns as well. Martin Curie-Cohen and colleagues surveyed nearly 400 physicians who utilize artificial insemination in dealing with infertility.[56] Curie-Cohen and his colleagues warned physicians and the public that the tendency to use the same donor to induce a series of pregnancies in small communities may create a danger of genetic defects through incest. As a protective measure to insure privacy, few doctors keep adequate records of donors and subsequent births; so this problem may go unnoticed and be difficult to solve. Physicians were also warned to conduct chromosome tests on donors to reduce chances of passing on genetic defects.

Notes and References

1   *Murray v. Vandevander*, 522 P.2d 302 (Okla. App. 1974).
2. *Roe v. Wade*, 410 U.S. 113 (1973).
3. *Murray v. Vandevander*, supra at 303.
4. *Roe v. Wade*, supra; See also, Am. Jur. 2d § 161, "A married woman in full possession of her faculties has the power, without the consent of her husband, to submit to a surgical operation upon herself."
5. *Murray v. Vandvander*, supra at 304.
6. *Skinner v. Oklahoma*, 316 U.S. 535 (1942); *Doe v. Doe*, 314 N.E.2d 128 (Mass. 1974).
7. *Ponter v. Ponter*, 135 N.J. 50 342 A.2d 574 (1975).
8. Id. at 577.
9. Id.; accord, *Karp v. Cooley*, 493 F.2d 408 (5th Cir. 1974).
10. *Ponter v. Ponter*, supra at 577.
11. *Planned Parenthood of Missouri v. Danforth*, 428 U.S. 52 (1976).
12. *Roe v. Wade*, supra; *Eisenstadt v. Baird*, 405 U.S. 438 (1972); *Griswold v. Connecticut*, 381 U.S. 479 (1965).
13. See, *Holton v. Crozer-Chester Medical Center*, 419 F. Supp. 334 (D.C. Pa. 1976).
14. *Hathaway v. Worcester City Hospital*, 475 F.2d 701, 706 (1st Cir. 1973); *Roe v. Wade*, supra; *Doe v. Bolton*, 410 U.S. 194 (1973).
15. *Poelker v. Doe*, 432 U.S. 519 (1977); but see, Cal. Health and Safety Code § 1258 forbidding any hospital that performs therapeutic sterilization from discriminating against those that are elective.
16. P.L. 93-45 Health Programs Extension Act, the Church Amendment or the "Federal Conscience Clause," 87 Stat. 91 § 401 (b).
17. *Chrisman v. Sisters of St. Joseph of Peace*, 506 F.2d 308 (9th Cir. 1974); *Taylor v. St. Vincent's Hospital*, 523 F.2d 75 (9th Cir. 1975).
18. *Taylor v. St. Vincent's Hospital*, id. at 77, quoting *Chrisman v. Sisters of St. Joseph of Peace*, supra at 312.
19. See, e.g. *Vaughn v. Shelton*, 514 S.W.2d 870 (Tenn. App. 1974); *Bowman v. Davis*, 356 N.E.2d 496 (Ohio 1976).
20. *Ziemba v. Sternberg*, 357 N.Y.S. 2d 265, 269 (1974).
21. *Zepeda v. Zepeda*, 41 Ill. App. 2d 240, 190 N.E.2d. 849, 855 (1963), cert. denied 379 U.S. 945 (1964).
22. Id. at 857–59.
23. *Park v. Chessin*, 60 A.D.2d 80, 400 N.Y.S. 2d 110 (1977).
24. Id. at 111.
25. Id. at 114.
26. *Stills v. Gratton*, 127 Cal. Rptr. 652 (1976).
27. *Gleitman v. Cosgrove*, 227 A.2d 689 at 692 (1967).
28. *Stewart v. Long Island College Hospital*, 58 Misc. 2d 432, 296 N.Y.S. 2d 41 (1968).
29. *Stewart v. Long Island College Hospital*, 313 N.Y.S. 2d 502, appeal dismissed 315 N.Y.S. 2d 863 and aff'd 332 N.Y.S. 2d 640 (1970). A. Berman vs. Allen, N.J. (June 26, 1979).
30. See, e.g. *Clegg v. Chase*, 391 N.Y.S. 2d (Sup. Ct. 1977); *Rieck v. Medical Protective Society*, 64 Wis. 2d 514, 219 N.W.2d 242; 11 Pa. D. & C.2d 41 (1957); *Ball v. Mundy*, 64 Wash. 2d 247, 391 P.2d 201 (1964).

31. *Custodio v. Bauer*, 251 Cal. App. 2d 303, 59 Cal. Rptr. 463 (1967); *Coleman v. Garrison*, 327 A.2d 757 (1974), aff'd 349 A.2d 8 (1975).
32. *Troppi v. Scarf*, 31 Mich. App. 240, 187 N.W.2d 511 (1971); *Ziemba v. Sternberg*, 45 A.D. 2d 230, supra at 357 N.Y.S. 2d 265 (1974); *Rivera v. State*, 404 N.Y.S. 2d 950 (1978); *Green v. Sudakin*, 81 Mich. App. 545, 265 N.W.2d 411 (1978); *Bishop v. Byrne*, 265 F. Supp. 460 (W.Va. 1967); *Sherlock v. Stillwater Clinic*, S. Ct. Minn., 260 N.W.2d 169 (1977).
33. *Sherlock v. Stillwater Clinic*, id.; *Rivera v. State*, id.; *Green V. Sudakin*, id.; *Bishop v. Byrne*, id.; *Custodio v. Bauer*, supra.
34. See, cases in note 14, supra.
35. *Troppi v. Scarf*, supra; *Ziemba v. Sternberg*, supra.
36. *Coleman v. Garrison*, supra; *Sherlock v. Stillwater Clinic*, supra; *Ziemba v. Sternberg*, supra.
37. See, *Shaheen v. Knight*, (Pa. 1957) 11 Pa. Dist. & Co. R.2d 41; *Gleitman v. Cosgrove*, 49 N.J. 22, 227 A.2d, supra at 689 (1967).
38. *Troppi v. Scarf*, supra at 511.
39. Id. at 518.
40. Id.
41. Id.
42. *Becker v. Schwartz*, 400 N.Y.S. 2d 119 (1977), aff'd (N.Y. Ct. App. Nos. 559 and 560, Dec. 27, 1978).
43. *Rivera v. State*, supra at 953.
44. Id. at 954.
45. Lutz, John R., Jr., Wrongful healthy life: to be or not to be, *American Bar Association Journal* 65:15 at 17, 1979.
46. *Chicago Tribune* 25 Mar. 1978.
47. Okla. Stat. Ann. ch. 24 § 552 (Supp. 1967).
48. Okla. Stat. Ann. ch. 24 § 553.
49. *Doornbos v. Doornbos*, unreported, Super. Ct. Cook County No 54 S. 14981, 23 Law Week 2308 (Ill. 1954), appeal dismissed 12 Ill. App. 2d 473, 139 N.E. 2d 844, cited in 25 ALR3d 1108.
50. *Orford v. Orford*, 49 Ont. L.15, 58 D.L.R. 251 (1921); *People v. Sorenson*, 66 Cal. Rptr. 7, 437 P.2d 495 (1968); see also, *Hoch v. Hoch*, unreported Ill. case (1945) discussed in 25 ALR 3d 1108.
51. Re Adoption of Anonymous, 74 Misc. 2d 99, 345 N.Y.S. 2d 430 (1977); accord, *Strnad v. Strnad*, 190 Misc. 786, 78 N.Y.S. 2d 390 (1948); contra, *Gursky v. Gursky*, 39 Misc. 2d 1083, 242 N.Y.S. 2d (1963); *People ex rel. Abajian v. Dennett*, 15 Misc. 2d 260, 184 N.Y.S. 2d 178 (1958) (dicta).
52. *People v. Sorenson*, supra; Re Adoption of Anonymous, supra.
53. *Gursky v. Gursky*, supra.
54. *Strnad v. Strnad*, supra.
55. Re Adoption of Anonymous, supra.
56. *Newsweek*, 93 (No. 13): 72, Mar. 26, 1979.

Part FIVE

DEATH WITH DIGNITY

Introduction

Death with dignity is not a new concept, but rather has taken different forms throughout history. The elderly members of primitive tribes willingly journeyed into the wilderness to die, releasing their fellow tribesmen from the burden of feeding them and traveling at their slow pace. Suicide was both socially acceptable and honorable during much of Western history. The ancient Greeks preferred drinking hemlock to dishonor. Roman philosophers espoused the view that to die at one's own time and choosing was a gift from God to ease the suffering of this life.[1] It was not until the Judeo-Christian influence pervaded the West that the view of suicide as a violation of the natural law became predominant.

Nevertheless, such notable figures as Sir Thomas More and Francis Bacon publicly asserted their views that patients suffering from painful and terminal diseases should be encouraged to commit suicide.[2] Bacon held the view that physicians should make all efforts not only to prolong life but also to mitigate pain when it might serve to "make a faire and easy passage."[3]

Some historians have pinpointed the turn of the nineteenth century as the time Western civilization did an abrupt about-face from viewing death as a family ritual that included both adults and children. Instead, death became something that had to be removed from a family setting. Today, typically, the family may still be responsible for financing the care of their dying member, but they have been relieved of the burden of the dying person's presence.[4] With its ability to prolong life, modern technology has lessened further the integrity of death. Although a new movement toward the hospice approach of caring for the dying in their own homes is growing, commonly people spend their last days in hospitals in a mass of wires and tubes hooked up to machines, which monitor their vital signs, distribute oxygen when needed, and keep their hearts beating and their lungs breathing.* Their urine is eliminated through catheters.

While such technology is certainly helpful and even miraculous where a disease is curable or the patient's condition is expected to improve, it proves to be tortuous, expensive, and inhumane for some patients. The line between prolonging life and prolonging a painful death is a difficult one to draw, and many doctors and judges are hesitant to draw that line unilaterally. Nevertheless, where to draw the line is a decision that medical staffs across the country make every day.

Just as the Supreme Court in *Roe v. Wade* was asked to decide when human life begins for purposes of constitutional recognition, two New Jersey courts in *Matter of Karen Quinlan* were asked to consider when human life ends.[5] The Quinlan case, because of widespread media coverage, brought to light many legal and medical issues surrounding death, such as the legal definition of death and the duty of a physician and hospital to prolong the life of a patient for whom there is no hope of recovery to a normal state of being. The Quinlan case and euthanasia cases before Quinlan reflect a double standard that is applied in both courts and hospitals in treating the terminally ill. The New Jersey Supreme Court grappled with this issue in the Quinlan case.

In the past, medical practitioners, using more limited technology, took a more simplified approach to deciding when someone had died: when someone's heart had stopped beating and the blood had stopped circulating, that person was pronounced dead. The rather inexact, unscientific approach to the pronouncement of death made the discernment of death a worry to many, including Edgar Allen Poe. Poe expressed his rather grim vision in *The Premature Burial*.[16]

Today, Poe would be happy to note that brain-death has been accepted by much of the medical profession as the operative definition of death. Since respirators can keep a body "breathing" and the blood circulating indefinitely, alternative criteria for death were created.

An Ad Hoc Committee of the Harvard Medical School set standards for brain death.[7] Their criteria for no cerebral function include the following:

- No response to pain or other stimuli
- No reflex action
- No spontaneous respiration or muscular movement for at least one hour
- A flat electroencephalogram. This latter test is confirmation; the diagnosis can be made from clinical signs alone.
- All tests are to be repeated at least 24 hours later with a finding of no change.

After death has been declared, the artificial life-support systems can be removed. The ad hoc committee also made efforts to define irreversible coma as a new criterion for death and, in so doing, further fueled the controversy over the accuracy and morality of their definition of death.

---

*The modern hospice movement started in England as institutional care for the dying. Lately, the hospice movement has begun to provide home care, too. A hospice may refer to an institution for inpatients, a hospital team that goes to the dying anywhere in the hospital, or a staff that works out of an office to help the dying in their homes.

†It is hard to say whether these stories were fictional events or whether Poe gathered them with some effort and persistence over the years. His morbid fear of being buried while still alive was not quieted by stories such as that of an artillery officer who suffered a skull fracture upon being thrown from an unruly horse. After the officer was buried with "indecent haste," a peasant sitting on the fresh and shallow grave felt a commotion underneath him. After the peasant at the gravesite had reopened the grave, revealing the coffin, not a few hearts "stopped briefly" as the occupant sat upright and gazed rather ungratefully at the crowd of mourners surrounding him. Since Poe himself was a victim of some disease that sent him into fits and left him comatose for long intervals, he worried that he might one day become a victim of premature burial. To ease his tortured mind, he fashioned a coffin with a latch spring operative from the inside cover and a vault that could be opened from within. Ironically, he died (or was buried, at least) while traveling away from home and never got to test his creation.

Notes and References

1. Steele, Walter W., Jr., and Hill, Bill, A legislative proposal for a legal right to die, *Criminal Law Bulletin*, 12:140 at 143, Mar.-Apr. 1976.
2. Id. at 144.
3. Bacon, Francis, "New Atlantis." In *Selected Writings of Francis Bacon*, 1955, quoted in Steele and Hill, A legislative proposal, supra.
4. Aries, Phillippe, *Western Attitudes Toward Death*, Translated by Patricia M. Ranum (Baltimore: Johns Hopkins University Press, 1974), pp. 12, 86.
5. *Roe v. Wade*, 410 U.S. 113 (1973); *Matter of Karen Quinlan*, 137 N.J. Super. 227; 348 A.2d 801 (1975), rev'd 70 N.J. 10, 335 A.2d 647 (1976).
6. Poe, Edgar Allen, "The Premature Burial." In *Collected Works of Edgar Allen Poe: Tales of Mystery and Horror*. Edited by Thomas A. Mabbot (Cambridge, Mass.: Harvard University Press, 1969), pp. 263–64.
7. Harvard Medical School, Ad Hoc Committee to Examine the Definition of Brain Death, A definition of irreversible coma, *Journal of the American Medical Association* 205:337-40, Aug. 5, 1968.

CHAPTER 15

The Duty to Prolong Life Reexamined

THE QUINLAN CASE

On April 15, 1975, Karen Ann Quinlan, aged 21, was admitted in a coma to the intensive care unit of Newton Memorial Hospital in Newton, New Jersey. Later, the coma was ascribed to two, 15-minute periods of apnea brought on by a mixture of alcohol and drugs. A mechanical respirator kept her breathing.

Several months later, her parents attempted to have her taken off the respirator, thought to be the only thing keeping her alive in a chronic state from which no recovery was anticipated. Their attempt brought to light many legal issues surrounding death and the authority of the family members and the attending physician to authorize the removal of a life-support system thought to be essential.

The first court to hear the appeal of Joseph Quinlan (Karen's father and later her guardian) to authorize removal of the respirator was the New Jersey Superior Court. At the time of the trial, Karen had been transferred from Newton Memorial Hospital to another hospital, St. Clare's. She was still in an intensive care unit and was still 21 years old. She was hooked up to a respirator. She received fluids intravenously and was fed through a nasogastric tube. Her body was in a fetal-like position and subject to bedsores. Antibiotics were being administered to prevent infection. She responded to painful stimuli and yawned occasionally in a spasm-like fashion, and her pupils dilated in response to light. At times, Karen breathed on her own.

Several doctors testified that she could not survive removal from the respirator at that time. The only change in her condition since admission to St. Clare's was from sleeping-comatose to sleep-awake-

187

comatose. She did not technically meet the definition of brain death because of her response to pain and light, and because the vegetative-regulative functions of her brain, including control of body temperature, breathing, blood pressure, heart rate, swallowing, and sleeping, were still intact. The sapient functions of the brain, which enable a human being to talk, see, feel, and think, were thought to be absent in Karen. This underscored her condition in an apparently persistent vegetative state with irreversible brain damage and no cognitive or cerebral functioning. There is much supposition in such a statement. For example, no one really knew whether Karen could feel or think.

The attorney general took the position that termination of respirator assistance would amount to criminal homicide. The attending physician, Robert Morse, believed that termination of respirator assistance would deviate from medical tradition, since use of the respirator was considered "ordinary" versus "extraordinary" means of prolonging life. Joseph Quinlan contended that since medical science held no hope for her recovery and since Karen would herself, if conscious, choose to terminate respirator assistance, there was no duty to keep her alive.[1]

The New Jersey Superior Court disagreed:

> There is a higher standard, a higher duty, that encompasses the uniqueness of human life, the integrity of the medical profession and the attitude of society toward the physician, and therefore the morals of society. A patient is placed, or places himself, in the care of a physician with the expectation that he [the physician] will do everything in his power, everything that is known to modern medicine, to protect the patient's life. He will do all within his human power to favor life against death.
>
> •
>
> The morality and conscience of our society places this responsibility in the hands of the physician. What justification is there to remove it from the control of the medical profession and place it in the hands of the courts?[2]

The court wanted the doctors to make the decision whether to terminate use of the respirator, deciding strictly from a medical-ethical standpoint. The judge was not convinced that Karen would herself choose to turn it off if conscious and competent to do so since "Karen Quinlan, while she was in complete control of her mental faculties to reason out the staggering magnitude of the decision not to be 'kept alive,' did not make a decision."[3]

Likewise, the court considered that there was hope, although remote, for recovery. Thus, there was a duty to continue life-assisting apparatus if, in the opinion of the treating physician, this should be done. The judge also was impressed with the fact that Karen was not suffering any pain. The superior court thus rejected Mr. Quinlan's plea to be appointed as guardian of Karen's person with the authority to consent to termination of respirator assistance. Karen was "alive" for legal purposes and thus termination of respirator assistance might constitute homicide, but even so, ending assistance would be a medical and not a judicial decision.

At the time the Supreme Court of New Jersey was presented with the *Quinlan* case, Karen was 22 years of age. The court was looking at the same record as the superior court, with the one exception that Karen's weight had dropped from 115 to 75 pounds. As to the statement by the lower court concerning the "hope" for recovery, the supreme court viewed the medical data and testimony as indicating that "[n]o form of treatment which can cure or improve that condition [chronic and persistent vegetative state] is known or available... and as nearly as can be determined... she can never be restored to cognitive or sapient life."[4]

The higher court also gave much attention to the testimony of one physician:

> Dr. Korein also told of the unwritten and unspoken standards of medical practice implied in the foreboding initials DNR (do not resuscitate), as applied to the extraordinary terminal case: "Cancer, metastatic cancer, involving the lungs, the liver, the brain, multiple involvements, the physician may or may not write DNR.... It could be said to the nurse: if this man stops breathing don't resuscitate him.... No physician that I know personally is going to try and resuscitate a man riddled with cancer and in agony and he stops breathing. They are not going to put him on a respirator.... I think that would be the height of misuse of technology."[5]

This particular testimony concerned the supreme court, since it implied a double standard, which did not sit well with the court. The judge did not think that continued use of the respirator in Karen's case was much different:

> We perceive no thread of logic distinguishing between such a choice on Karen's part and a similar choice which, under the evidence in this case, could be made by a competent patient terminally ill, riddled by cancer and suffering great pain; such a patient would not be resuscitated or put on a respirator in the example by Dr. Korein, and a fortiori would not be kept against his will on a respirator.[6]

The court went on to accept Dr. Korein's testimony as being representative of current medical-ethical standards:

> [I]t is perfectly apparent from the testimony we have quoted of Dr. Korein, and indeed so clear as to almost be judicially noticeable, that humane decisions against resuscitative or maintenance therapy are frequently a recognized de facto response in the

medical world to the irreversible, terminal, pain-riddled patient, especially with familial consent. And these cases, of course, are far short of "brain death."

• •

We glean from the record here that physicians distinguish between curing the ill and comforting and easing the dying; that they refuse to treat the curable as if they were dying or ought to die, and that they have sometimes refused to treat the hopeless and dying as if they were curable.... [M]any of them have refused to inflict an undesired prolongation of the process of dying on a patient in irreversible condition when it is clear that such "therapy" offers neither human or humane benefit.

• •

One would think that the use of the same respirator or like support could be considered "ordinary" in the context of the possibly curable patient but "extraordinary" in the context of the forced sustaining by cardio-respiratory processes of an irreversibly doomed patient.[7]

Simply stated, the court deciphered that medical ethics imposes no duty on a physician to use extraordinary life-prolonging treatment of terminally ill patients with no hope of recovery. The respirator in Karen's case was considered by the court to be extraordinary.

Aside from the medical-ethics issue, the court examined the constitutional right of privacy, which is broad enough to encompass a woman's right to terminate her pregnancy if she so chooses. The court likewise found that it is "broad enough to encompass a patient's decision to decline medical treatment under certain circumstances."[8] The court allowed Joseph Quinlan to assert this right on Karen's behalf.

Apparently, the court was convinced that if Karen were to have a lucid interval, she would choose to terminate the artificial life-support system, basing her decision on the irreversibility of her condition. Although recognizing that the state has an interest in preserving life and protecting susceptible individuals, the court found that if Karen were able and did choose to discontinue the extraordinary life-prolonging treatment, the state could not compel her to "endure the unendurable, only to vegetate a few measurable months with no realistic possibility of returning to any semblance of cognitive or sapient life."[9]

The Quinlans were granted their wish. Joseph Quinlan was named Karen's guardian. He had the authority to order the appointment of a new physician (one who would agree that the respirator should not be used, based on the medical decision that there could be no reasonable possibility of Karen's returning to a cognitive state). The court ruled that the ethics committee of the hospital must concur, and that no civil

or criminal liability would attach to any of the above named partici-
pants in the decision.[10]

Karen was taken off the respirator. She is still alive. Since the
respirator was thought to be necessary, her survival questions an
important belief: just how expert are the experts who say that there is
no hope? After all, there are many established instances of supposedly
hopelessly ill patients, including some who were in a coma for several
years, who have made miraculous recoveries.

The Quinlan decision was followed by two recent cases involving
the terminally ill: *Perlmutter v. Florida Medical Center* and *Superintendent of Belchertown State School v. Saikewicz.*[11]

Perlmutter v. Florida Medical Center was the case of a 73-year-old
man who was suffering from an incurable disease. He was being kept
alive by a mechanical respirator attached to a tracheostomy tube. In
great pain, he had attempted to remove the respirator himself several
times, but medical personnel had stopped him. He petitioned the court
for a declaratory judgment (a judicial action that states the rights of
parties) of his right to choose to die from natural causes and to choose
that extraordinary, expensive, and painful mechanical means of
prolonging his life be discontinued. The court held, relying on
Quinlan, that as a matter of fact and law, no state or medical interest
was sufficient to upset the plaintiff's decision and that no civil or
criminal liability would ensue for the hospital and medical staff who
turned off the respirator.

Superintendent of Belchertown State School v. Saikewicz was
concerned with a 67-year-old man with leukemia and an intelligence
quotient of 10. The court upheld the decision of his guardian to
withhold consent for chemotherapy for his ward's leukemia. The
defendant-guardian argued that, although the chemotherapy might
prolong his ward's life, the fear and pain involved with the treatment
would make his life unendurable, and the confusion surrounding it
would be inhumane. The court denied authorization for the chemotherapy, since extraordinary measures for prolonging life would, in
the opinion of the court, really prolong the suffering.

The current status of medical ethics on the question of withholding
treatment was stated as follows: "Physicians should not use extraordinary means of prolonging life or its semblance when after careful
consideration, consultation, and the application of the most well-
conceived therapy, it becomes apparent that there is no hope of
recovery for the patient. Recovery should be defined as meaning life
without intolerable suffering."[12]

ISSUES IN LEGALIZED EUTHENASIA

Several authors have expressed concern about reasoning that, in their
opinion, legalizes euthanasia. The phrase "extraordinary means of
prolonging life" seems too obscure for such a delicate decision,
especially since the *Quinlan* court noted that what is ordinary in one

set of circumstances can be considered extraordinary in another.

In "A Legislative Proposal for a Legal Right to Die," Steele and Hill discuss several early euthanasia cases where strong public sentiment in favor of those being tried led to jury acquittals or commuted sentences.[13] Their concern is mainly one of guidance.

As Kamisar aptly noted, the "caring" relative may not be exactly fulfilling the wishes of the dying person, who might just want to stick it out despite the pain.[14] He discussed one case of the daughter of a man named Paight, who was dying of cancer. Abhorring the thought that her father would suffer a painful death as her other relatives had in such circumstances, she shot him to death. Kamisar said sardonically,

> It is true that Mother Paight said approvingly of her mercy-killing daughter that "she had the old Paight guts," but it is no less true that Father Paight had no opportunity to pass judgment on the question. He was asleep, still under the anesthetic of the exploratory operation which revealed the cancer in his stomach when his daughter, after having taken one practice shot in the woods, fired into his left temple. Is it not just possible that Father Paight would have preferred to have had the vaunted Paight intestinal fortitude channelled in other directions, e.g., by his daughter bearing to see him suffer?[15]

It is precisely this situation and such others as *Perlmutter, Quinlan,* and *Saikewicz* that Steele and Hill are concerned with:

> Everyone concedes that advances in medicine provide a choice between allowing life to end and extending life far beyond what the body and mind would tolerate if left to their own devices. Medicine's ability in this respect gives rise to a new phenomenon—the need to die. And as the need to die becomes better recognized, pressure builds to legally facilitate it. Ignoring the problem and relying, in the main, on jury nullification to do justice will not suffice much longer. Soon we will be forced to choose between two courses: to fully enforce the law of criminal homicide [which includes euthanasia] as now written or to pass new laws permitting self-chosen death under enumerated circumstances.
>
> Already, choices between terminating life and extending life are made daily, "governed only by the dictates of conscience and social pressure on one extreme and the law of homicide on the other." How much longer can we afford to be without procedures and definitive rules for guidance when these decisions are made? We are ill-served if we allow the subject of self-chosen death to remain taboo. Indeed, life is sacrosanct, so much so that its termination deserves all of the reason and analysis we can bring to it.[16]

They propose a change in homicide laws, such that under certain guidelines, "aiding suicide" would be legalized.

Kamisar makes an interesting argument that voluntary euthanasia (legalized) would serve as the thin edge of a wedge that might be driven into our structures of human rights and protections, eventually leading to infanticide and genocide. The Steele article concludes with an expression of Kamisar's concern:

> Among all the arguments against self-death, the strongest are those which posit that legalized self-death would be abused. Indeed, those who are responsible for the growth and ultimate fruition of a legally sanctioned right to die bear a heavy responsibility because, over time, a right to die may be transmuted into a duty to die. Such a transmutation would prove the arguments of those who state that man must never vary from the tradition of the sacrosanct character of human life; for once that tradition is broken, there is no stopping its progression to genocide.[17]

LIVING WILLS AND THE NATURAL-DEATH ACTS

The California Legislature passed the "Natural Death Act," which became effective January 1, 1977. California was the first state to move toward codifying the *Quinlan* decision and giving the guidelines needed to satisfy such persons as Steele and Hill. Other states were quick to follow, including Arkansas, North Carolina, New Mexico, Nevada, Texas, Idaho, and Oregon; and most states have now passed or are in the process of passing such legislation. Basically, these acts give terminally ill patients the legal right to express their wish to not have their lives prolonged by extraordinary methods.

Under the California Act, the following formalities are required for the patient's directive to be legally binding:[18]

1. The patient must be an adult and of sound mind (emotionally and mentally competent).
2. The patient must have been diagnosed as terminally ill at least two weeks prior to signing the directive.
3. The directive must be executed with will formalities including the patient's signing the directive in the presence of two witnesses who are unrelated to him or her and are not in a position to benefit financially from the patient's death.
4. The patient cannot be pregnant at the time.

The directive reads, in part, as follows:

I, _____, being of sound mind, willfully, and voluntarily make known my desire that my life shall not be artificially prolonged under the circumstances set forth below, do hereby declare:
1. If at any time I should have an incurable injury, disease, or illness certified to be a terminal condition by two physicians, and where the application of life-sustaining procedures would serve only to artificially prolong the moment of my death and where my physician determines that my death is imminent whether or not

life-sustaining procedures are utilized, I direct that such procedures be withheld or withdrawn, and that I be permitted to die naturally.[19]

The act provides for easy revocation. There is no civil or criminal liability for any physician, nurse, or other health care personnel who comply with the directive. Section 7194 provides that anyone who forges or falsifies the directive of another or withholds evidence of revocation of the directive with the intent that life-sustaining procedures be terminated contrary to the patient's wishes shall be guilty of unlawful homicide. Some legal commentators believe such legislation is counterproductive. Horan believes that such legislation adds nothing new to the law and, if anything, serves to inhibit rather than increase the physician's ability "to solve with dignity and grace the problem of the dying patient."[20] Already, adults of sound mind have the right to refuse medical treatment unless a third person with equal and countervailing rights is involved. Jehovah's Witness cases, previously discussed in the section on "The Right to Refuse Treatment" (Chapter 8), illustrate that point.

Developing case law also has upheld the right of a guardian or the next of kin to refuse treatment on behalf of an incompetent patient.[21] Thus, a patient already has the right to refuse "extraordinary treatment" or other treatments, according to case law and the law of informed consent.

Likewise, Horan notes that no civil or criminal liability arising out of stopping a terminally ill patient's treatment has attached against a physician or a hospital. The very reason which supposedly prompted this legislation was the fear of malpractice suits. In Horan's opinion, this fear is unfounded.

Under the California Act, doctors who previously relied on their own sound judgment and on the wishes of patients and their relatives in deciding the proper course of treatment or its termination now have to comply with what Horan views as a complicated law requiring an array of decisions the doctor should make and is not always qualified to make. The physician now has to determine whether or not the patient is "of sound mind," a decision that most psychiatrists are hesitant to make. There also is the problem that most patients will sign the directive before they are "qualified" by having been diagnosed as terminally ill at least 14 days before signing. Horan advises,

[I]f the patient is competent and alert the doctor should disregard the directive and obtain an informed consent from the patient to terminate the treament. If the patient is not competent and alert, then 7191(c) requires the physician to make an inordinate investigation into the surrounding circumstances concerning the execution of that directive. Who needs such a statute? Certainly not the doctors. Nor does it help the patient or his concerned family.[22]

The statute also requires the witnesses to be unrelated to the patient. Horan remarks,

> How in the world is any physician supposed to know that the witnesses are not related to the declarant, nor are they getting any portion of his or her estate when he or she dies?... Why should the attending physician be involved in matters of this sort when his job is to take care of a human being who is in a terminal condition—certainly the most psychologically difficult time of most people's lives.[23]

Horan suggests different wording for the statute: "Life-sustaining measures may be terminated by the attending physician when, in his judgment, based upon a reasonable degree of certainty according to usual and customary standards of medicine, it is proper to do so."[24]

It will take some time and application before legislation in this area is perfected. Whether Horan is correct in his assumption that such legislation is unnecessary and counterproductive remains to be seen. The very existence of cases such as *Quinlan* and *Perlmutter* demonstrates that physicians and prosecutors are not certain that the law precludes civil and criminal liability in the termination of life-prolonging treatment.

What is of paramount importance is that physicians, nurses, legislatures, and all others involved with the terminally ill have enough respect for life so that all attempts will continue to "make a faire and easy passage," but in its own good time.

Notes and References

1. *In the Matter of Karen Quinlan*, 348 A.2d 818 (1975).
2. Id.
3. Id. at 819.
4. In the Matter of Karen Quinlan, 355 A2d at 655 (1976).
5. Id. at 657.
6. Id. at 663.
7. Id. at 668–69.
8. Id. at 664, where there is no hope of cure.
9. Id. at 663.
10. Id. at 671.
11. Perlmutter v. Florida Medical Center, Fla. Cir. Ct. 17th Jud. Dist. Broward City (7/11/78) 47 Law Week 2069; Superintendent of Belchertown State School v. Saikewicz, 370 N.E.2d 417 (Mass. 1978).
12. Superintendent of Belchertown State School v. Saikewicz, id. at 2312.
13. Steele, Walter W., Jr., and Hill, Bill, A legislative proposal for a legal right to die, Criminal Law Bulletin, 12:140, at 151,152, Mar.-Apr. 1976.
14. Kamisar, Yale, Some non-religious views against proposed mercy-killing legislation, Minnesota Law Review 42:969, 1019–21, n. 168–88, cited in Steele and Hill, A legislative proposal, id. at 151–52.
15. Kamisar. id. at 1020; Miss Paight was acquitted on grounds of temporary

insanity, *New York Times* 8 Feb. 1950.

16. Steele and Hill, A legislative proposal, supra at 154–55.
17. Id. at 164.
18. Cal. Health and Safety Code ch. 3.9 § 7188 et seq. (1977).
19. Id. at § 7188.
20. Horan, Dennis J., The right to die: legislative and judicial developments, *The Forum* 13(2): 488 at 491 Winter 1978.
21. *In the Matter of Karen Quinlan*, supra; *Superintendent of Belchertown State School v. Saikewicz*, supra; *Dockery et al. v. Dockery* (No. 51439 Ch. Ct.) Tenn. Ct. App. declined to rule on merits, since Mrs. Dockery had died in the interim; cited in Horan, id. at 490, n. 9.
22. Horan, The right to die, supra at 494.
23. Id. at 494.
24. Id. at 492.

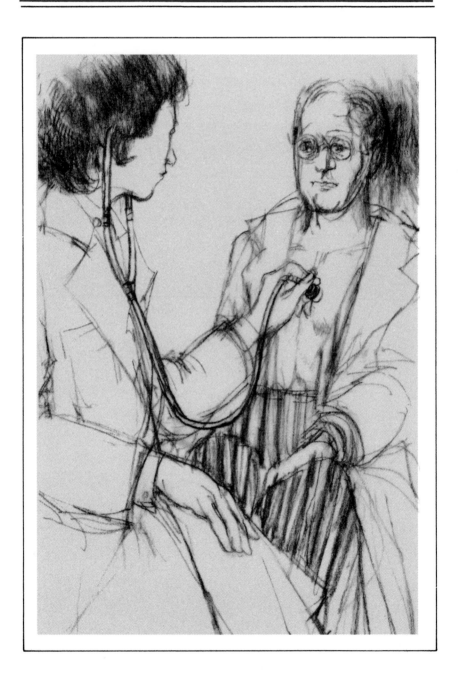

Part SIX

A TREND—EXPANDED ROLE, FUNCTIONS, AND RESPONSIBILITY OF THE NURSE

Introduction

While health care consumers and providers have been fighting over procedures and rights, nurses have been struggling to change their image as handmaidens to physicians.

Although physicians often cast nurses in a subservient role, legislatures and consumers, to say nothing of nurses themselves, have demonstrated that they see nurses as more independent providers of health care services.

While demands on nurses to perform more duties and exercise more independent judgment have increased, it has become apparent that all too often they are functioning beyond the scope of the law. Many legislatures have recognized the need to define this expanding role and have acted to protect nurses with laws that recognize these expanded functions.

The following examination focuses on the evaluation of legislation designed to recognize this expanding role and to accordingly protect the nurse in practice, and on the future as nurses' practical and legal positions change.

The activism of the 1960s and 1970s has precipitated a social reawakening and consequent legal response. Awakened regard for human rights in the various sectors of society has carried over to health care providers and patients. The long-existing basic rights of individuals are now being implemented during their status as patients. The courts and the legislatures of our various states have responded to this reawakening and to the problems and social dilemmas created by major advances in medical science.

The response of the law still lags and sometimes regresses in many of these areas. The combination of consumerism among patients and the judicial liberalization of the laws regarding malpractice litigation has increased law suits and malpractice awards. The insurance industry has responded with sharply increased premiums for malpractice insurance. In many states, reactionary legislation to limit patients' rights has resulted from this insurance phenomenon.

A new awareness of the legal implications of practice has also occurred in the nursing profession. As the scope and responsibilities of nursing practice have enlarged, the law has lagged. As a result, in many instances, nurses are functioning outside the scope allowed by nurse practice acts.

It is almost axiomatic that the nurse's main concern is the patient and the patient's needs, whether physical, emotional, social, or spiritual. Only a few of the nurse's functions may be considered dependent.

In most hospital situations, the nurse is present to guide and teach the patient, and, in the process, the patient is taught to care for himself and, when necessary, to reestablish self-esteem. This learning process sometimes may be painful physically or emotionally. For example, a patient learning to cough after a chest operation may feel considerable pain.

Ujhely, in *Determinants of the Nurse-Patient Relationship*, considers the real concern to be "sustaining the patient."[1] The nurse may be seen chiefly in the role of providing a suitable and optimal climate for restoring the patient to health. Compassion can be conveyed to the patient and can lay the foundation for the emotional climate that is essential in the process of getting well.

The most accessible member of the health care team and the one best able to assist a patient in establishing an often painful adjustment is the nurse who has seen the patient through the trials of recovery. The nurse is the one who alerts the hospital that the patient's condition has worsened and interprets the patient's clinical findings to other members of the health care team.

Possibly, a clergyman may assume some responsibility in sustaining the patient but is unlikely to be present when the patient needs help most. Thus, it is the nurse's role to aid patients in their adjustment to living within the limitations of their reduced capabilities. It is also the nurse's responsibility to be alert to violations in health care and to question whether a patient's condition is being compromised.

Several recent medical malpractice cases, some of which were discussed in earlier chapters, illustrate with distressing clarity the bizarre and sometimes disastrous results arising from overzealous or indifferent treatment of some common diseases. Even when care providers have the best of intentions and have applied the most modern therapy, human error has entered with disturbing results. In many instances, the nurse has served as a sentinel of impending danger and has been instrumental in averting disastrous consequences.

Nurses in expanded roles are now called upon to perform independent functions requiring a degree of professional judgment that was seldom contemplated a few years ago. Speaking of the expanded nursing role, Mauksch said, "Granted that some nurses have practiced, partly or totally, like this in the past, the profession as a whole certainly has not."[2]

The expanded functions are not recognized in most nurse practice acts. The nurse, therefore, has become more susceptible to the charge of malpractice and the resulting litigation. As the entire health care team is being sued more often, the nurse, as an integral part of the health care team, is more likely to be called as a witness in suits initiated against the others. Furthermore, these new functions often result in the nurse's having to confront the social and legal dilemmas resulting from such contemporary issues as abortion, contraception, euthanasia, drug abuse, and child abuse.

STATUTORY DEFINITIONS AND SPECIALIZATION

Traditionally, the major decision making as to treatment has been left to physicians. Although the member of the health care team who has the closest contact with the patient, the nurse has lower status than the physician in terms of responsibility, authority, and recognition from other health care professionals and some segments of society. Thus, nurses often have been viewed as an extension of the physician, assuming a dependent role.

A dependent, supportive role is reflected in the majority of nurse practice acts and state legislative acts defining the legal scope of allowable and acceptable nursing practice. The traditional nurse practice act distinguishes the registered professional nurse from the licensed practical nurse, who meets a lesser educational standard and whose work does not require the same level of skill, judgment, and knowledge as that required of the professional nurse. The definition of professional nursing in many state laws, both new (as in Illinois) and old and since revised (as in Iowa) focuses on the "observation, care and counsel of the ill," "the maintenance of health or prevention of illness," and "the administration of medications and treatments as prescribed by a licensed physician or dentist."[3]

Nurses' care of patients is "under medical direction" and they cannot make independent medical diagnoses or prescribe medical, therapeutic, or other corrective measures.[4] The nurse's role, under many state nurse practice acts that define the scope of acceptable practice, in some respects, remains a dependent one.

Notes and References

1. Ujhely, Gertrud, *Determinants of the Nurse-Patient Relationship* (New York: Springer Publishing Co., 1968) p. 93.
2. Mauksch, Ingeborg G., Nursing is coming of age... through the practitioner movement, *American Journal of Nursing* 75:1836, Oct. 1975.
3. Ill. Rev. Stat. ch. 91 §35.35 (1975); Kan. Stat. § 65-1113 (1975); N.C. Gen. Stat. ch. 90 § 18; N.D. Century Codes ch. 43 § 12-01 (1953); Iowa Code ch. 152 § 152.1 (1949); Vt. Stat. tit. 26 ch. 31 § 1725-1729.
4. Ohio Rev. Codes § 4723.06 (1968).

CHAPTER 16

The Expanded Role of the Nurse

The increased demands on the time of physicians, the existence of a segment of the population that lacked access to adequate medical care, the assertiveness of state nurses associations, the upgrading of professional nursing education, the realities of the nurse's role in health care, and the growing awareness of women in general and women as nurses—in particular their capabilities and need for autonomy—have resulted in the expansion of the role of the nurse in health care as an independent arm of the health care team.

The California revised Nurse Practice Act begins with the following statement, perhaps expressing most succinctly the rationale and history behind the expanded role of the nurse:

> [T]he legislature recognizes that nursing is a dynamic field, the
> practice of which is continually evolving to include more
> sophisticated patient care activities. It is the intent of the
> Legislature... to provide clear legal authority for functions and
> procedures which have common acceptance and usage. It is the
> legislative intent also to recognize the existence of overlapping
> functions between physicians and registered nurses.[1]

The American Nurses' Association and its various state constituencies have continually pressed state legislators and licensing commissions to allow nurses to expand their care activities and responsibilities. They view the nurse as having the responsibility for professional decision making involving both diagnosis of health problems and prescription of corrective measures based on such diagnosis. The goal of nursing, as expressed in a statement by the Illinois Nurses Association to the Health Care Licensure Commission in 1972, is to continue "to expand its responsibilities to extend needed health care services and to prevent unnecessary fragmentation of patient care."

ANA CERTIFICATIONS

The expanded role and specialization of the nurse are reflected in several other areas. Nurses are becoming certified under the auspices of the American Nurses' Association in various fields of nursing practice. The American Nurses' Association was certifying the following 11 nursing specialities early in 1979: adult and family nurse practitioner, school nurse practitioner, community health nursing, gerontological nursing, nursing of acute and chronically ill children, pediatric nurse practitioner, high-risk perinatal nursing, medical-surgical nursing, clinical specialist in medical-surgical nursing, psychiatric and mental health nursing, and clinical specialist in psychiatric and mental health nursing. Late in the year, ANA began certification in nursing administration and nursing administration—advanced.[2] Specialty groups in nursing have developed competing certification processes. The standards established by the American Nurses' Association are aimed at upgrading the profession to insure excellence in the quality of nursing care offered in each particular field.

Requirements of the American Nurses' Association for eligibility for certification include current state licensure, a minimum of two to three years of practice as a registered nurse, and current engagement in the clinical practice of nursing in the field of certification. The candidate must pass an objective examination to assess her knowledge of basic concepts and interpretation and application of principles and values of current nursing practice in the specific field of certification. Evidence of endorsement by colleagues, excellence in clinical performance, and continuing education must be submitted. Certification must be updated every five years to ensure continuous upgrading of knowledge and skills in the field. The effect of specialization has done much to improve the nurse's self-image and patient care as well.

The effect of specialization and the increased responsibility and independence that follow perhaps best reflect the expanded role of the nurse. As more and more demands are made on the time of physicians, many functions formerly viewed as solely within the realm of physicians are now being shared with other health care personnel, mostly nurses. By statute, state legislatures also have created several new health care provider roles that, in fact, are expanded or modified nursing roles. They have also created, by statute, physician's assistants roles.

ROLES IN HEALTH CARE DEFINED BY STATUTE

The Nurse Practitioner

The title nurse practitioner accurately reflects the "nurse of the future" as envisioned by health care planners in one institution. At Mt. Sinai Hospital Medical Center, Chicago, they visualize one specialist, the community health care practitioner, as one whose practice should resemble but not replace that of the family doctor.[3]

States that have passed legislation to recognize the expanded role of the nurse have opened the door to nurse practitioners without actually creating such a position. In Illinois, the last sentence in the definition of professional nursing reads, "The foregoing shall not be deemed to include those acts of medical diagnosis or prescription of therapeutic or corrective measures which are properly performed only by physicians."[4]

Current legislation such as physician's assistants acts delegating performance of medical diagnosis and prescription of certain therapeutic or corrective measures to medical personnel other than physicians has been interpreted as having cleared the way for the role of the nurse to include anything not stated specifically to be solely in the realm of the physician.[5] It is doubtful that such a broad interpretation would withstand judicial scrutiny, but it demonstrates the general mood and desire of the nursing professional with regard to the expanded role.

Several states have adopted legislation directed to the professional position of nurse practitioner. New Hampshire defines the advanced registered nurse practitioner (ARNP) as a registered nurse with credentials determined by the board of nursing that indicate specialized preparation enabling the nurse practitioner to "function in collaborative relationships with physicians as well as in private practice."[6] Oregon defines a nurse practitioner as a registered nurse who has been certified by the Oregon State Board of Nursing "to practice in an expanded specialty role within the practice of nursing."[7] Florida, also by statute, recognizes certification for an advanced or specialized nurse practitioner.[8]

The Oregon State Board of Nursing has set standards for the education, practice, certification, and continuing education of the nurse practitioner. Application requirements include a current Oregon registered nurse's license, completion of a certificate or degree program appropriate in the specialty area, and certain continuing education requirements. Requirements depend on whether the applicant has stopped practicing, has not yet practiced in the expanded role, or completed the educational program two or more years earlier. A professional performance review is also required. The nurse practitioner's patient care is evaluated according to standards of practice established by a team that includes two or three nurse practitioners and a physician. Also, by 1981, in addition to the foregoing requirements, such a nurse must have a bachelor's degree with a major in nursing. By January 1, 1986, a master's degree will be required. The specialized, in-depth educational program and faculty requirements are also set and include supervised clinical experience.

The role of the nurse practitioner is to provide primary health care, after the care has been initiated by the physician in a variety of settings. The nurse practitioner is primarily responsible for the provision and management of personal health services that usually include promotion and maintenance of health, prevention of illness and disability, managment of health care during acute and chronic phases of illness, and guidance and counseling of individuals and families with appropriate referral to physicians and other health care providers and community resources.

The categories of specialty areas covered by the primary care administrative role include (but are not limited to) family nurse practitioner, pediatric nurse practitioner, adult nurse practitioner, psychiatric-mental health practitioner, nurse midwife, women's health care nurse practitioner, school health nurse practitioner, and school and college health nurse practitioner. (These headings are similar to the ANA certifications.)

The scope of practice as defined by administrative rule includes managing mental and physical health care in the specialty areas through integration of health maintenance, disease prevention, phy-sicial diagnosis, and treatment of common episodic and chronic problems (including pregnancy) in primary health care, the nurse practitioner working in collaboration with physicians and other health care professionals and agencies.

This position, created by statute, gives a nurse the potential to function more independently of a physician than most other health care providers. The nurse practitioner is given freedom to perform far beyond the traditional role of the registered professional nurse. She may legally perform additional functions similar to those of a phy-sician's assistant but with an important difference. The nurse does not require direct supervision and control of a physician. This expanded specialty role provides, more than any other, the freedom for indi-vidual nurses to use their education, skills, and knowledge to perform as vital and autonomous members of the health care team.

Nurse Anesthetists The category of nurse anesthetist has existed for some time and was one of the first expanded nursing roles. A few states, such as Louisiana, define the position as a registered nurse who has completed an educational program in a nationally accredited school of anesthesia, is nationally certified, and administers anes-thetics and ancillary services under the direction and supervision of a licensed physician or dentist.[9] This definition expands the role of the nurse to that of a person who independently administers drugs that can be dangerous to a patient.

Nurse Midwives The role of the nurse in obstetrics recently has been expanded in several states, including California. The Nurse-Midwives Act in California gives the nurse-midwife authority "to attend cases of normal childbirth and to provide prenatal, intrapartum and post-partum care, including family planning care, for the mother, and immediate care for the newborn."[10]

The Oregon State Board of Nursing has taken steps and set standards necessary to ensure that the nurse practitioner of maternal-child care has the requisite education, skills, and background to perform in this new and demanding role. The nurse is directed by statute to be under the supervision of a licensed obstetrician. "Supervision" under the statute, however, does not require the physical presence of the physician. Thus, the nurse's role in childbirth has been expanded from that of sustaining the patient and family with traditional nursing care, assisting the physician, and supervising the labor and delivery rooms to independent and autonomous direction of the childbirth process.

In 1979, the Tennessee Board of Nursing revoked the license of a registered nurse for practicing as a nurse midwife "without appropriate education or credentials. ... In order to practice in Tennessee, a nurse-midwife must have two years' experience as an R.N. and must pass a certification examination given by the ACNM [American College of Nurse-Midwives], after having attended an approved school of nurse-midwifery."[11]

The Physician's Assistant

For various purposes, several states have created by statute the role of the physician's assistant. In Illinois, it is "to encourage and promote the more effective utilization of the skills of physicians by enabling them to delegate certain health tasks."[12] Other states have stated in such legislation a concern with "the growing shortage and geographic maldistribution of health care services" in their states.[13]

In general, the state statutes that permit the physician's assistant to function have given the state board of medical examiners the authority to define the scope of their activities. All the states, however, require the physician's assistant to work under the responsible supervision and control of a licensed physician in the office where the physician maintains his primary practice, when the physician is present in that office, or in a hospital where the physician is a staff member and present.

All states define supervision as "the easy availability or physical presence of the licensed physician for consultation and direction of their actions." Also, most states expressly disallow the exercise of any independent judgment for purposes of diagnosis and treatment of patients. Illinois limits the number of allowable assistants to one per physician. All acts expressly preclude the release of physicians from legal liability for the acts of their assistants.

Notes and References

1. Cal. Codes § 2725 (1974).
2. McCarty, Patricia, Certification process complex but rewarding, The American Nurse 11:7, 20, June 20, 1979; Over 400 apply for certification in administration, The American Nurse 11:3, Sept. 20, 1979.

3. *The Record*(Chicago: Mt. Sinai Hospital Medical Center) July–Aug. 1973, p. 2.
4. Ill. Rev. Stat. ch. 91 § 35.35 (1975).
5. Statement by Joan Bundly, Illinois Nurses Association, Mar. 16, 1978.
6. N.H. Rev. Stat. 326-B:10 (1975).
7. Ore. Rev. Stat. § 678.010 (1975).
8. Fla. Stat. ch. 464 § 464.106 (1976).
9. La. Civil Code ch. 37 § 930 (1976).
10. Cal. Codes art. 2.5 § 2746.5 (1974).
11. Tennessee Board of Nursing Revokes Non-Certified Midwife's RN License (News), *American Journal of Nursing* 79:574, Apr. 1979.
12. Ill. Rev. Stat. ch. 91 § 211 (1976).
13. Neb. Rev. Stat. ch. 71-1 § 107.15 (1973); Fla. Stat. ch. 458 § 457.135 (1) (1976); Cal. Codes § 3500 (1975).

CHAPTER 17

Nurse Practice Acts, and the Expanded Role

THE NEW NURSE PRACTICE ACTS

Because of the perseverance of state nursing associations and the increasingly expanded role of the nurse, many states have revised their nurse practice acts to reflect the nurse's growing independence. Many of these amendments, however, will not become effective until future dates; and many still limit, in varying degrees, the autonomy granted the nurse. Sixteen states maintain the traditional model for the nurse, excluding definitions that allow independent diagnosis or treatment.[1] As a result, nurse practitioners are organizing to lobby for federal and state legislation to establish criteria for certifying nurse practitioners and to develop standards for preparation and third-party reimbursement for services. Thus, the nurse, especially the nurse practitioner who is performing under expanded role in states without applicable legislation, is functioning beyond what is allowed by the pertinent nurse practice acts.

States with recently updated nurse practice acts include California, New York, North Dakota, Florida, Minnesota, South Dakota, Iowa, and Oregon. Other state nurse practice acts will be in effect in 1980, 1981, and 1982. The focus in the nurse practice acts in the states that recently updated them has turned to independent diagnosis and treatment rather than the traditional functions of observation, and supportive and restorative care, which are now within the realm of licensed practical nurses. The new statutes are carefully designed to define the boundaries of diagnosis; and several specifically make reference to nursing diagnosis, which includes the "identification of and discrimination between physical and psychosocial signs and symptoms essential to effective execution and management of the nursing care."[2] In a manner similar to the Nurse Practice Act of North Dakota, most of these states define the practice of the registered professional nurse as follows:

[Practice] is the performance of acts requiring the specialized knowledge, judgment, and skill based on principles of the biological, physical, behavioral, and social sciences in:

1. The maintenance of health and prevention of illness.
2. Diagnosing human responses to actual or potential health problems.
3. Collaboration in the implementation of the total health care regimen and execution of a medical regimen as prescribed or authorized by a licensed physician or dentist, and the performance of such additional acts which are recognized by the nursing profession, in connection with the medical profession, as proper to be performed by registered nurses who have had additional specialized preparation and are authorized by the board... to perform such acts.[3]

The new statutory provisions allow the nurse to diagnose certain health problems. They further recognize collaboration between the physician and the nurse that is so necessary for the provision of adequate health care. A collateral result is the legislative recognition of the upgraded status, which legitimizes, under law, the broadened practice.

The expanded role of the nurse in specialization is also recognized in the North Dakota Statute, with the enabling clause, "and such additional acts which are recognized... as proper to be performed by nurses... with specialized preparation."[4]

California and Minnesota use slightly different wording in their Nurse Practice Acts. California emphasizes the sharing of functions between physicians and registered nurses to provide for collaboration between the two professions. The California statute addresses the role of the nurse in both direct and indirect patient care services and, when defining allowable functions, uses the phrase "including, but not limited to" to provide an opening for the further expansion of the nurse's role. The expanded role is outlined in sections (c) and (d), which provide for the following:

1. The performance, according to standardized procedures, of basic health care, testing and prevention procedures, including, but not limited to, skin tests, immunization techniques, and the withdrawal of human blood from veins and arteries
2. Observation of signs and symptoms of illness, reactions to treatment, general behavior, or general physical condition, and (1) determination of whether such signs, symptoms, reactions,

*behavior, or general appearance exhibit abnormal character-
istics; and (2) implementation. Based on observed abnormal-
ities appropriate reporting, or referral, or standardized procedures, or changes in treatment regimen in accordance with
standardized procedures, or the initiation of emergency
procedures.*[5]

The Act goes on to define standardized procedures as "policies and
protocol which are developed through the *collaboration* among ad-
ministrators and health professionals, including physicians *and*
nurses."[6] (Emphasis added.)

The California Statute gives the nurse a wide range of functions and
allows for independent and autonomous diagnosis and treatment on a
limited level. It also emphasizes the collaboration among the professions, an area that has been of mounting concern to nurses over the
years in their attempts to upgrade their image as professionals.

To the definition of professional nursing, the Minnesota Nurse
Practice Act adds the phrase, "includes both independent nursing
functions and delegated medical functions which may be performed in
collaboration with other health team members." The Minnesota Act
goes on to say that "independent nursing function may also be
performed autonomously." This further opens the door to a degree of
independence and autonomy before not included in the nursing
profession.[7]

Although many states have amended the nurse practice acts, and a
few have gone far to expand the definition of professional nursing,
nurses may find themselves in a dilemma in those states where such
legislation is not yet in effect or where no such legislation has been
passed. The independent and expanded role of the nurse is an
indisputable fact brought about by necessity. Nevertheless, until state
legislatures respond to this reality *in clear terms* giving nurses the
statutory sanction to move forward, nurses will continue to practice in
a twilight zone that is beyond legal sanction.

CONTINUING EDUCATION AND THE EXPANDED ROLE

With the emergence of the expanded role and the increase in professional independence and autonomy, nurses are increasingly faced
with the problem of keeping pace with current trends. Skills and
knowledge have to be kept up-to-date and continuously reinforced.

Today, many nurses, especially those functioning in highly technical areas, find themselves in situations demanding in-depth knowledge but may have only a superficial education in those areas.[8] The
inactive nurse is faced with an even more serious problem when she
returns after being away from nursing anywhere from two to 20 years.

Many state nurses associations have been urging state legislatures to
require continuing education for relicensing for a nurse who has been
inactive for a specified number of years.

A new version of the Nurse Practice Act went into effect in Utah in May 1979. The new Act defines inactive status. "A nurse who doesn't practice for five years automatically becomes inactive and must fulfill certain mandatory continuing education requirements and take a licensing examination before being readmitted to active status."[9]

The state nurses associations' concern is not only for the improvement of professional competency but also for nurses to upgrade the quality of patient care and for stimulating colleagueship with other health care professionals. In addition, the state nurses associations want to instill confidence in nurses and other members of the health care team in the new, expanded role of the nurse. The nursing profession is moving toward accountability for the quality of nursing care delivered to patients.[10] Continuing education as a requirement for all practicing nurses may soon be the rule rather than the exception.

For years, the issue of continuing education has been debated by various factions in nursing and medical associations as well as in legislatures. Problems arising from the concept include availability, quality and cost of programs (along with facilities), faculties, and compensation for nurses who participate. Many nurses are hampered by geography, particularly those living in rural areas, and by time, particularly career nurses with families.

The issue of who will pay for the programs has arisen, and the state nurses associations are arguing that the individual nurse should not bear this burden alone. Also, programs in continuing education must meet the needs of new graduates as well as nurses who have practiced a long time or who have been inactive.

Many of the state nurses associations have responded to these problems by developing voluntary continuing education programs, giving nurses the option and the motivation to upgrade their education. Certificates recognizing completion of continuing education programs are given, and the names of individual nurses who complete the programs are published statewide and, in many cases, presented to the nurses' employers. States with voluntary programs will offer such programs to the state legislatures as models in the event that mandatory continuing education is required. The American Nurses' Association has prepared guidelines and criteria for continuing education programs. Most states follow them to insure transferability of recognition and interchange of records from state to state.[11]

In several states, mandatory continuing education is required for relicensing of nurses. In California, nurses must prove that in the two years prior to applying for relicensing they have kept abreast of current trends by completing courses of continuing education relevant to their particular fields, or that they meet other standards deemed equivalent by the California Board of Nursing Education and Registration. This law became effective July 1, 1978. As an alternative, applicants may take an objective examination to test their knowledge of recent developments in the field.[12]

The statute further requires the board of nursing to make a variety of forms of continuing education available including, but not limited to, academic studies, workshops, inservice education, institutes, seminars, lectures, conferences, extension studies, and home-study programs. A maximum of 30 hours may be required by the board in California.[13] Thus, the California legislature has attempted to address several problems by making available a variety of forms of continuing education to those nurses limited by time and geography and to ensure that a variety of needs are satisfied.

Minnesota enacted legislation (effective January 1, 1978) that requires mandatory continuing education for relicensing and, for inactive nurses, relicensing after five years of not actively practicing nursing. The board of nursing is authorized to establish the procedures and minimal requirements for such programs, free of legislative direction of the kind specified in California.[14]

Florida will likewise require mandatory continuing education as a condition for renewal of a license to practice (effective March 1, 1980).[15] The minimum number of hours per year will be 15.

Kansas has enacted legislation requiring continuing education for relicensing (effective July 1, 1978).[16] The legislation directs the board of nursing to "consider any existing programs of Continuous Education currently being offered to such licensees by medical facilities," in establishing the requirements. In this case, the legislature is attempting to deal with current availability and quality of such programs in terms of mandatory requirements for continuing education.

Many other state nurses associations have urged or are urging requirements for mandatory continuing education, including Illinois (already in effect), Michigan, New York, Rhode Island, and Texas. Three states have passed mandatory continuing education for relicensure for specific groups.[17] Oregon and Nebraska mandate relicensure for those inactive for five years or more, and New Hampshire mandates it for advanced registered nurse practitioners.

Finally, several states including Oregon, Colorado, Louisiana, and South Dakota, have included enabling clauses in their nurse practice acts that give the board of nursing the authority to institute mandatory continuing education at its discretion. An example of such a clause provides that a license "shall be renewed by [the nurse's] . . . meeting other such requirements of the board prior to the expiration of said license."[18] The South Dakota Statute reads, "The board may also require continuing education for the renewal of licenses."[19]

A pattern seems to be evolving in the state legislatures with current nursing practices, not only in the definition of allowable scope of practice, but also in regard to the standards of education for licensing. The expanding function of nurses often requires practice beyond statutory boundaries, as well as beyond their knowledge and skill to perform expected services. Until state legislatures enact realistically broadened practice acts and practical requirements for continuing education, nurses will run the risk of performing outside legal boundaries and, in many instances, beyond their competencies.

Self-motivation to improve may not be enough to guarantee the required competence of a nurse in a specialized field, although voluntary programs of continuing education are a step in the right direction. Mandatory programs may have to be developed to insure high quality nursing in the expanded role as well as mutual respect and collaboration among all health care professionals. Mandatory educational requirements must be set for nurses certified in the various specialites and, at the very least, for those nurses who have been away from the profession for a number of years.

THE FUTURE DIRECTION OF THE PERMISSIBLE SCOPE OF PRACTICE UNDER THE LAW

In reviewing various nurse practice acts and the legislation providing for nurse practitioners and physicians' assistants, one sees emerging a slow but steady recognition by the law of the reality of what is, in effect, the expanded role of nursing. Indeed, the reality of present health care needs and requirements makes it necessary for the nurse to perform more independent functions than are actually permitted by most nurse practice acts. The consequences of the lag in the majority of states to broaden the scope of permissible practice under law is to expose those nurses performing in an expanded role to the penalties prescribed for unauthorized practice. In the event of malpractice litigation, a nurse may also be held to a higher standard of performance than nurses practicing with broadened statutory boundaries.

If one who is—to borrow words from Francis Bacon—"skillful in precedents, wary in proceeding, and understanding in the business of the court" may act as a "finger of a court" and point the way, the way would be this: Nurses could better serve both their own profession and the public by taking the lead in formulating uniform nationwide standards to guide the states in the revision of the nurse practice acts.[20] Then, nurses should exert themselves to secure legislation that would result in the implementation of nurse practice acts that would broaden the scope of nursing practice.

Nurse practice acts that would better protect nurses and society would incorporate the following principles:

- They would broaden the scope of nursing practice to conform to the existing practice of nursing in which contemporary nurses are now engaged and for which they have been educated.
- Desirable statutes would also allow for an even broader scope of practice for nurse specialists who are appropriately certified by a qualified professional body.
- Statutes would protect society by requiring continuing education. This would eliminate the inept nurse and prevent the

return of a nurse after several years absence until she overcomes inadequate skills.

Such legislation would eliminate the confusion resulting from statutory designations of nurse practitioners and other special health care providers who, in essence, have nursing as an educational base, with additional concentration in certain specialty areas. Past experience, however, suggests that such an approach will be slow in developing.

Notes and References

1. Ellis, Barbara, Future evolution of nursing role contingent on legislation, *Hospitals J.A.H.A.* 52:81–82, Feb. 1, 1978.
2. Consol. Laws of N.Y. § 6901 (1)(1972); Ore. Rev. Stat. § 678.010 (2)(1975).
3. N.D. Cent. Code.
4. N.D. Cent. Code 43-12.1-03 (1977); see also, Fla. Stat. § 464.021 (2) (a) (1975), repealed as of 7-1-78; Consol. Laws of N.Y. § 6902 (1) (1972); S.D. Codified Laws § 36-9-3 (1976); Iowa Code § 152.1 (2) (1976).
5. Cal. Codes § 2725 (c) (d) (1974).
6. Cal. Codes § 2725 (c) (d) (2) (1974).
7. Minn. Stat. § 148.171 (3) (1974).
8. Meyer, Linn, Educational requirements raise controversy for health personnel, *Hospitals J.A.H.A.* 51:119–20, 122, 124–25, Apr. 1, 1977.
9. Practice Act Changes Applauded in Utah (News), *The American Journal of Nursing* 79:1182, 1202, July 1979.
10. McClure, Margaret, Can we bring order out of the chaos of nursing education? Margaret McClure says... *American Journal of Nursing* 76:100–03, Jan. 1976.
11. The status of continuing education: voluntary and mandatory, *The American Journal of Nursing* 77:410–16, Mar. 1977.
12. Cal. Codes § 2311.5 (a) (1976).
13. Cal. Codes § 2811.5 (b) (1976).
14. Minn. Stat. ch. 1. 148.231 (1) and (5) (1976).
15. Fla. Stat. ch. 464-464.018 (effective July 1, 1979).
16. Kan. Stat. 76-1117 (1976).
17. Ore. Rev. Stat. 678.050 (c) (1953); Rev. Stat. of Neb. ch. 1.71 § 1,132.20 (1976); N.H. Rev. Stat. ch. 326-B § 10 (1975).
18. La. Civil Code ch. 1.37 § 922 E (1) (1966).
19. S.D. Codified Laws 36-9-58 (1967).
20. Bacon, Francis, "Of Judicature," In *Complete Essays of Francis Bacon* (New York:Belmont Books, 1962), p. 165.

Glossary of Legal Terms and Abbreviations

Abbreviations of Court Names

App. Appellate
Cir. Ct. Circuit court (state)
Cir. Ct. App. Circuit court of appeal(s) (federal)
Crim. App. Court of criminal appeals
D. District court (state)
Dist. Ct. District court (state)
F.2d Federal reporter, second series—case reporter for the decisions of the United States Circuit Court of Appeals
F. Supp. Federal supplement—case reporter for the decisions of the United States District Court
Juv. Ct. Juvenile court
Mun. Ct. Municipal court
N.E.2d North Eastern, second series—area reporter for state court decisions of the north eastern states
P. Ct. Probate court
Super. Ct. Superior court
Sup. Ct. Supreme Court

Explanatory Phrases in Case Citations

aff'd The confirmation by an appellate court of the judgment, order or decree in a lower court
cert. denied The denial of certiorari which is an appellate proceeding requesting a reexamination of the action of an inferior

court. Generally, the procedure by which litigants seek the review of the United States Supreme Court

et seq. A reference to pages which follow the initial page designated

ex rel. Upon relation or information referring to legal proceedings that are instituted by the attorney general, or other proper person, in the name and behalf of the state, and on the information and at the instigation of an individual who has a private interest in the matter

id. Reference to a citation to the same authority as that in the immediately preceding citation

in re Refers to "in the matter of; concerning." A method of entitling a judicial proceeding in which there are no adversary parties but there is something tangible, concerning which judicial action is to be taken such as an estate, etc. It is also used as a designation of a proceeding where one party makes an application in his own behalf.

mandate A demand, usually from an appeals court, resulting from a decision directing the lower court to take specified action with regard to a case that has been heard on appeal

modified To change incidental or subordinate aspects of an order or a judicial conclusion

prob. juris noted Acknowledgment of the jurisdiction of a court to exercise power in probate, i.e. the power to administer the law with regard to wills, settlement of decedent's estate, and the supervision of guardianship of minor children

sub nom. Under the name or under the title of

supra Refers back to an authority which has been fully cited

Definition of Legal Terms

adversary proceedings A proceeding in which there are opposing parties and which is contested

amicus curiae Latin term meaning a friend of the court. Generally used to describe a party who has no right to appear in a suit but is allowed to do so after application and by permission of the court to protect his interest

assumption-of-risk Generally used to describe a defense to a law suit in which the plaintiff allegedly assumed the consequences of the claimed injury

case of first impression A legal action presenting issues in controversy for which there is no prior judicial precedent

certiorari The name of the writ by which a party seeks a further review of a case by a higher court, usually the United States Supreme Court

class certification The order of a court which provides that the parties who initiated the case may proceed as representatives of all members of a group or class of people who are similarly situated to those who have initiated the action

decision on the merits A decision of the court which disposes of the case on the primary issues raised by the parties

declaratory judgment An order of court which declares the rights of the parties or declares the applicable law without specifically ordering anything to be done

dicta The expressions of a judge in an opinion which do not specifically affect the resolution or determination of the case

John or Jane Doe (also Roe) The name of a fictitious party, either plaintiff or defendant. When identifying a plaintiff, it is generally under circumstances to present a test case involving an issue affecting many such persons. When identifying a defendant, it is to attempt to prevent the statute of limitations from running against an unidentified party.

discovery The proceedings by which the attorneys in behalf of their parties through depositions and written questions (interrogatories) learn of the facts of the case and the evidence to be presented at the trial

emancipated minor A person who has not yet reached majority under the law but, because of marriage or acts of self-sustenance, is given adult status under the law

en banc Literally, means "from the bench"; generally, refers to a court actually ruling from the bench

evidentiary hearing Any proceeding, whether administrative or judicial, in which evidence is presented with regard to specified issues

guardian ad litem A person appointed by the court to prosecute or defend for a minor

habeas corpus A writ directing a person in authority to release a prisoner

hearing on the merits Any court or administrative hearing in which the subject, not collateral issues, is the main issue in the legal controversy

infant A person who has not as yet reached the age at which he can act for himself under the law

injunction A writ issued by a court forbidding a party defendant from doing a specified act

in loco parentis A person who stands in the place of a parent with a parent's rights, duties, and responsibilities

merits The strict legal rights of the parties

order A ruling entered by a court

parens patriae Generally used to refer to the state as having the sovereign power of guardianship over persons under disability

qualified immunity A limited exemption from serving in an office or performing duties that are generally required of other citizens.

Usually used to describe an order entered by a court providing that a person may testify without having that testimony used against him in a subsequent criminal proceeding

remand To send back. Generally used to describe the action of a reviewing court in returning the case to the lower court for the purpose of having some specified action taken

scienter Having knowledge of a particular state of facts

statutory Relating or required by a specific statute

sum Summary or abstract of a case or treatise

summary judgment The entry of a judgment disposing of a case on affidavits or depositions prior to a trial

tort A civil wrong or injury

vacate, to set aside Usually used to describe the action of a court in setting aside an order or judgment previously entered

Medical Glossary
for Laymen

apnea Temporary suspension of breathing

dermabrasion Removal of such skin defects as scars by abrading the skin with brushes or sandpaper

electroshock or electroconvulsive therapy (EST) Use of electric current to the brain to induce convulsions to treat psychotic disorders, particularly depression

Fallopian tubes A pair of slender tubes (the oviducts) leading to the body cavity of the uterus, which transport ova from the ovaries to the uterus

group psychotherapy In psychiatry, a group of patients led by a therapist discuss their problems in an attempt to solve them through group interactions.

hydrocephalic Having hydrocephalus, an accumulation of serous fluid in the cranium due to obstructed flow, causing pressure and often causing enlargement of the head

hysterectomy Surgical removal of the uterus

hysterotomy Surgical incision into the uterus, as in a Caesarean section

laminectomy Surgical removal of one or more laminae (bony spinal processes which join behind the body of the vertebra to form the vertebral or neural arch)

milieu therapy In psychiatry, the treatment of mental disorders by creating an environment that enhances other forms of therapy, for instance, by providing recreational facilities or giving patients a voice in policies that affect them

nasogastric tube A tube inserted through the nose into the stomach for such purposes as feeding a patient or removing fluid or gas

prostaglandins A whole family of physiologically potent compounds that occur naturally in many tissues (first found in semen) and that cause varied physiological responses, including stimulating labor-like contractions of the uterus after an intravenous dose

psychoanalysis A doctrine and technique developed by Sigmund Freud for treating a variety of emotional disorders, particularly neuroses, by bringing to conscious manipulation ideas and experiences from the unconscious part of the mind

ruptured disk or herniated disk Between adjacent vertebrae are disks of fibrocartilage, each with a soft, pulpy, elastic center called the nucleus pulposus. When herniated, the nucleus pulposus protrudes into the fibrocartilage and may cause mild to severe pain by impinging on nearby nerves

scoliosis A lateral curvature of the spine

spinal fusion The surgical fusion of two or more vertebrae to immobilize part of the spine as treatment for such conditions as herniated disk or deformity from severe arthritis

tracheostomy or tracheotomy Surgical incision into the trachea to establish and maintain the airway

vas deferens The convoluted duct through which sperm pass from the testis to the penis

Bill of Rights and Amendment 14, Section 1 Constitution of the United States of America

ARTICLE [I]†

Congress shall make no law respecting an establishment of religion, or prohibiting the free exercise thereof; or abridging the freedom of speech, or of the press; or the right of the people peaceably to assemble, and to petition the Government for a redress of grievances.

ARTICLE [II]

A well regulated Militia, being necessary to the security of a free State, the right of the people to keep and bear Arms, shall not be infringed.

ARTICLE [III]

No Soldier shall, in time of peace be quartered in any house, without the consent of the Owner, nor in time of war, but in a manner to be prescribed by law.

---

*All the amendments except the Twenty-first Amendment were ratified by State Legislatures. The Twenty-first Amendment, by its terms, was ratified by "conventions in the several States." Only the Thirteenth, Fourteenth, Fifteenth, and Sixteenth Amendments had numbers assigned to them at the time of ratification.

ARTICLE [IV]

The right of the people to be secure in their persons, houses, papers, and effects, against unreasonable searches and seizures, shall not be violated, and no Warrants shall issue, but upon probable cause, supported by Oath or affirmation, and particularly describing the place to be searched, and the persons or things to be seized.

ARTICLE [V]

No person shall be held to answer for a capital, or otherwise infamous crime, unless on a presentment or indictment of a Grand Jury, except in cases arising in the land or naval forces, or in the Militia, when in actual service in time of War or public danger; nor shall any person be subject for the same offence to be twice put in jeopardy of life or limb; nor shall be compelled in any criminal case to be a witness against himself, nor be deprived of life, liberty, or property, without due process of law; nor shall private property be taken for public use, without just compensation.

ARTICLE [VI]

In all criminal prosecutions, the accused shall enjoy the right to a speedy and public trial, by an impartial jury of the State and district wherein the crime shall have been committed, which district shall have been previously ascertained by law, and to be informed of the nature and cause of the accusation; to be confronted with the witnesses against him; to have compulsory process for obtaining witnesses in his favor, and to have the Assistance of Counsel for his defence.

ARTICLE [VII]

In Suits at common law, where the value in controversy shall exceed twenty dollars, the right of trial by jury shall be preserved, and no fact tried by a jury shall be otherwise re-examined in any Court of the United States, than according to the rules of the common law.

ARTICLE [VIII]

Excessive bail shall not be required, nor excessive fines imposed, nor cruel and unusual punishments inflicted.

ARTICLE [IX]

The enumeration in the Constitution, of certain rights, shall not be construed to deny or disparage others retained by the people.

ARTICLE [X]

The powers not delegated to the United States by the Constitution, nor prohibited by it to the States, are reserved to the States respectively, or to the people.

ARTICLE XIV*

Section I. All persons born or naturalized in the United States, and subject to the jurisdiction thereof, are citizens of the United States and of the State wherein they reside. No State shall make or enforce any law which shall abridge the privileges or immunities of citizens of the United States; nor shall any State deprive any person of life, liberty, or property, without due process of law; nor deny to any person within its jurisdiction the equal protection of the laws.

---

†The first 10 amendments (termed articles), together with 2 others that failed of ratification, were proposed to the several States by resolution of Congress on September 25, 1789. The ratifications were transmitted by the Governors to the President and by him communicated to Congress from time to time. The first 10 amendments were ratified by 11 of the 14 States. Virginia completed the required three fourths by ratification on December 30, 1791. The legislatures of Massachusetts, Georgia and Connecticut ratified them on March 2, 1939, March 18, 1939, and April 19, 1939, respectively.

A Patient's Bill of Rights

The American Hospital Association presents *A Patient's Bill of Rights* with the expectation that observance of these rights will contribute to more effective patient care and greater satisfaction for the patient, his physician, and the hospital organization. Further, the Association presents these rights in the expectation that they will be supported by the hospital on behalf of its patients as an integral part of the healing process. It is recognized that a personal relationship between the physician and the patient is essential for the provision of proper medical care. The traditional physician-patient relationship takes on a new dimension when care is rendered within an organizational structure. Legal precedent has established that the institution itself also has a responsibility to the patient. It is in recognition of these factors that these rights are affirmed.

1. The patient has the right to considerate and respectful care.
2. The patient has the right to obtain from his physician complete current information concerning his diagnosis, treatment, and prognosis in terms the patient can be reasonably expected to understand. When it is not medically advisable to give such information to the patient, the information should be made available to an appropriate person in his behalf. He has the right to know, by name, the physician responsible for coordinating his care.
3. The patient has the right to receive from his physician information necessary to give informed consent prior to the start of any procedure and/or treatment. Except in emergencies, such information for informed consent should include but not necessarily be limited to the specific procedure and/or treatment, the

medically significant risks involved, and the probable duration of incapacitation. Where medically significant alternatives for care or treatment exist, or when the patient requests information concerning medical alternatives, the patient has the right to such information. The patient has also the right to know the name of 'the person responsible for the procedures and/or treatment.

4. The patient has the right to refuse treatment to the extent permitted by law and to be informed of the medical consequences of his action.

5. The patient has the right to every consideration of his privacy concerning his own medical care program. Case discussion, consultation, examination, and treatment are confidential and should be conducted discreetly. Those not directed involved in his care must have the permission of the patient to be present.

6. The patient has the right to expect that all communications and records pertaining to his care should be treated as confidential.

7. The patient has the right to expect that within its capacity a hospital must make reasonable response to the request of a patient for services. The hospital must provide evaluation, service, and/or referral as indicated by the urgency of the case. When medically permissible, a patient may be transferred to another facility only after he has received complete information and explanation concerning the needs for and alternatives to such a transfer. The institution to which the patient is to be transferred must first have accepted the patient for transfer.

8. The patient has the right to obtain information as to any relationship of his hospital to other health care and educational institutions insofar as his care is concerned. The patient has the right to obtain information as to the existence of any professional relationships among individuals, by name, who are treating him.

9. The patient has the right to be advised if the hospital proposes to engage in or perform human experimentation affecting his care or treatment. The patient has the right to refuse to participate in such research projects.

10. The patient has the right to expect reasonable continuity of care. He has the right to know in advance what appointment times and physicians are available and where. The patient has the right to expect that the hospital will provide a mechanism whereby he is informed by his physician or a delegate of the physician of the patient's continuing health care requirements following discharge.

11. The patient has the right to examine and receive an explanation of his bill, regardless of source of payment.

12. The patient has the right to know what hospital rules and regulations apply to his conduct as a patient.

No catalog of rights can guarantee for the patient the kind of treatment he has a right to expect. A hospital has many functions to perform, including the prevention and treatment of disease, the education of both health professionals and patients, and the conduct of clinical research. All these activities must be conducted with an overriding concern for the patient, and, above all, the recognition of his dignity as a human being. Success in achieving this recognition ensures success in the defense of the rights of the patient.

INDEX

Date Due